Survival

GLOBAL POLITICS AND STRATEGY

Volume 63 Number 1 | February–March 2021

'Trump deployed the lost-cause narrative brilliantly, transplanting it in the fertile soil of his electoral defeat. It engaged the gears of resentment and stoked anxieties spurred by the collision of an ideology of rugged individualism and the experience of personal failure.'

Steven Simon, Trump's Insurrection and America's Year of Living Dangerously, p. 10.

'Dissuasion of this sort … did not work in 1939–40. Germany, a revisionist power fully aware that it could not win a war of attrition, was not deterred from occupying Poland, subsequently trouncing the combined forces of France and Britain on the European continent in May–June 1940.'

François Heisbourg, Europe Can Afford the Cost of Autonomy, p. 26.

'Promoters of the grey-zone idea have opened conceptual space that they are unable to fill. By claiming that grey-zone challenges are neither fully peace nor fully war, they redefine those concepts without clarifying how they are to be understood.'

Chiara Libiseller and Lukas Milevski, War and Peace: Reaffirming the Distinction, p. 105.

Survival

GLOBAL POLITICS AND STRATEGY

Volume 63 Number 1 | February–March 2021

Contents

Cover: Lev Radin/ Pacific Press/LightRocket via Getty Images

Survival GLOBAL POLITICS AND STRATEGY

A house divided

On the cover
Rioters attempting to enter the US Capitol in Washington DC clash with police on 6 January 2021.

On the web
Visit www.iiss.org/ publications/survival for brief notices on new books on War, Conflict and the Military, Russia and Eurasia, and Asia-Pacific.

Survival editors' blog
For ideas and commentary from *Survival* editors and contributors, visit www.iiss.org/blogs/ survival-blog.

Survival
GLOBAL POLITICS AND STRATEGY

The International Institute for Strategic Studies

2121 K Street, NW | Suite 600 | Washington DC 20037 | USA
Tel +1 202 659 1490   Fax +1 202 659 1499   E-mail survival@iiss.org   Web www.iiss.org

Arundel House | 6 Temple Place | London | WC2R 2PG | UK
Tel +44 (0)20 7379 7676   Fax +44 (0)20 7836 3108   E-mail iiss@iiss.org

14th Floor, GBCorp Tower | Bahrain Financial Harbour | Manama | Kingdom of Bahrain
Tel +973 1718 1155   Fax +973 1710 0155   E-mail iiss-middleeast@iiss.org

9 Raffles Place | #49-01 Republic Plaza | Singapore 048619
Tel +65 6499 0055   Fax +65 6499 0059   E-mail iiss-asia@iiss.org

Survival Online www.tandfonline.com/survival and www.iiss.org/publications/survival

Aims and Scope *Survival* is one of the world's leading forums for analysis and debate of international and strategic affairs. Shaped by its editors to be both timely and forward thinking, the journal encourages writers to challenge conventional wisdom and bring fresh, often controversial, perspectives to bear on the strategic issues of the moment. With a diverse range of authors, *Survival* aims to be scholarly in depth while vivid, well written and policy-relevant in approach. Through commentary, analytical articles, case studies, forums, review essays, reviews and letters to the editor, the journal promotes lively, critical debate on issues of international politics and strategy.

Editor **Dana Allin**
Managing Editor **Jonathan Stevenson**
Associate Editor **Carolyn West**
Assistant Editor **Jessica Watson**
Production and Cartography **John Buck, Kelly Verity**

Contributing Editors

Ian Bremmer	**Toby Dodge**	**John L. Harper**	**Jeffrey Mazo**	**Angela Stent**
Rosa Brooks	**Bill Emmott**	**Matthew Harries**	**'Funmi Olonisakin**	**Ray Takeyh**
David P. Calleo	**Mark Fitzpatrick**	**Erik Jones**	**Teresita C. Schaffer**	**David C. Unger**
Russell Crandall	**John A. Gans, Jr**	**Hanns W. Maull**	**Steven Simon**	**Lanxin Xiang**

Published for the IISS by
Routledge Journals, an imprint of Taylor & Francis, an Informa business.

About the IISS The IISS, a registered charity with offices in Washington, London, Manama and Singapore, is the world's leading authority on political–military conflict. It is the primary independent source of accurate, objective information on international strategic issues. Publications include *The Military Balance*, an annual reference work on each nation's defence capabilities; *Strategic Survey*, an annual review of world affairs; *Survival*, a bimonthly journal on international affairs; *Strategic Comments*, an online analysis of topical issues in international affairs; and the *Adelphi* series of books on issues of international security.

SUBMISSIONS

To submit an article, authors are advised to follow these guidelines:

- *Survival* articles are around 4,000–10,000 words long including endnotes. A word count should be included with a draft.
- All text, including endnotes, should be double-spaced with wide margins.
- Any tables or artwork should be supplied in separate files, ideally not embedded in the document or linked to text around it.
- All *Survival* articles are expected to include endnote references. These should be complete and include first and last names of authors, titles of articles (even from newspapers), place of publication, publisher, exact publication dates, volume and issue number (if from a journal) and page numbers. Web sources should include complete URLs and DOIs if available.
- A summary of up to 150 words should be included with the article. The summary should state the main argument clearly and concisely, not simply say what the article is about.
- A short author's biography of one or two lines should also be included. This information will appear at the foot of the first page of the article.

Please note that *Survival* has a strict policy of listing multiple authors in alphabetical order.

Submissions should be made by email, in Microsoft Word format, to survival@iiss.org. Alternatively, hard copies may be sent to *Survival*, IISS–US, 2121 K Street NW, Suite 801, Washington, DC 20037, USA.

The editorial review process can take up to three months. *Survival*'s acceptance rate for unsolicited manuscripts is less than 20%. *Survival* does not normally provide referees' comments in the event of rejection. Authors are permitted to submit simultaneously elsewhere so long as this is consistent with the policy of the other publication and the Editors of *Survival* are informed of the dual submission.

Readers are encouraged to comment on articles from the previous issue. Letters should be concise, no longer than 750 words and relate directly to the argument or points made in the original article.

ADVERTISING AND PERMISSIONS

For advertising rates and schedules

USA/Canada: The Advertising Manager, Taylor & Francis Inc., 530 Walnut Street, Suite 850, Philadelphia, PA 19106, USA Tel +1 (800) 354 1420 Fax +1 (215) 207 0050.

UK/Europe/Rest of World: The Advertising Manager, Routledge Journals, Taylor & Francis, 4 Park Square, Milton Park, Abingdon, Oxfordshire OX14 4RN, UK Tel +44 (0) 207 017 6000 Fax +44 (0) 207 017 6336.

SUBSCRIPTIONS

Survival is published bimonthly in February, April, June, August, October and December by Routledge Journals, an imprint of Taylor & Francis, an Informa Business.

Annual Subscription 2021

	UK, RoI	US, Canada Mexico	Europe	Rest of world
Individual	£172	$290	€ 233	$290
Institution (print and online)	£620	$1,085	€ 909	$1,142
Institution (online only)	£527	$922	€ 773	$971

Taylor & Francis has a flexible approach to subscriptions, enabling us to match individual libraries' requirements. This journal is available via a traditional institutional subscription (either print with online access, or online only at a discount) or as part of our libraries, subject collections or archives. For more information on our sales packages please visit http://www. tandfonline.com/page/librarians.

All current institutional subscriptions include online access for any number of concurrent users across a local area network to the currently available backfile and articles posted online ahead of publication.

Subscriptions purchased at the personal rate are strictly for personal, non-commercial use only. The reselling of personal subscriptions is prohibited. Personal subscriptions must be purchased with a personal cheque or credit card. Proof of personal status may be requested.

Dollar rates apply to all subscribers outside Europe. Euro rates apply to all subscribers in Europe, except the UK and the Republic of Ireland where the pound sterling rate applies. If you are unsure which rate applies to you please contact Customer Services in the UK. All subscriptions are payable in advance and all rates include postage. Journals are sent by air to the USA, Canada, Mexico, India, Japan and Australasia. Subscriptions are entered on an annual basis, i.e. January to December. Payment may be made by sterling cheque, dollar cheque, euro cheque, international money order, National Giro or credit cards (Amex, Visa and Mastercard).

Survival (USPS 013095) is published bimonthly (in Feb, Apr, Jun, Aug, Oct and Dec) by Routledge Journals, Taylor & Francis, 4 Park Square, Milton Park, Abingdon, OX14 4RN, United Kingdom.

The US annual subscription price is $1,023. Airfreight and mailing in the USA by agent named WN Shipping USA, 156-15, 146th Avenue, 2nd Floor, Jamaica, NY 11434, USA. Periodicals postage paid at Jamaica NY 11431.

US Postmaster: Send address changes to Survival, C/O Air Business Ltd / 156-15 146th Avenue, Jamaica, New York, NY11434.

Subscription records are maintained at Taylor & Francis Group, 4 Park Square, Milton Park, Abingdon, OX14 4RN, United Kingdom.

ORDERING INFORMATION

Please contact your local Customer Service Department to take out a subscription to the Journal: **USA, Canada:** Taylor & Francis, Inc., 530 Walnut Street, Suite 850, Philadelphia, PA 19106, USA. Tel: +1 800 354 1420; Fax: +1 215 207 0050. **UK/Europe/Rest of World:** T&F Customer Services, Informa UK Ltd, Sheepen Place, Colchester, Essex, CO3 3LP, United Kingdom. Tel: +44 (0) 20 7017 5544; Fax: +44 (0) 20 7017 5198; Email: subscriptions@tandf.co.uk.

Back issues: Taylor & Francis retains a two-year back issue stock of journals. Older volumes are held by our official stockists: Periodicals Service Company, 351 Fairview Ave., Suite 300, Hudson, New York 12534, USA to whom all orders and enquiries should be addressed. *Tel* +1 518 537 4700 *Fax* +1 518 537 5899 *e-mail* psc@periodicals.com *web* http://www.periodicals. com/tandf.html.

The International Institute for Strategic Studies (IISS) and our publisher Taylor & Francis make every effort to ensure the accuracy of all the information (the "Content") contained in our publications. However, the IISS and our publisher Taylor & Francis, our agents, and our licensors make no representations or warranties whatsoever as to the accuracy, completeness, or suitability for any purpose of the Content. Any opinions and views expressed in this publication are the opinions and views of the authors, and are not the views of or endorsed by the IISS and our publisher Taylor & Francis. The accuracy of the Content should not be relied upon and should be independently verified with primary sources of information. The IISS and our publisher Taylor & Francis shall not be liable for any losses, actions, claims, proceedings, demands, costs, expenses, damages, and other liabilities whatsoever or howsoever caused arising directly or indirectly in connection with, in relation to or arising out of the use of the Content. Terms & Conditions of access and use can be found at http://www.tandfonline.com/page/terms-and-conditions.

The issue date is February–March 2021.

The print edition of this journal is printed on ANSI-conforming acid-free paper.

Trump's Insurrection and America's Year of Living Dangerously

Steven Simon

When Donald Trump was elected president of the United States in 2016, two books came to mind more or less spontaneously. One was British historian Norman Cohn's *The Pursuit of the Millennium*, the other Polish-American novelist Isaac Bashevis Singer's *Satan in Goray*.[1] These books are no longer widely read. The world moves on while ageing writers remain in the grip of works they encountered while young and impressionable. Cohn's book about medieval and early-modern millenarian movements in Europe was originally published in 1957, not long after the wars against German fascism and Japanese militarism had ended, and as the Cold War was peaking. Singer's book emerged in English in 1955, long before he was awarded the Nobel Prize in Literature. It had been serialised in Yiddish during the interwar years in Poland, shortly after Adolf Hitler became chancellor of neighbouring Germany. Both books explored patterns of eschatological behaviour. In each, disasters had bred messianic expectations that were destined to be disappointed. Cohn's history dwelt on Anabaptists, Flagellants, Ranters and other revolutionary movements from the Crusades through the English Civil War. Singer's allegorical novella depicted a town in late seventeenth-century rural Poland, ravaged by the pogroms of 1648, then swept away by the rise of the false Messiah, Shabtai Zvi, and

Steven Simon is a professor in the practice of international relations at Colby College and a contributing editor to *Survival*. He was US National Security Council senior director for the Middle East and North Africa from 2011 through 2012. His book *The Long Goodbye: The US and the Middle East from the Islamic Revolution to the Arab Spring* will be published this year.

Survival | vol. 63 no. 1 | February–March 2021 | pp. 7–16   https://doi.org/10.1080/00396338.2021.1881247

subsequently devastated by his conversion to Islam. It was hard not to see Trump as such a false messiah, enchanting a beleaguered population possessed of an apparently inexhaustible capacity for cognitive dissonance.

As the Trump administration enjoyed its share of successes and then as it declined during the pandemic, the messianic dimension of his presidency and its antinomian temper were harder to ignore. Academic observers pointed to the cult-like nature of his leadership and the mass hypnosis that seemed to envelop his constituents. If Cohn were still with us, he would doubtless cast the widespread conviction of Trump's supporters that he actually won the 2020 election as a typical eschatological response to cognitive dissonance, reconciling the belief in Trump's invincibility with his electoral defeat. Their readiness to risk COVID-19 infection to demonstrate their faith in the new messiah was both impressive and disgusting. Trump's contempt for rules smacked of the messianic notion that a new world could not emerge without the destruction of existing norms. Gershom Scholem, the great scholar of messianic movements, dubbed this impulse 'redemption through sin'.[2]

Grains of truth

Trump's base certainly saw existing norms as a barrier to a better world. It's not as though his constituents were completely wrong about this. Since the 1980s, they had increasingly been colonised by a self-congratulatory global elite celebrating a new ethos of capital mobility that inexorably eviscerated manufacturing in the United States. The emergence of this entitled aristocracy, as it saw itself, was linked to the reform of management theory. Corporate stewards were not morally responsible for the health of a company and the labour it employed, but answerable only to shareholders whose sole concern was the value of their stock. This revolution altered the structure of firms, which largely eliminated middle management, and transformed corporate compensation. The great compression of the post-war years gave way to a widening – and now astronomical – gap between the pay earned by senior executives and that earned by workers.

The new dispensation undermined unionisation and collective bargaining, moved entire industries offshore and generated a tax structure that displaced the country's fiscal burden onto a stagnant middle class. This left corporations and wealthy individuals even wealthier, the national income gap wider, the beneficiaries of these arrangements politically empowered and government deprived of the resources required for discretionary spending. A new ideological superstructure was devised to justify this arrangement, anchored by the not-so-new trickle-down theory, which purported to show that tax relief for the rich would generate new investment and raise employment levels. The theory was comprehensively wrong, as a parade of mainstream economists has shown. The collapse of discretionary spending, squeezed by the defence budget on one side and entitlement programmes on the other, left few resources for the development of human capital or physical infrastructure. Good jobs became a thing of the past. Social and economic advancement, especially in rural areas, was just another golden-age myth. Wages shrank and social ills multiplied, including drug abuse fuelled by callous investors in Big Pharma. Then came the crash of 2008, triggered by the investment elite, which, predictably, was bailed out by tax revenues collected not from the wealthy but rather from people who were being crushed by the avalanche.[3]

Harder truth

This was, to repeat, a plausible narrative with significant elements of truth. Things were not, however, quite that simple. Among those who descended on the US Capitol on 6 January 2021 were a woman from Texas who had flown to Washington in a private jet and a young man whose father was a Jewish judge from Brooklyn, New York.[4] As in many other revolutions, the petite bourgeoisie is leading the charge. And it is they who embodied European fascism in the last century. From a comparative standpoint, counter-terrorism scholars would be happy to talk your ears off about the leadership role played by technical professionals in al-Qaeda. Whatever it is that upended Americans' sense of cosmic justice, it wasn't just busted unions.

It seems clear, certainly in retrospect, how Trump's unlikely victory in 2016 came to be. Many would point out that he had lost the popular vote. It is true that urbanised populations were both better off than their rural counterparts and less likely to be seduced by messianic overtures. They also tend to be less religiously oriented. But the US electoral system favours rural, less populated states and does not confer victory on the winner of the popular vote. And religion matters. Evangelicals constitute a significant bloc, which maps almost entirely on to the Republican Party. Democrats' denunciation of their hypocrisy was always misconceived. From an evangelical perspective, God chooses imperfect vessels to embody His will. Trump may have paid prostitutes and bragged about grabbing women 'by the pussy', but the biblical King David, the root of Jesse and ancestor of Jesus Christ, murdered Uriah the Hittite, Bathsheba's husband, so he could freely bed her.

Trump had another thing going for him: the long and sordid history of American racism. In the aftermath of the Civil War, reunification was an urgent political and strategic necessity. Yet the war had killed hundreds of thousands on both sides. The South was largely destroyed. Union commander General Ulysses S. Grant demanded that Virginia's Shenandoah Valley be so thoroughly desolated that 'crows flying over it for the balance of the season will have to carry their provender with them'.[5] And, of course, slaves, the foundation of the Southern economy, had been freed. To facilitate reconciliation, the victors halted Reconstruction, permitted the disenfranchisement and suppression of the black population, and turned a blind eye to the propagation of a new narrative of the 'lost cause', in which Southerners were the better men, defeated in defence of a superior civilisation by a mongrelised industrial-capitalist class.[6] This post-conflict compromise worked well enough, such that the US could field national armed forces in numbers sufficient to subdue powerful enemies in two world wars. But the wounds never really healed, as regional voting patterns demonstrate. And the bargain was purchased at the cost of the country's black citizens.

Trump deployed the lost-cause narrative brilliantly, transplanting it in the fertile soil of his electoral defeat.[7] It engaged the gears of resentment and stoked anxieties spurred by the collision of an ideology of rugged individualism and the experience of personal failure. He had a lot to work with. The projected enemy was the financial elite whose aim was to replace the white population with people of colour to whom the wealth of the nation would be transferred. In the Charlottesville riot of 2017, the battle cry of the alt-right was 'Jews will not replace us'. Although Jews were the natural focus of these born-and-bred anti-Semites, their infamous claim was misdirected. There was nonetheless an elite class responsible in some measure for their misery, which made the rest of the myth all the more credible. The anger had been building for decades. *The Turner Diaries*, the 1978 novel that became required reading for counter-terrorism officials after the 1995 bombing of the Oklahoma City federal building by a so-called Christian Patriot, depicted a country in which whites were subjugated and were forced to carry out a guerrilla campaign that would spark a race war.[8] A century-old militia culture now dominated, as far as we know, by the Boogaloo Bois, the Proud Boys, the Oath Keepers, the Three Percenters and others, provides an infrastructure for insurrection. This was the movement that Trump beckoned to 'stand back and stand by' in the first presidential debate in September 2020.[9]

These groups have prioritised recruitment in the military and law enforcement. Shortly after the 6 January breach of the Capitol, the Joint Chiefs of Staff issued a message to all military personnel that they were pledged to defend the Constitution and that Joseph R. Biden would soon be their commander-in-chief – an alarming suggestion that contrary views had been brewing among those in uniform.[10] Early reports suggest that police officers at the Capitol cooperated with violent intruders.[11] And Trump, as Jonathan Stevenson has argued, had effectively used federal law-enforcement officers as his personal militia in suppressing Black Lives Matter protests in several cities.[12] Germany also faces a problem with radicalisation in the ranks, while Russia and others provide safe space for training radicals prepping for racial Armageddon.[13] Unlike Germany, weapons acquisition in the US is virtually unregulated.

Unprecedented political crisis
Following the lethal spectacle of 6 January, the United States is in uncharted political waters. A survey taken from 8–11 January indicated that 74% of Republicans credited allegations of voter fraud.[14] Another poll conducted on 11 January revealed that 70% of Republicans believed those attempting to block certification of the electoral-college ballots were 'protecting

democracy'. Some 73% believe that Trump, too, is protecting democracy. More reassuringly, most Republican respondents disapproved of the storming of the Capitol.[15]

Both Republicans and Democrats believe that democracy is under threat, but naturally differ on the source of the danger. At the extreme right of the spectrum, Senator Josh Hawley of Missouri says that man can legislate only in accord with the revealed will of Jesus Christ, who has sole dominion over creation, and that the United States is a Christian nation.[16] On this point, Hawley is analogous to Salafist Muslims, who oppose secular democracy. More moderate Republicans have come to see Trump as a liability who had served his purpose by gutting the US tax structure, dismantling regulation and channelling a vast amount of COVID-19 relief to big companies, while leaving small businesses with derisory payments. Whoever replaces Trump as the *de jure* Republican standard-bearer will have to ride the tiger he unleashed.

The Democratic Party is an unstable coalition of identitarian factions, which the Biden administration will have to satisfy. They range from a more cautious but still hungry and entitled Wall Street to progressives who harbour pent-up demands for racial, social and economic justice certain to antagonise the right just as Reconstruction mobilised white resistance so long ago. It is generally believed that the wave of Sunni radicalism that ultimately led to 9/11 was set in motion by the 1979 Islamic Revolution in Iran, which uncaged a Shia triumphalism profoundly threatening to Sunni elites in Arab states where they had held sway over Shi'ites for generations.[17] The slow progress of American minorities towards equal treatment, which progressives justifiably wish to consummate, is stirring analogous passions that will resist conciliation.

Prior to summer 2020, Trump was arguably on course to win the 2020 election by prevailing in the electoral college. Biden's win was secured by the COVID-19 deaths of 220,000 Americans, over half of the total US casualties in the Second World War. What happens now?

Typically, in a two-party system, political interactions are shaped by game theory's prisoner's dilemma. Will one of the players conclude that the gains of defection will exceed the gains of cooperation? Where cooperation is the bet over and over again, trust generally evolves, making defection ever more unlikely. Over at least the past two decades, however, Republicans have begun to calculate that the gains from cooperation are shrinking and that their better option is to defect. In recent years, these choices have become starker, such as when Republicans refused to consider Barack Obama's appointee Merrick Garland for the Supreme Court. The crisis of 6 January, spawned by contested election results, was the logical extension. Cooperation no longer served the party's purposes. In the short to medium term, the Democrats, for their part, would be foolish to cooperate. Accordingly, little can be done to restore the trust that had been built up over the preceding century. These considerations do not portend an easy way back to political balance for the American republic.

*   *   *

Two possible narratives have arisen in the wake of the 6 January invasion of the Capitol. In the first one, the fever has broken and the United States is now on a path to recovery. Republicans are looking at the carnage and doubting whether it was worth it. A new pattern of cooperation will emerge. The second, far grimmer scenario is that the country remains in a state of civil instability, on the verge of a decisive breakdown in consensual government. The unprecedented nature of the 6 January catastrophe makes predictions risky. But given the systemic factors at work, the surer bet would be on the second possibility.

The idea that Republicans, like Dorothy in *The Wizard of Oz*, have suddenly awakened from an awful dream, murmuring 'there's no place like home', is at odds with the fact that majorities of House Republicans and handfuls of Senate Republicans voted to reject the ballots of Arizona and Pennsylvania electors after the Capitol had been trampled by the mob that Trump incited, and just ten representatives subsequently voted to impeach him. Although there is reason to be sceptical about the allegedly pivotal role played by social media in this crisis and the Trump presidency more broadly – the revolutions of 1848 spread across Europe in a matter of months in a pre-digital era – the cyber sphere will continue to fuel conspiracy-driven paranoia. The tensions pulsating through society and politics will make it harder to manage the challenges of climate change and the pandemic, and to rationally allocate national resources to cope with their effects. Divisions are likely to sharpen.

In this context, the Democrats' razor-thin edge in the Senate and slim advantage in the House; the factionalisation of the Democratic Party; Republicans' cynical portrayal of debt prompted by COVID-19 as a danger posed by Democratic big-government zealots; and the possibility that Trump can continue to command his followers from his Mar-a-Lago exile cast a long shadow over the Biden presidency. These factors could prevent Biden from performing well enough to maintain Democratic control of Congress – especially given the long-standing trend in US politics whereby a new incumbent loses control of Congress in the midterm elections – or prevail in the 2024 presidential election. Republicans, as a matter of per-ceived necessity, are apt to remain committed to a strategy of minority rule. And minority rule almost inevitably devolves into violence – as indeed it did on 6 January – or at least the threat of violence.

There remains a genuine possibility that Biden, Speaker of the House Nancy Pelosi and Senate Majority Leader Chuck Schumer can enforce tight party discipline and legislate something like a Green New Deal paid for by Carter-era tax rates, a slimmer defence budget and the cooperation of cor-porate elites spooked by 6 January. Investment in education, public health, infrastructure and organised labour might give the Biden administration some traction and take the wind out of the right-wing radicals' sails. But it's far from a sure thing.

Notes

1   Norman Cohn, *The Pursuit of the Millennium: Revolutionary Millenarians and Mystical Anarchists of the Middle Ages* (London: Secker & Warburg, 1957); and Isaac Bashevis Singer, *Satan in Goray* (New York: Farrar Straus & Giroux, 1955).

2   See Gershom Scholem, 'Redemption Through Sin', in Gershom Scholem, *The Messianic Idea in Judaism and Other Essays on Jewish Spirituality*, rev. ed. (New York: Schocken, 1995).

3   See generally Thomas Piketty, *Capital in the Twenty-first Century* (Cambridge, MA: Belknap Press, 2014).

4   See Marie Fazio, 'Notable Arrests

After the Riot at the Capitol', *New York Times*, 17 January 2021 (updated), https://www.nytimes.com/2021/01/10/us/politics/capitol-arrests.html.

5   Quoted in, for example, Jed Morrison, 'Sheridan's Ride', *New York Times*, 21 October 2014, https://opinionator.blogs.nytimes.com/2014/10/21/sheridans-ride/.

6   The original articulation of the myth was Edward A. Pollard's *The Lost Cause: A New Southern History of the War of the Confederates*, first published in 1867. On its durability and erosion, see David W. Blight, *Race and Reunion: The Civil War in American Memory* (Cambridge, MA: Belknap Press, 2002). The myth is debunked in Gary W. Gallagher and Alan T. Nolan (eds), *The Myth of the Lost Cause and Civil War History* (Bloomington, IN: Indiana University Press, 2000).

7   See Karen L. Cox, 'What Trump Shares with the "Lost Cause" of the Confederacy', *New York Times*, 8 January 2021, https://www.nytimes.com/2021/01/08/opinion/trump-confederacy-lost-cause.html.

8   Andrew Macdonald, *The Turner Diaries* (Charlottesville, VA: National Vanguard Books, 1978). On 11 January 2021, Amazon removed the book from its website. See Alexandra Alter, 'How "The Turner Diaries" Incites White Supremacists', *New York Times*, 12 January 2021, https://www.nytimes.com/2021/01/12/books/turner-diaries-white-supremacists.html.

9   See, for example, Naomi Nix, 'Trump Tells Violent, Far-right Group: "Stand Back and Stand By"', Bloomberg, 30 September 2020, https://www.bloomberg.com/news/articles/2020-09-30/trump-proud-boys-debate-stand-back-stand-by.

10 See, for instance, Eric Schmitt, 'Military Chiefs Remind Troops of Their Oath After Fallout from Assault on Capitol', *New York Times*, 12 January 2021, https://www.nytimes.com/2021/01/12/us/politics/joint-chiefs-capitol-constitution.html.

11 See, for example, Peter Nickeas, Annie Grayer and Ryan Nobles, '2 Capitol Police Officers Suspended and At Least 10 More Under Investigation for Alleged Roles in Riot', CNN, 12 January 2021, https://edition.cnn.com/2021/01/11/politics/capitol-police-officers-suspended-tim-ryan/index.html.

12 Jonathan Stevenson, 'Trump's Praetorian Guard', *New York Review of Books*, 22 October 2020, https://www.nybooks.com/articles/2020/10/22/trump-law-order-praetorian-guard/.

13 See Shelby Butt and Daniel Byman, 'Right-wing Extremism: The Russian Connection', *Survival*, vol. 62, no. 2, April–May 2020, pp. 137–52; and The Soufan Center, 'White Supremacy Extremism: The Transnational Rise of the Violent White Supremacist Movement', September 2019, https://thesoufancenter.org/wp-content/uploads/2019/09/Report-by-The-Soufan-Center-White-Supremacy-Extremism-The-Transnational-Rise-of-The-Violent-White-Supremacist-Movement.pdf.

14 Vox/Data for Progress Survey, 8–11 January 2021, https://www.filesforprogress.org/datasets/2021/1/dfp_vox_election_trust.pdf.

15 'January 11, 2021 – 74% of Voters Say Democracy in the U.S. Is Under Threat, Quinnipiac University National

Poll Finds; 52% Say President Trump Should Be Removed from Office', Quinnipiac University Poll, 11 January 2021, https://poll.qu.edu/images/polling/us/us01112021_usmk38.pdf.

16 See Katherine Stewart, 'The Roots of Josh Hawley's Rage', *New York Times*, 11 January 2021, https://www.nytimes.com/2021/01/11/opinion/josh-hawley-religion-democracy.html.

17 See, for instance, Daniel L. Byman, 'The Iranian Revolution and Its Legacy of Terrorism', Brookings Institution, 24 January 2019, https://www.brookings.edu/blog/order-from-chaos/2019/01/24/the-iranian-revolution-and-its-legacy-of-terrorism/.

Forum: Can Europe Defend Itself?

Editor's Note

Throughout Donald Trump's term as the United States' president, his coolness towards the country's NATO allies and warmth towards Russian President Vladimir Putin cast increasing doubt on America's willingness to support the allies against a Russian military challenge in Europe. In April 2019, the IISS's team of defence and military analysts published a research paper arguing that European NATO allies, without US help, would be hard-pressed to repel and reverse, with conventional forces, Russia's conquest of Lithuania and part of Poland, which the team considered a plausible scenario that was representative of the threats and challenges currently facing European NATO militaries.[1] The IISS further estimated 'that European NATO members would have to invest between US$288 billion and US$357bn to fill the capability gaps generated by this scenario'.[2] In 'Europe Can Defend Itself', published in the last issue of *Survival*, Barry R. Posen argued that the IISS's scenario was unrealistically demanding because only a subsequent Russian campaign to reclaim Eastern Europe and threaten Germany would strategically justify the initial conquest hypothesised by the IISS. Employing the same analytic techniques used by the IISS, he argued that an autonomous European capability for defending against such a campaign was, in fact, 'within reach'. The editors of *Survival* invited the IISS team and three other experts to critique Professor Posen's position, and Professor Posen to respond.

Survival | vol. 63 no. 1 | February–March 2021 | pp. 17–18   https://doi.org/10.1080/00396338.2021.1881248

Notes

[1] Douglas Barrie et al., 'Defending Europe: Scenario-based Capability Requirements for NATO's European Members', IISS Research Paper, April 2019, https://www.iiss.org/blogs/research-paper/2019/05/defending-europe.

[2] *Ibid.*, p. 3.

Europe's Defence Requires Offence

Douglas Barrie, Ben Barry, Henry Boyd, Nick Childs and Bastian Giegerich

In the last issue of *Survival*, Barry Posen offered a thoughtful analysis of the ability of NATO's European members to defend themselves against a conventional Russian military attack without US support.[1] Posen, who has argued that 'NATO's founding mission has been achieved and replaced with unsuccessful misadventures', supports the view that European allies should be responsible for their own security, freeing up the US to focus on other contingencies.[2]

His *Survival* article argues that Europe is nearly ready. He contrasts his assessment with a 2019 research paper written by several members of the IISS Defence and Military Analysis Programme (DMAP) and specifically a scenario contained therein that deals with the defence of European NATO territory against a state-level military attack by Russia.[3] In this scenario, tensions between Russia and NATO members Lithuania and Poland escalate into war after the US has left NATO. This war results in the Russian occupation of Lithuania and some Polish territory seized by Russia. Invoking Article V, the European members of NATO develop plans to reassure Estonia, Latvia, Poland and other front-line NATO member states by deterring further Russian aggression. European NATO also prepares and assembles forces for a military operation to restore Polish and Lithuanian government control over their territories. The IISS assessed that European

Douglas Barrie is IISS Senior Fellow for Military Aerospace. **Ben Barry** is IISS Senior Fellow for Land Warfare. **Henry Boyd** is IISS Research Fellow for Defence and Military Analysis. **Nick Childs** is IISS Senior Fellow for Naval Forces and Maritime Security. **Bastian Giegerich** is IISS Director of Defence and Military Analysis.

Survival | vol. 63 no. 1 | February–March 2021 | pp. 19–24   https://doi.org/10.1080/00396338.2021.1881249

NATO members would have to invest between $288 billion and $357bn, spread over a number of countries and years, to fill the capability gaps generated by this scenario. These investments would establish a NATO Europe force level that would likely allow it to prevail in a limited regional war in Europe against a peer adversary, in this case Russia.

Posen contends that the IISS paper presents an unnecessarily hard test of European capabilities and is thus predisposed to find European shortfalls which – given his view of NATO and the US role in it – presumably would fuel an unwelcome argument that European dependencies on US capabilities are inevitable. Posen's article suggests that using a methodology similar to the IISS study's but allowing for 'changes in a limited number of important assumptions' paired with 'modest but analytically defensible changes in estimates of each side's available forces' leads to a different result, whereby the European members of NATO are roughly up to the task.[4] Posen argues that the question the IISS assessment asks – could NATO without the US return the situation to the status quo ante in the face of limited Russian aggression resulting in the occupation of part of NATO territory? – is the wrong one. 'What we really want to know', he says, 'is, if Europe alone were responsible for providing the military forces to stop a Russian campaign to reconquer its Soviet-era empire in Eastern Europe – and threaten the ultimate prize, which is Germany – could it do so?'[5]

Posen's article makes important and elegantly presented points about the utility of campaign analyses like the IISS's, and highlights the lack of hard information on NATO readiness. But overall, his article misses the point. He changes the question and then moves the goalposts. Naturally the result is different. But is it relevant?

The IISS team deliberately constructed a challenging scenario because we feel it is a reasonable assumption that any attacker would want to make life difficult for NATO. From our point of view, a Russian plan involving the use of military force would most likely entail seizing some territory very quickly, declaring a ceasefire and opening negotiations with NATO while posturing to deter a NATO attack and split off irresolute states among NATO members. If NATO attacked, Russia would seek to inflict a maximum number of casualties, and use its long-range strike capabilities for attacks deep in NATO homelands to weaken resolve and split the Alliance. If the NATO attack failed, it would be a political victory for Russia, and NATO would probably be finished as a military alliance. If NATO did not attack because Russia was successful in deterring it from doing so, and the violation of NATO territory went unanswered, NATO would likely be finished as well. To preclude a severely damaged or more likely dissolved NATO, NATO Europe would have to fight offensively and would need the capabilities to win.

Under Posen's alternative scenario, NATO's mission changes from an offensive one to a defensive one, and the Russian objective from dealing a fatal blow to NATO to rebuilding a Soviet empire that includes Germany. NATO would implicitly concede the loss of the Baltics as inevitable and would try to force Russia to capitulate by harassing it 'around its periphery'.[6] Why Russia would adopt such far-reaching goals, Posen does not explain. Russia's recent uses of force in Georgia (2008), Ukraine (since 2014) and Syria (since 2015) – and the decision not to intervene militarily in the Armenia–Azerbaijan war of 2020 – do not suggest overreach. The military-modernisation programme that Russia began in 2008 – and that Posen does not sufficiently address – produced a much more capable force, but one that is geared towards short and decisive campaigns relatively close to home.[7] Why would the Russian leadership do what it is not preparing for? Why should NATO expect its opponent not to play to its own strengths while allowing NATO to play to its strengths? Why should NATO cohesion be assumed to hold when some member states are effectively written off?[8] Are European forces equipped to harass Russia effectively? Posen does not address any of these key questions.

Europe would have to fight offensively

He needs his alternative scenario to produce an outcome suggesting that 'Europe can defend itself' to fit with his grand strategic position of US restraint.[9] On the terms he has defined, we agree with his overall conclusion; however, we disagree on analytical details and, more importantly, believe Posen has started in the wrong place. Posen, for his part, probably would agree with our assessment on the terms we have defined, but considers them to be the wrong terms. Posen's writing is nuanced enough to not suggest explicitly that the IISS assessment was designed to show Europe cannot defend itself and needs the protective umbrella of the US indefinitely, but he implies that the 2019 IISS paper is being used for that purpose.[10] That paper in fact acknowledged the enduring importance of the US military contribution, but also explicitly stated that the analysis should not be taken to suggest Europe is structurally unable to defend itself.[11] Some €350bn is a lot of money, of course, but at the time the 2019 paper was finalised, the gap between NATO's 2%-of-GDP spending goal and what European NATO members actually spent was about $100bn per year. (In the meantime, the COVID-19 pandemic has shrunk GDPs.) As explained in the IISS paper, it would take between ten and 20 years to fill all the capability gaps, and the investment would correspondingly be spread over a number of years. But the IISS does not suggest that European shortfalls are inevitable or cannot be fixed. As both the IISS and Posen recognise, they are the result of political choices and thus can be remedied by political choices. Leaving aside the issue of whether it is more useful to set a more demanding test or a less demanding one, there are several analytical judgements on which Posen and the IISS team disagree.

It is certainly legitimate to debate the overall level of Russian military readiness and strength. The IISS paper makes optimistic but plausible assumptions in this regard. On paper, Russian brigades are smaller than German or British ones, but larger than Polish equivalents (and those of a number of other NATO member states). Russian brigades should be expected to have fewer armoured vehicles, but will bring much more artillery and air-defence assets, which are organic to the units. A similar comparison applies to a generic Russian battalion tactical group and a generic NATO battlegroup. The latter will have more personnel and armour but less artillery. Russian divisions are roughly equivalent – on paper – to two or three average NATO brigades in terms of manpower. Posen mistakenly suggests that the IISS report claims that Russian divisions are instead much larger than this, and thus justifies his own assessed reduction in overall Russian forces. He succeeds in winding back the level of Russian capability this way, but he is off the mark. The Russian armed forces have practised swiftly mobilising for and executing complex, but limited, missions. They are not stuck in 2008, as Posen seems to think, but in fact have come a long way since then.

Posen suggests that it would be a strong move for European powers to harass Russia around its periphery in order to force concessions. Arguably, Russia's armed forces – in particular, its maritime forces – are better equipped to undertake diversionary and harassing actions than European forces are. In his scenario, Posen implies that it would be straightforward to set up a defensive umbrella over Poland.[12] But from what bases and supported by what European tanker and airborne early-warning aircraft? Posen touches on these European vulnerabilities only in passing. We further note that the large stocks of stand-off cruise missiles that could wreck the Russian effort through attrition in a way envisioned by Posen are held largely by the US, not the Europeans. Russia can outgun and out-range European land forces.

Posen, for his part, suggests that the IISS paper is too pessimistic regarding the readiness and availability of European forces. Yet

> *Russia can outgun European land forces*

there is very little open-source evidence to suggest that being optimistic about the readiness of European forces is reasonable. The readiness challenges of the German armed forces are well rehearsed and publicised. The readiness of UK land forces has diminished, such that British Army divisions can now field only half the planned combat power of that declared in the 2015 Strategic Defence and Security Review. NATO exercises have begun to test rapid mobilisation and strategic deployments, but aside from the US Army, the IISS has not observed any NATO state conducting regular armoured- or mechanised-brigade field exercises. NATO's record thus lines up poorly against Russia's focus on rapid and large-scale mobilisation in its exercise activity. We also set a force-ratio requirement high enough to ensure a good chance of success for NATO; it would seem foolish not to, given the fractured nature of political support for operations and the practical reality that no one would want to go into a fight equipped to lose.

It is interesting that Posen suggests that Russia's seizing part of the Baltics and part of Poland – as in the IISS scenario – would 'make Europeans angry', motivating them to deny Russia the option of ending the war there.[13] To us it seems more plausible that some Europeans would be angry, some might be scared and others might think fighting is not worth the trouble. Alliance cohesion has not been a NATO strong suit in recent years.

The IISS picked a scenario that would be tough for NATO Europe so that capabilities could be stress-tested. Posen has demonstrated that the outcome of this kind of campaign analysis depends on the scenario and that one that is more favourable and still feasible from NATO's point of view can be constructed. On that point, there is no disagreement.

Notes

1   Barry R. Posen, 'Europe Can Defend Itself', *Survival*, vol. 62, no. 6, December 2020–January 2021, pp. 7–34.

2   Barry R. Posen, 'Trump Aside, What's the U.S. Role in NATO?', *New York Times*, 10 March 2019, https://www.nytimes.com/2019/03/10/opinion/trump-aside-whats-the-us-role-in-nato.html.

3   Douglas Barrie et al., 'Defending Europe: Scenario-based Capability Requirements for NATO's European Members', IISS Research Paper, April 2019, https://www.iiss.org/blogs/research-paper/2019/05/defending-europe.

4   Posen, 'Europe Can Defend Itself', pp. 12, 19.

5   *Ibid.*, p. 23

6   *Ibid.*, pp. 13, 17–18.

7   IISS, *Russia's Military Modernisation: An Assessment*, IISS Strategic Dossier (Abingdon: Routledge, 2020).

8   Posen seems to think the IISS team considers the Baltics to be indefensible. The 2019 paper does not say that.

9   See Barry R. Posen, *Restraint: A New Foundation for U.S. Grand Strategy* (Ithaca, NY: Cornell University Press, 2014).

10 Posen, 'Europe Can Defend Itself', pp. 8–9.

11 IISS, *Russia's Military Modernisation*, p. 42.

12 Posen, 'Europe Can Defend Itself', p. 22.

13 *Ibid.*, p. 17.

Europe Can Afford the Cost of Autonomy

François Heisbourg

In assessing the current balance of inputs between Europe and its potential foes, there exists a risk of underestimating the shortcomings of Europe's defence capabilities. While Barry Posen is clearly correct in stating that Europe's main security problem is Russia, Europe has other possible adversaries in Africa, the Eastern Mediterranean and the Middle East. Although none of these are in Russia's league, they would factor into a major crisis with Russia. For instance, Turkey could seriously hinder Europe's ability to focus all of its assets against Russia.

State of play

It is no doubt true that Europe spends much more on its military forces than Russia. But the difference is not as substantial as suggested. Given Russia's large and competent domestic defence-industrial base and comparatively low manpower and infrastructure costs, its defence budget is best assessed in purchasing-power-parity terms, thus as up to $160 billion, as indicated in Posen's article.[1] This is much less than NATO Europe's $266bn (excluding Turkey).[2] But in short-warning/short-war scenarios, this gap may count for less than in a war of attrition, which Russia, with a GDP the size of Spain's, cannot afford.

François Heisbourg is IISS senior adviser for Europe and special adviser of the Paris-based Fondation pour la Recherche Stratégique (FRS). He is author of *Le Temps des Prédateurs: La Chine, les États-Unis, la Russie et Nous* [The Age of the Predators: China, the United States, Russia and Us] (Odile Jacob, 2020).

Survival | vol. 63 no. 1 | February–March 2021 | pp. 25–32   https://doi.org/10.1080/00396338.2021.1881250

The limits of standardisation and inter-operability also should not be underestimated. Not all studies on this score are as methodologically opaque as the one Posen cites from the European Parliament.[3] In 2013, McKinsey & Company, the international consultancy, produced a report in cooperation with the Munich Security Conference that estimated the annual cost of such inefficiencies in peacetime to be €13bn ($16bn at 2020 exchange rates), which was 30% of European defence-procurement spending at the time.[4] Their wartime impact would presumably be materially higher and would be measured in blood as well as treasure.

Finally, it is small consolation that, according to Posen, the US military machine is possibly even more inefficient at management and support than Europe's. With a defence budget of nearly $700bn, the US has the leeway to cope with poor cost efficiency: in battle, what counts is mission effectiveness. The appropriate comparison here, as in the case of standardisation, is not the one between the Europeans and the United States, but the one between Europe and Russia. Such a study would be well worth undertaking.

In sum, Europe's starting point is arguably somewhat weaker than Posen suggests, and there are grounds for the 'general pessimism' he rightly mentions.

The virtues of a hard scenario

Posen's basic objection to the IISS's scenario is that 'from the point of view of Europe's ability to defend itself, the IISS's deck is stacked'.[5] The IISS scenario is indeed extremely demanding and posits both a failed initial defence and, some months later, a successful counter-offensive to free con-quered territory. It thus goes beyond Posen's basically defensive scenario, which condemns Russia to an unwinnable war of attrition. This prospect has the supposed virtue of dissuading Russia from seizing low-hanging fruit in the Baltics.

Dissuasion of this sort, however, did not work in 1939–40. Germany, a revisionist power fully aware that it could not win a war of attrition, was not deterred from occupying Poland, subsequently trouncing the combined forces of France and Britain on the European continent in May–June 1940.[6] In April 1940, a striking propaganda poster had graced the walls of Paris, with a map displaying the globe-straddling span of the British and French democracies and their imperial possessions, surrounding a comparatively small and isolated Germany, the visual message underscored by the ringing declaration 'Nous vaincrons parce que nous sommes les plus forts' – 'We will be victorious because we are the strongest'.[7] This bravado hardly discouraged Adolf Hitler's panzers from entering Paris two months later, and it took five more years of war and misery for the sanguine French assessment, which was in fact accurate for what it was worth, to be vindicated, with considerable help from the United States and the Soviet Union. Similarly, Japan struck in December 1941 not because it thought it could win a war of attrition but because it knew it couldn't. Wars of aggression all too often begin out of a sense of actual or eventual weakness.

A convincing, rapidly deployable conventional counter-offensive capability may have greater deterrent value than a purely defensive force. For the public debate as well as decision-makers, a key virtue of the IISS scenario is that it gives a rough costing of the most demanding contingency – one in which, to upend founding NATO secretary-general Lord Ismay's purported axiom about NATO's purpose, the US is not kept in, the Russians are not kept out, and Europe including Germany, far from being kept down, shows the Russians the way back to the homeland by brute force.[8] This allows analysts to set an outer limit for measuring the cost of European strategic autonomy, at least in terms of conventional military capabilities.

Here the figures look terrible at first blush: the IISS estimates at $228–357bn the expenditures necessary to enable NATO to deal with the IISS scenario. Yet this level of expenditure is hardly beyond Europe's capacity. The suggested time frame is 20 years.[9] Front-loading part of this investment and concentrating it over a shorter period than posited by the IISS would lead to extra annual expenditure of less than $25bn, or a comparatively modest 0.15% of NATO Europe's combined GDP. Since NATO Europe spent about 1.5% of its GDP on defence in 2019, such an increase would fit with no particular difficulty into the 2%-of-GDP target NATO set itself for 2025. Sticking to that 2% objective would therefore allow Europe to ensure strategic autonomy in financial terms under even the most demanding of circumstances – at least in a conventional framework, and on the basis of pre-COVID-19 GDPs.

Enter nuclear deterrence

Russia is a nuclear superpower on a scale matched only by the United States. This doesn't mean that France and the United Kingdom are nuclear weaklings. France's arsenal alone is comparable to China's. Each European nuclear power is presumably capable of deterring threats against its own vital interests. But Russia may not readily credit French or British claims to extend deterrence along US lines to non-nuclear European allies. Such scepticism on Russia's part could negatively impact Europe's ability to prevail in high-end scenarios. Indeed, the nuclear factor is a missing link in both the IISS's and Posen's analysis.

The risk of war in Europe cannot be analysed independently of the nuclear factor. Even in Russia's shooting-free and operationally elegant seizure of the Crimea in 2014, the Kremlin imparted brutal reminders of the nuclear aspects of the unfolding crisis. Government-backed Russian television presenter Dmitry Kiselyov pointedly referenced Russia's ability to turn the United States into radioactive ash on his weekly current-affairs show early in the crisis, and Russian President Vladimir Putin subsequently emphasised the importance of nuclear deterrence on state-run media.[10] Since then, Russia's large-scale *Zapad* military exercises focused on the West have been bracketed by tests of strategic nuclear-delivery systems, notably the RS-24 *Yars* (SS-27 mod. 2) intercontinental ballistic missile.[11] Whatever the West's plans, Russia does not envision even low-key military operations in the European theatre independently of an implicit Russian nuclear threat.

Extended deterrence to counter Russian nuclear coercion would be a necessary feature of any successful attempt to dissuade or counter Russian military aggression. There has been much talk in recent years of an expansion of France's deterrent role, a development I favour. However, it could only be effective if three conditions arose. Firstly, France itself would have to be ready to expand its nuclear missions. Secondly, France's non-nuclear European allies would have to be ready to do their part to facilitate such an expansion. Thirdly, Russia would of course have to consider France's willingness to undertake such missions if commensurately provoked to be credible. The first condition is under consideration in Paris.[12] The second one is far from certain, notably with respect to Germany. Russia would presumably take seriously such an expansion of French nuclear roles if they were accompanied by an increase of French nuclear capabilities and new force dispositions – for instance, by the rotational presence of French dual-capable aircraft outside of French territory.

It goes almost without saying that such a reconfiguration would cost serious money – though substantially less than that required for high-end conventional scenarios – and call for quite difficult, even agonising, political decisions in European capitals. In any case, Europe for the time being is unlikely to be able to field the functional equivalent of the US nuclear deterrent, including in the NATO operational context, in which US B-61 nuclear weapons are currently based in Belgium, Germany, Italy and the Netherlands, and nuclear missions currently involve most NATO European air forces either directly or in conventional support roles.

Defence spending in the age of COVID-19

The COVID-19 pandemic has unleashed an unprecedented torrent of public spending in order to mitigate and eventually reverse the so-called corona depression. France's 10% increase in public expenditures in 2020 is not untypical among industrialised countries. Much of the money has been earmarked for capital investment, notably as part of the €750bn European recovery plan or the EU's seven-year (2021–27) budget. In France and the UK, NATO Europe's two most militarily powerful countries, defence spending is set to benefit from this trend. The UK has announced an additional £16.5bn in defence spending over the next four years, while France has recently decided on a 4.5% (€1.7bn) increase in 2021.[13] Posen is on the mark in anticipating a shift of skilled labour from the hard-hit civilian aerospace sector to the defence-industrial base.

In addition, the geo-economic impetus to reshore Chinese-based value chains will favour dual-capable technological investment in Europe and the United States. In parallel, the Committee on Foreign Investment in the United States and related bodies will discourage China's acquisition and expatriation of critical technologies, and European countries are now establishing their own restrictions on sensitive technologies. In combination, these trends stand to narrow the big European gaps in maintenance and

readiness while broadening the innovation base of Europe's defence industry. Although the pandemic-related spending boom will eventually taper
off, the immediate effect may buoy rather than depress defence spending.

The ratcheting back of the EU's European Defence Fund from an initially planned €13.3bn to less than €7bn over the 2021–27 period has been
rightly deplored. The same may be said of the EU's Action Plan on Military
Mobility, to which less than €1.7bn has been allocated. But truth be told, prior
to the pandemic the EU was only beginning to create new funding streams
in light of national budgets. The new pot of European money will largely
be used to implement force standardisation through the European Defence
Fund, while the mobility plan, by optimising the regulatory scheme and the
defence infrastructure, will ease the rapid and timely movement of forces
from one end of the European continent to the other – a capability without
which neither the IISS nor the Posen scenario could be implemented in a
time-urgent manner. With these new facilities, the EU as such can add substantial value to NATO and European defence, even if increases in national
defence budgets remain critical.

Strategic autonomy, however it is funded, is not unaffordable, whether
the ultimate frame of reference is the IISS scenario or the Posen option.
European efforts should and can materially enhance both transatlantic and
European defence, whether NATO is the prime mover or European allies
and partners operate, politically and strategically, under their own steam.

Notes

1   Barry R. Posen, 'Europe Can Defend
     Itself', *Survival*, vol. 62, no. 6, December
     2020–January 2021, p. 26, note 9.
2   Derived from 2019 estimates in
     International Institute for Strategic
     Studies (IISS), *The Military Balance*
     (Abingdon: Routledge, 2020).
3   Posen, 'Europe Can Defend Itself', p. 10.
4   McKinsey & Company, 'The Future
     of European Defence: Tackling
     the Productivity Challenge', 2013,
     https://www.mckinsey.com/~/media/

     mckinsey/industries/public%20
     and%20social%20sector/our%20
     insights/enlisting%20productivity%20
     to%20reinforce%20european%20
     defense/the%20future%20of%20
     european%20defence.pdf.
5   Posen, 'Europe Can Defend Itself', p. 23.
6   On the state of the German economy
     on the eve of the Second World War
     and the Third Reich's awareness of
     its economic limitations, see Adam
     Tooze, *The Wages of Destruction:*

The Making and Breaking of the Nazi Economy (London: Allen Lane, 2006).

[7] The line is from a speech by Paul Reynaud broadcast on the radio on 10 September 1939, when he was France's minister of finance. The poster was printed after he became prime minister in March 1940. An image of the poster is accessible at Google Arts and Culture, https://artsandculture. google.com/culturalinstitute/ beta/asset/nous-vaincrons-parce-que-nous-sommes-les-plus-forts-souscrivez-aux-bons-d-armement/ sAHoaiqIiDxTzw.

[8] The remark widely but not reliably attributed to Lord Ismay is that the purpose of NATO is 'to keep the Russians out, the Americans in, and the Germans down'. See, for example, Geoffrey Wheatcroft, 'Who Needs NATO?', *New York Times*, 15 June 2011, https://www.nytimes.com/2011/06/16/ opinion/16iht-edwheatcroft16.html.

[9] Douglas Barrie et al., 'Defending Europe: Scenario-based Capability Requirements for NATO's European Members', IISS Research Paper, April 2019, https://www.iiss.org/ blogs/research-paper/2019/05/ defending-europe.

[10] On Kiselyov's extraordinary statement, see Lidia Kelly, 'Russia Can Turn U.S. to Radioactive Ash: Kremlin-backed Journalist', Reuters, 16 March 2014, https://uk.reuters.com/article/ us-ukraine-crisis-russia-kiselyov/

russia-can-turn-u-s-to-radioactive-ash-kremlin-backed-journalist-idUS-BREA2F0XF20140316. On Putin's messaging, see Laura Smith-Spark, Alla Eshchenko and Emma Burrows, 'Russia Was Ready to Put Nuclear Forces on Alert Over Crimea, Putin Says', CNN, 16 March 2015, https://edition.cnn. com/2015/03/16/europe/russia-putin-crimea-nuclear/index.html.

[11] See Bruno Tertrais, 'Does Russia Really Include Limited Nuclear Strikes in Its Large-scale Military Exercises?', Survival Editors' Blog, IISS, 15 February 2018, https://www. iiss.org/blogs/survival-blog/2018/02/ russia-nuclear.

[12] See Élysée, 'Speech of the President of the Republic on the Defense and Deterrence Strategy', 7 February 2020, https://www.elysee.fr/en/ emmanuel-macron/2020/02/07/speech-of-the-president-of-the-republic-on-the-defense-and-deterrence-strategy.

[13] See Peter Roberts, 'Britain's Defences: The Biggest Spending Boost Since the Cold War', RUSI, 19 November 2020, https://rusi.org/commentary/ britain-defences-biggest-spending-boost-cold-war; and Ministère des Armées, 'Projet de loi de finances 2021: engagements tenus pour le budget de la défense', 29 September 2020, https://www.defense.gouv.fr/ actualites/articles/projet-de-loi-de-finances-2021-engagements-tenus-pour-le-budget-de-la-defense.

Europe Cannot Defend Itself: The Challenge of Pooling Military Power

Stephen G. Brooks and Hugo Meijer

Detailed examinations of Europe's autonomous defence capacity have great value for addressing a series of policy questions on European security as well as for advancing the ongoing scholarly debate over US grand strategy. The existing literature features a wide range of articles on what European 'strategic autonomy' is or should be, but there has been a dearth of research on what specifically is required for Europe to autonomously defend itself in a potential conflict with Russia.

Accordingly, Barry Posen's article 'Europe Can Defend Itself' is a crucial contribution.[1] The piece critically evaluates a path-breaking 2019 campaign analysis by the International Institute for Strategic Studies (IISS).[2] The IISS study concluded that Europe would lack the autonomous capacity to effectively respond to a hypothetical Russian conquest of Lithuania and parts of northwest Poland if the United States pulled out of NATO. Posen disagrees, arguing that it would be more sensible for Europe to adopt a defensive strategy rather than seeking to quickly regain the lost territory.

We agree with Posen's assessment that Europe would need significantly fewer forces if it were to adopt a defensive strategy in this scenario. We see his article as having great value moving forward, since the cost and benefits of a defensive European military strategy should now be seriously debated.

Stephen G. Brooks is a professor of government at Dartmouth College and author of four books, including *America Abroad: The United States' Global Role in the 21st Century* (Oxford University Press, 2016). **Hugo Meijer** is CNRS Research Fellow at Sciences Po's Center for International Studies (CERI) and Founding Director of The European Initiative for Security Studies (EISS). He co-edited (with Marco Wyss) *The Handbook of European Defence Policies and Armed Forces* (Oxford University Press, 2018).

Survival | vol. 63 no. 1 | February–March 2021 | pp. 33–40   https://doi.org/10.1080/00396338.2021.1881251

However, we concur with the top-line finding of the IISS report and see no empirical basis for accepting Posen's conclusion that 'as far as conventional defence is concerned, European defence autonomy is not an unachievable and unaffordable goal. Indeed, it is within reach.'[3] Posen does not specify what time frame he has in mind for Europe's achieving defence autonomy, but other writings of his suggest that he thinks it would probably be a matter of just a few years.[4] In our assessment, it is inconceivable that Europe could achieve defence autonomy so soon, or even within a decade.

There are many reasons for our scepticism, including persistently diverging threat perceptions and strategic priorities across Europe, as well as severe military capacity shortfalls that will take a long time to close.[5] Here, we will focus on just one specific issue: Europe's inability to pool and effectively employ military power.

The lack of European integrated command structures

Europe is not a single country, which substantially curtails its capacity to orchestrate its own defence. As a 2018 European Parliament report notes, 'it is precisely because European defence is fragmented by the decisions of 27 political and military chiefs of staff, duplicates the same research, the same programs and the same capabilities and has no chain of command that it is, collectively, inefficient'.[6] Posen does briefly address and reject two arguments for why Europe might 'get less for its total defence spending than would a single country'.[7] But he is just scratching the surface regarding why Europe's defence whole is less than the sum of its parts. If we recognise a more complete set of reasons why European countries cannot pool and effectively employ military power, Posen's conclusion that Europe is primed for defence autonomy crumbles.

For one thing, as Posen notes, the IISS study assumes the NATO command structure 'has passed intact to the Alliance (less the US complement) and is available to coordinate the operation. The authors rightly observe that without this assumption, the Europeans would have a difficult time managing a large operation, as the "shadow" structures maintained by the EU probably are not sufficiently developed to run a large operation.'[8] While Posen rigorously challenges a large range of assumptions of the IISS study, he leaves this particular assumption untouched and incorporates it into his analysis.

But how likely is it that Europeans can effectively use NATO's command structure if the US leaves? Even if all European countries were highly like-minded, attaining sustained cooperation among so many states through a unified command structure would be extremely difficult once America's leadership within NATO were removed. Yet Europeans are not highly like-minded: the European security-studies literature has demonstrated that Europe's capacity to either create or maintain an integrated military structure has been, and will continue to be, constrained by diverging interests, organisational cultures and strategic priorities.[9]

Recognising the significant constraints on the useability of a European command structure is critically important, especially given that Russia is a unitary actor. A 2019 report of the French Senate stresses that 'compared to other European countries, Russia enjoys a considerable but not quantifiable advantage: unity of command. The Russian army has one commanding authority, one hierarchy, one language, and one equipment range. Obviously, on the operational level, these are very important assets.'[10]

Europe's wanting C4ISR

An additional consideration is command, control, communications, computers, intelligence, surveillance and reconnaissance (C4ISR). The modern battlefield is vastly different than it was in past eras, and C4ISR – often referred to as the 'nervous system' of modern militaries – is essential for gathering information and for processing, disseminating and using it to formulate and implement complex plans.[11]

Europe's development of the independent C4ISR capacity required to be able to autonomously defend against Russia would face major, long-term challenges. For one thing, Europeans would need large amounts of new C4ISR systems (including reconnaissance and communication satellites; early-warning and control aircraft; sensor systems; and air, naval and land command-and-control platforms), the most complex of which take an extremely long time to develop. Europeans would not, of course, need to duplicate America's entire C4ISR architecture, which has been designed to project and protect massive military force throughout the world. But NATO's 2011 military involvement in Libya showed how heavily reliant Europeans were on America's C4ISR capacity in the areas of intelligence collection and analysis, target acquisition and reconnaissance, among others. This experience demonstrates that they would need far better C4ISR systems than they have now to take on Russia, which is no Libya.

Additionally, Europeans would need to assemble military personnel who could effectively use these C4ISR systems in conjunction with their military forces. A recent study has shown that the employment of C4ISR systems calls for highly skilled and highly trained military personnel that are difficult to recruit and retain.[12] Many European militaries, though relatively small, have in recent years strained to recruit sufficient personnel, especially for skilled positions.[13]

Even given enough recruits with the right capacity, training them would be a daunting task. Gaining the skill to effectively use weapons systems in a coordinated manner is complex and taxing. It has taken US military personnel an extraordinarily long time to develop the requisite abilities. As Posen himself emphasised in a 2003 article, America's 'development of new weapons and tactics depends on decades of expensively accumulated technological and tactical experience'.[14] European militaries would be hard-pressed to develop the needed collective skills due to differences in operational culture, level of ambition and language.[15]

Russia's edge in employing military power

Beyond the fact that Russia, as a single country, is not plagued by the coordination challenges that hamper the ability of a group of countries to build an integrated command structure and to sustain the development and deployment of a C4ISR capacity, its history is significant. Russia is the descendent state of the Soviet Union, which created a formidable military-industrial base with a huge cadre of highly trained personnel; this provided a strong foundation for Moscow's current military infrastructure. Russia substantially modernised and expanded its forces in the 2010s and now has a robust capacity for managing complex military operations. A comprehensive 2019 RAND Corporation report concluded that the Kremlin has 'a

Figure 1: **Military satellites**

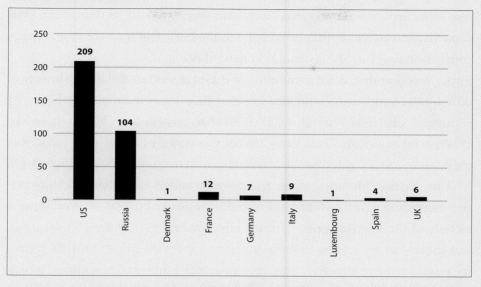

Source: Union of Concerned Scientists, UCS Satellite Database, available at https://www.ucsusa.org/resources/satellite-database. The data shows the combined total of Low Earth Orbit (LEO), Medium Earth Orbit (MEO), Geosynchronous Earth Orbit (GEO) and Elliptical Orbit (EO) military satellites.

modern, whole-of-government C4ISR infrastructure that will enable Russia to pursue its vision of net-centric or "non-contact warfare"' and that these 'advances in long-range strike, Russia's command and control and information gathering systems are fundamental in their ability to compete directly with the West and dominate regional adversaries'.[16] Other studies have offered similar assessments of Russia's C4ISR capacity.[17]

Military satellites are a key indicator of how far ahead Russia is compared to Europe in terms of C4ISR infrastructure. The gap in military satellites is shown in Figure 1. Any European effort to move beyond the continent's current base of 40 satellites and deploy the level needed to effectively counter Russia would take an extremely long time to mount given that the development lead time for military satellites is around 20 years.[18]

* * *

There are many reasons for pessimism regarding Europe's prospects for defence autonomy. In this article, we have highlighted one particular challenge: Europe's inability to pool and effectively employ military power due to its lack of an integrated command structure and its deficient C4ISR capacity. In our view, this provides a sufficient basis for rejecting Posen's conclusion that Europe is primed to defend itself.

As noted above, a large number of existing studies detail the immense difficulties Europeans would face in either creating or maintaining their own command structure. This situation could change, of course. But analysts like Posen who maintain Europeans are on the verge of being able to defend themselves are obligated to show how they can overcome these difficulties.

The existing literature does not provide sufficiently detailed information regarding exactly what kind of C4ISR capacity Europeans would need to defend themselves, or how much effort would be required to secure it. But there is every reason to think that developing a sufficient C4ISR capacity would require a truly formidable amount of time and resources, which would be possible only if there were very extensive and sustained political coordination and defence-industrial cooperation. These have consistently proven elusive within Europe. Those contending that Europeans can defend themselves must delineate what C4ISR systems Europe specifically requires and show that developing them, as well as finding and training the personnel to use them, is actually 'within reach'.

Acknowledgements

For their helpful comments, we thank Julien Demotes-Mainard, Andrea Gilli, Mauro Gilli, Alexander Lanoszka, Luis Simón and Katarzyna Zysk.

Notes

1 Barry R. Posen, 'Europe Can Defend Itself', *Survival*, vol. 62, no. 6, December 2020–January 2021, pp. 7–34.

2 Douglas Barrie et al., 'Defending Europe: Scenario-based Capability Requirements for NATO's European Members', IISS Research Paper, April 2019, https://www.iiss.org/blogs/research-paper/2019/05/defending-europe.

3 Posen, 'Europe Can Defend Itself', p. 24.

4 Barry Posen, 'From Unipolarity to Multipolarity: Transition in Sight?', in G. John Ikenberry, Michael Mastanduno and William C. Wohlforth (eds), *International Relations Theory and the Consequences of Unipolarity* (Cambridge: Cambridge University Press, 2011), esp. p. 323.

5   We have written a separate article, soon to be published, which outlines all these considerations in detail. See Hugo Meijer and Stephen Brooks, 'Illusions of Autonomy: Why Europe Cannot Provide for Its Own Security Even if the US Pulls Back', *International Security*, forthcoming in 2021. We draw here on two small sections of this article.

6   European Parliament, Directorate General for External Policies, Policy Department, 'EU Defence: The White Book Implementation Process', December 2018, pp. 58–9, https://www.europarl.europa.eu/RegData/etudes/STUD/2018/603871/EXPO_STU(2018)603871_EN.pdf.

7   Posen, 'Europe Can Defend Itself', p. 9.

8   *Ibid.*, p. 14.

9   See, for example, Jolyon Howorth, *Security and Defence Policy in the European Union* (Basingstoke: Palgrave Macmillan, 2014), pp. 96–7; and Luis Simón, 'Neorealism, Security Cooperation, and Europe's Relative Gains Dilemma', *Security Studies*, vol. 26, no. 2, April 2017, pp. 197–211.

10   Sénat de France, 'European Defence: The Challenge of Strategic Autonomy', Information Report no. 626, 3 July 2019, p. 33, http://www.senat.fr/rap/r18-626-2/r18-626-2_mono.html.

11   See, for example, Frans Osinga, 'The Rise of Military Transformation', in Terry Terriff, Frans Osinga and Theo Farrell (eds), *A Transformation Gap? American Innovations and European Military Change* (Stanford, CA: Stanford University Press, 2010), pp. 14–34.

12   Andrea Asoni et al., 'A Mercenary Army of the Poor? Technological Change and the Demographic Composition of the Post-9/11 US Military', *Journal of Strategic Studies*, January 2020.

13   See, for example, UK National Audit Office, Comptroller and Auditor General, 'Ministry of Defence: Ensuring Sufficient Skilled Military Personnel', 18 April 2018, pp. 18–25, https://www.nao.org.uk/wp-content/uploads/2018/04/Ensuring-sufficient-skilled-military-personnel.pdf.

14   Barry Posen, 'Command of the Commons: The Military Foundation of US Hegemony', *International Security*, vol. 28, no. 1, Summer 2003, p. 10.

15   See, for example, Sylvain Paile, 'The European Military Higher Education Stocktaking Report', European Security and Defence College, May 2010, http://www.emilyo.eu/sites/default/files/Gell%20Scientific%20Publications/2010%20Paile%20Stocktaking%20Report_0.pdf.

16   Andrew Radin et al., *The Future of the Russian Military: Russia's Ground Combat Capabilities and Implications for U.S.–Russia Competition* (Washington DC: RAND Corporation, 2019), pp. 47, 54, https://www.rand.org/content/dam/rand/pubs/research_reports/RR3000/RR3099/RAND_RR3099.pdf.

17   See, for example, Roger N. McDermott, 'Russia's Electronic Warfare Capabilities to 2025: Challenging NATO in the Electromagnetic Spectrum', International Centre for Defence and Security, September 2017, pp. 3, 28, https://icds.ee/wp-content/uploads/2018/ICDS_Report_Russias_Electronic_Warfare_to_2025.pdf.

18   See Innovation Finance Advisory, 'The Future of the European Space Sector: How to Leverage Europe's

Technological Leadership and Boost Investments for Space Ventures', Report for the European Commission, 2019, p. 87, https://www.eib.org/attachments/thematic/future_of_european_space_sector_en.pdf.

In Reply: To Repeat, Europe Can Defend Itself

Barry R. Posen

The European members of NATO and the United States are at a fateful moment, when each must reconsider the resilience of the transatlantic security bargain. The US faces significant economic, social and global geo-strategic challenges that will require it to set rigorous strategic priorities, or risk failure as resources are spread too widely and thinly. Europe, in the aftermath of COVID-19 and Brexit, and facing an energetic and intrusive China, an obstreperous Russia and a restless North African littoral, also confronts serious challenges. Europeans, in particular, should be asking themselves whether the extent of their reliance on the US is prudent. And Americans should be asking themselves whether the acceptance of primary responsibility for European security is the most effective use of what will be increasingly scarce resources.

To these ends, I commend the IISS study 'Defending Europe' for opening the discussion of the adequacy of European forces for a self-reliant security strategy, especially in the realm of expensive conventional military forces. Could Europe go it alone? This is a complicated matter, and as noted in the article of mine under discussion, the IISS analysis asks only a basic question: could Europe give Russia a run for its money in a very demanding counter-offensive contingency that they argue is central to European security? Their answer was 'no'. If not, then what would it take to do so? Their answer was

Barry R. Posen is the Ford International Professor of Political Science in the Security Studies Program at the Massachusetts Institute of Technology. He is the author of numerous articles and three books, including *Restraint: A New Foundation for US Grand Strategy* (Cornell University Press, 2014).

Survival | vol. 63 no. 1 | February–March 2021 | pp. 41–49   https://doi.org/10.1080/00396338.2021.1881252

'a lot'. I argued that using the team's analytic techniques and assumptions, but a different, and I believe more strategically representative, defensive scenario, Europe could indeed give Russia a run for its money.

Before proceeding further, I will state clearly what careful readers of *Survival* will already have discerned: none of the three responses to my argument challenge its analytically derived conclusions.[1] This is not to say that we can be sure that NATO Europe would be successful in a defensive scenario. And it is not to contend that European forces require no repairs. I argued simply that Europeans have the force structure – brigades and fighter squadrons – to defend themselves, using the IISS team's own standards. The European members of NATO could impose a long attrition war on Russia, in which Europe could mobilise its superior resources: over three times the population and five to ten times the economic output of Russia. What arguments, then, do these three pessimistic critiques offer?[2]

Three arguments are marshalled mainly to defend the apparently entrenched consensus that Europe is doomed to dependency on the US. Firstly, Europeans are natural appeasers; at the first sign of trouble, a NATO shorn of the US will collapse like a house of cards. Secondly, without US leadership and command-and-control hardware, the Europeans would be incapable of managing allied forces for a war with Russia. Thirdly, Europe's substantial advantages in money and personnel and its greatly superior economy and population don't matter. A fourth consideration is outside the scope of a discussion of conventional forces, but as François Heisbourg notes, it would be central to European autonomy: how will nuclear deterrence be managed?

The IISS team: bandwagoning versus balancing

The IISS team says that, should the European alliance lose control of one or more states in the east and not be able promptly to restore the situation, the alliance would collapse. Thus, a massive infusion of offensive armoured striking power into the present order of battle is required – at least 32 additional armoured brigades, or roughly the equivalent to the late Cold War German Army but fully modernised.[3] The picture the IISS analysts paint is both dark and strange. If one or more Baltic states were to fall to Russian aggression, other Eastern European countries whose citizens know what it is like to live under the Russian boot, and who clamoured for NATO and European Union membership, would quickly abandon their sole protector. The larger European states such as Germany, which in particular benefits greatly from not having Russian troops on its immediate border, would instead stand down, allowing Russia to dominate Eastern Europe again. Other European states further afield would simply shrug, ignoring the stark evidence of Russia's aggressive intent.

Students of international politics have a term for this feared cascade of falling political dominoes: bandwagoning with the aggressor. The phenomenon is not unknown, but it is uncommon. If bandwagoning were the rule, Europeans would all speak French or German or Russian, as at least one of these aspiring European hegemons would have succeeded in its day. Far more common is balancing against the aggressor – that is, joining with other threatened states to build a coalition of resistance against aspiring hegemons.[4] States value their sovereignty and those that can will often fight for it. Even small and isolated states often balance if they think there is a chance of success. Europeans today do prefer passing the buck to the US to get their protection on the cheap. But absent that option, balancing is likely. The existence of an up-and-running European military coalition makes balancing a reasonable option. One cannot rule out the possible political collapse on which the IISS team built its military scenario and force requirements. But, if this is their considered and expert assessment of the actual commitment of Europeans to defend their independence and liberties, US supporters of the transatlantic relationship should sombrely take note. In the eyes of the IISS team, the European allies are, per Thomas Paine, summer soldiers and sunshine patriots.

Brooks and Meijer: alliance management and C4ISR

It is not news that military coalitions face management problems. Stephen Brooks and Hugo Meijer believe that a European alliance unaided by the US would face insurmountable difficulties, and Heisbourg seems to agree. Military coalitions work for four main reasons: shared interest, discussed above; a unified command structure; the experience and habits of cooperation; and the sufficiency of a command, control, communications, computers, intelligence, surveillance and reconnaissance (C4ISR) infrastructure for the type of war that the coalition plans to fight. Although shortfalls and obstacles surely exist in these areas, the European alliance would be well placed to address them.

Both the IISS team's scenario and my own posit that the European alliance would inherit NATO's existing command structure, though without American officers or US military equipment.[5] Brooks and Meijer seem to assume that a US departure would produce the dissolution of the entire extant command structure, and that the Europeans would have to start from scratch. Why they assume this is unstated. In any case, their fight, as they admit, is with the IISS team as much as it is with me, as our analyses share this assumption, though the defensive scenario I advance is likely less demanding on the C4ISR front than the rapid counter-offensive that the IISS team deems essential.

Europeans have also been working together as allies for 70 years. The habits of cooperation, knowledge of one another's strengths and weaknesses, skills needed to surmount language barriers, and deeper knowledge of one another's military commanders have been laboriously developed. And there has been a sustained, if constantly challenging, effort to produce common doctrine and standard procedures.[6]

In addition, Brooks and Meijer intimate that the Europeans lack the autonomous C4ISR capability to run a war. The 'military satellite' ledger they offer is somehow meant to convey the parlous state of Europe relative to Russia. But it tells us nothing especially useful, because what we would like to know is what each side needs to address its particular military problems. Overall, Russia has much more challenging C4ISR problems than Europe, partly because its nuclear deterrent, especially its land-based intercontinental-ballistic-missile force, lives in the gunsights of the US military, which is postured to try to eliminate them in the event of a nuclear war. The Russian military also has to cover a vast landmass. In any case, the IISS's *Military Balance 2020*, and Brooks and Meijer's own source, the Union of Concerned Scientists, tell a more nuanced story than the summary table. Europeans have invested in autonomous capability. According to the IISS, the European states deploy nearly as many intelligence-gathering satellites as Russia.[7] Furthermore, the authors include in the Russian count the GLONASS navigation satellites but oddly exclude from the European count the *Galileo* constellation of two dozen navigation satellites in commission.[8] Russia does have many more military-communications satellites than Europe, but one suspects that its very different strategic situation is the explanation.

Heisbourg: relative inputs and nuclear deterrence

It is hard to know what to make of Heisbourg's ironically mistitled contribution, 'Europe Can Afford the Cost of Autonomy'. After his confirmatory review of the usual factors that make Europe particularly inefficient, one wonders what resources Europe would need to muster to defend itself. Europe already outmatches Russia in key military inputs, including spending and personnel. Sceptics about Europe's potential for military autonomy obscure or explain away these facts. In addition to the standard arguments, Heisbourg embraces the newly popular admonition that we must compare defence inputs on the basis of purchasing power parity, not exchange rates, bringing European NATO's favourable spending advantage down from roughly 4:1 to 1.7:1, or $266 billion for Europe to $160bn for Russia.[9] Even if we accept this adjustment, a major gap favouring Europe remains. Europe would need to be wildly inefficient to turn this into a net deficiency so grave that it would, in the apparent view of the IISS team and Brooks and Meijer, take 20 years of significantly increased military spending to rectify. Heisbourg concludes that 'Europe's starting point is arguably somewhat weaker' than I suggest, and on account of this he shares the 'general pessimism' that I observe in the other commentators. He may be as pessimistic as he wishes, but not on the basis of inferior inputs.

Insofar as my article is titled 'Europe Can Defend Itself', Heisbourg is free to introduce the subject of nuclear deterrence. At the same time, I stated clearly that I would not discuss the issue even though it does indeed require serious discussion. My only reference to nuclear weapons was the comment that France and Britain are both nuclear-weapons states, and that Russia would need to take this into account in a decision to launch a war, and in its strategy for the conduct of war. Does 'existential extended deterrence' exist in an alliance that includes nuclear and non-nuclear states? What would it deter? Would the members of such a coalition need to take any special steps to make extended deterrence more credible? These are all questions of judgement, which can be informed by theory and experience, but there are no clear and comfortable answers. The extended-nuclear-deterrence relationship between the US and Europe has itself always been a fraught proposition.

Looking beyond my original article, I venture two observations. Firstly, Europeans would be unwise to attempt to revive the original US–NATO strategy of substituting the threat of nuclear escalation for resilient conventional forces. Under US pressure, the Alliance gradually abandoned this strategy between 1960 and 1975, and built up its power of conventional resistance. Once the Soviet Union developed the credible ability to strike the US mainland under most conditions, nuclear first use began to look less attractive to the United States. When the guarantor is vulnerable, it is difficult to make believable the commitment to fire first on another's behalf.

Furthermore, as Heisbourg correctly argues, Europeans have to consider how they can make extended deterrence credible. This has a diplomatic component and a military one. Europeans should stress that nuclear attacks by aggressor states deserve nuclear responses. If the United Kingdom and France remain the sole nuclear-weapons states in the European alliance, their nuclear diplomacy must regularly communicate why such a response, however risky, could still be in their interests. Observable military measures may also be necessary. Heisbourg offers several creative ideas. The most obvious measures are those employed today involving NATO's 'tactical nuclear weapons', which are owned by the US but often slung under European aircraft. A turn of the US 'key' turns the ally into a new nuclear power, and Russia can never know the conditions under which this would occur, which adds considerable uncertainty to any decision for war. France, the UK or both could consider using similar 'dual key' arrangements with some of their European partners.[10]

*   *   *

The IISS study did a service by moving the public discussion of the military aspects of European security beyond the Baltic-defence contingency. But the Baltic counter-offensive scenario is unrepresentative of the contributions that extant European forces and Europe's superior mobilisation base could make to deterring a Russian challenge and defending against that challenge. I offered a different way of looking at the problem, one that more completely reflects Europe's strengths and takes better account of political and strategic realities. I did not and do not minimise Europe's present shortcomings, though I am frustrated by the lack of high-resolution data about them and ongoing or planned efforts to find remedies.[11] In particular, addressing obvious readiness deficiencies should take priority in new European defence spending.

Finally, several authors chose to remind *Survival* readers that I advocate a more restrained grand strategy for the US, and thus a more autonomous security posture for Europe. Since I doubt regular *Survival* readers needed any such warning, this point presumably was meant to engender scepticism in any uninitiated reader who might have stumbled across 'Europe Can Defend Itself'. But an alternative strategic standpoint does seem to be a prerequisite for probing the conventional wisdom on European military weakness. The time is ripe to do so, because it should be obvious to Europeans that strategic dependence on the US is not as safe a refuge as it once appeared, and to Americans that US resources are not inexhaustible.

Acknowledgements

Thanks to Jolyon Howorth and Joshua Shifrinson for their helpful comments.

Notes

1   The IISS team's response instead reiterates the existence of European readiness issues, which I also discussed. See Barry R. Posen, 'Europe Can Defend Itself', *Survival*, vol. 62, no. 6, December 2020–January 2021, p. 8. And indeed, I used their readiness assumptions in my analysis. I suggested three different reasons that Europe's ability to defend could be up to the task. Firstly, only marginal improvements in the readiness of extant European units are needed to produce an acceptable force ratio. Secondly, Russia would likely experience problems in mobilising and

sustaining an 18-brigade force in offensive operations that would somewhat diminish the plausible size of the attacking force. Thirdly, meaningful numbers of extant European infantry units could and would be added to Europe's order of battle in a defensive scenario. Any or all of these adjustments leave Europe well placed to defend itself by the IISS team's own force-ratio criteria. See Posen, 'Europe Can Defend Itself', p. 21, Table 3.

2   In the interest of brevity, I address only the major arguments of the three critiques. Readers should not infer that I agree with points left undiscussed.

3   The IISS team is sanguine about the affordability of this effort, noting that the capital costs, at least of the major items of combat equipment, though high, could be easily accommodated if NATO countries spent 2% of GDP on defence. They shouldn't be. The additional forces they propose would be very expensive to own and operate. If the US Army were trying to add an armoured brigade, it would typically need an additional 17,000 personnel within the unit itself and in related supporting units. The operation and support costs would come to $2.8bn per year. We do not have corresponding estimates for European forces, but for developed societies, the costs of fielding high-technology forces with professional soldiers are presumably similar. If so, the 32 additional brigades needed to bring European forces up to the 1.5:1 force ratio could require almost 600,000 personnel, and $90bn annually to operate. I doubt that the European personnel and financial

costs would be quite this high, but they would nonetheless be substantial. See Congressional Budget Office, 'Interactive Force Structure Tool', last updated 15 August 2018, https://www.cbo.gov/publication/54351#info. The IISS team chose not to address this fundamental question. See Douglas Barrie et al., 'Defending Europe: Scenario-based Capability Requirements for NATO's European Members', IISS Research Paper, April 2019, endnote 32, https://www.iiss.org/blogs/research-paper/2019/05/defending-europe.

4   See Stephen M. Walt, *The Origins of Alliances* (Ithaca, NY: Cornell University Press, 1987), pp. 17–33. Though he argues that balancing is much more common than bandwagoning, Walt is sceptical, on deductive grounds, that weak states balance. For the view that weak states do balance, see Eric J. Labs, 'Do Weak States Bandwagon?', *Security Studies*, vol. 1, no. 3, 1992, pp. 383–416. John Mearsheimer argues that threatened states choose from two major strategies, buck-passing and balancing. In the former, they find someone else to counter an aggressor. Europeans prefer that the US be that someone else. In the absence of a buck catcher, states generally balance. John J. Mearsheimer, *The Tragedy of Great Power Politics* (New York: W. W. Norton & Co., 2014), pp. 138–40, 155–66.

5   See North Atlantic Treaty Organization, 'Military Structure', https://www.nato.int/cps/en/natohq/structure.htm.

6   See, for example, the 'NATO Standardization Office Public Web

Site', https://nso.nato.int/nso/SOSite/ default.html, which lists 1,159 laboriously negotiated standardisation agreements, many of which are classified. (See also the 'NATO Standarization Document Database' at https://nso.nato.int/nso/nsdd/listpromulg.html.) This is not to argue that NATO faces no standardisation and inter-operability problems; it is to say that the institution is constantly working to assess and overcome them.

7   See IISS, *The Military Balance 2020* (Abingdon: Routledge for the IISS, 2020), pp. 104, 109, 118, 145–6, 157 and 195, for a breakdown of French, German, Italian, Spanish, British and Russian satellites. The Europeans are credited with 15 intelligence, surveillance and reconnaissance satellites, Russia with 17 such satellites. Suggesting that European cooperation in the intelligence realm has been more intensive than most had believed is Bart Jacobs, 'Maximator: European Signals Intelligence Cooperation, From a Dutch Perspective', *Intelligence and National Security*, vol. 35, no. 5, April 2020, pp. 659–68.

8   See European GNSS Service Centre, 'Constellation Information', https://www.gsc-europa. eu/system-service-status/ constellation-information.

9   As I noted in 'Europe Can Defend Itself', endnote 9, I am unpersuaded that purchasing power parity (PPP) does more accurately represent Russian military inputs, and suggest that the median between the Russian defence budget at PPP and at prevailing exchange rates – roughly $110bn – is a more reasonable estimate.

10   From this perspective, Germany's decision to purchase the American F-18E *Super Hornet* fighter as its future contribution to NATO's tactical nuclear capability is a mistake. Germany should buy the French *Rafale* for this mission. The US certified the European-built *Tornado* for tactical nuclear delivery, and it can do the same for the *Rafale*. Having the *Rafale* would provide a stepping stone in reserve towards an all-European dual-key arrangement with France.

11   See Posen, 'Europe Can Defend Itself', pp. 8, 23–4.

Noteworthy

A house divided

'There's nothing wrong with saying that, you know, that you've recalculated … I just want to find 11,780 votes.'

> *Departing US president Donald Trump speaks with Georgia Secretary of State Brad Raffensperger on 2 January 2021, in an apparent bid to change the result of the 2020 presidential election during run-off Senate elections in Georgia.*[1]

'Our elections have occurred. Recounts and audits have been conducted. Appropriate challenges have been addressed by the courts. Governors have certified the results. And the electoral college has voted. The time for questioning the results has passed; the time for the formal counting of the electoral college votes, as prescribed in the Constitution and statute, has arrived.

[…]

Transitions, which all of us have experienced, are a crucial part of the successful transfer of power. They often occur at times of international uncertainty about U.S. national security policy and posture. They can be a moment when the nation is vulnerable to actions by adversaries seeking to take advantage of the situation.

Given these factors, particularly at a time when U.S. forces are engaged in active operations around the world, it is all the more imperative that the transition at the Defense Department be carried out fully, cooperatively and transparently. Acting defense secretary Christopher C. Miller and his subordinates – political appointees, officers and civil servants – are each bound by oath, law and precedent to facilitate the entry into office of the incoming administration, and to do so wholeheartedly. They must also refrain from any political actions that undermine the results of the election or hinder the success of the new team.

We call upon them, in the strongest terms, to do as so many generations of Americans have done before them.'

> *From a* Washington Post *op-ed published on 3 January and signed by all ten living former US secretaries of defense.*[2]

'When I was born in 1947, two years after the second world war ended, Austria was in the middle of a famine. Growing up, I was surrounded by broken men drinking away their guilt over their participation in the most evil regime in history. They were part of a system that murdered 6m Jews along with at least 5m other innocent people, tortured and experimented on human beings and started a war that caused 75m deaths. Not all of them were rabid anti-Semites or Nazis. Many just went along step by step down the road toward greater and greater evil because it was the easiest path.

I don't believe America is capable of those depths of evil, but I do believe we should remember the dire consequences that choosing selfishness and cynicism over service and hope can have. I want to be sure that we don't take those fateful steps.'

> *Former governor of California and Hollywood actor Arnold Schwarzenegger calls on Trump and other Republicans to stop resisting the legitimate outcome of the presidential election.*[3]

Survival | vol. 63 no. 1 | February–March 2021 | pp. 50–52   https://doi.org/10.1080/00396338.2021.1881253

'Let's have trial by combat.'

Rudy Giuliani, Trump's attorney, disputes the election results at a rally in Washington on 6 January, shortly before a violent mob stormed the US Capitol, where members of Congress were preparing to certify that Joe Biden won the election.[4]

'It is up to Congress to confront this egregious assault on our democracy … We're going walk down to the Capitol, and we're going to cheer on our brave senators, and congressmen and women. We're probably not going to be cheering so much for some of them because you'll never take back our country with weakness. You have to show strength, and you have to be strong.'

President Trump speaks at the same rally.[5]

'Hang Mike Pence!'

Rioters chant threats directed at the US vice president while breaking into the Capitol. A man who was later arrested for having unlawfully entered the Senate chamber explained that 'once we found out Pence turned on us and that they had stolen the election, like, officially, the crowd went crazy. I mean, it became a mob.'[6]

'This is not dissent. It's disorder. It's chaos. It borders on sedition. The world is watching.'

President-elect Joe Biden comments on the riot.[7]

'What happened here today was an insurrection incited by the president of the United States. Those who choose to continue to support his dangerous gambit by objecting to the results of a legitimate, democratic election will forever be seen as being complicit in an unprecedented attack against our democracy. Fairly or not, they'll be remembered for their role in this shameful episode in American history. That will be their legacy … The best way we can show respect for the voters who are upset is by telling them the truth!'

US Senator Mitt Romney speaks in the Senate chamber after the violence was contained.[8]

'The announcement of the state of the vote by the president of the Senate shall be deemed a sufficient declaration as persons elected president and vice president of the United States.'

Outgoing US vice president Mike Pence, in his capacity as president of the US Senate, affirms at 3.41am on 7 January 2021 that Joe Biden and Kamala Harris will be the president and vice president of the United States as of 20 January 2021, despite the objections of some members of Congress.[9]

'They may have been hunting for Pence and [House Speaker Nancy] Pelosi to stage their coup, but every one of us in this room right now could have died.'

Representative Jamie Raskin speaks in favour of impeaching Trump for a second time on 13 January 2021.[10]

'The president of the United States summoned this mob, assembled the mob, and lit the flame of this attack. There has never been a greater betrayal by a president of the United States of his office and his oath to the Constitution.'

Representative Liz Cheney.[11]

'On January 6, 2021, pursuant to the 12th Amendment to the Constitution of the United States, the Vice President of the United States, the House of Representatives, and the Senate met at the United States Capitol for a Joint Session of Congress to count the votes of the Electoral College. In the months preceding the Joint Session, President Trump repeatedly issued false statements asserting that the Presidential election results were the product of widespread fraud and should not be accepted by the American people or certified by State or Federal officials. Shortly before the Joint Session commenced, President Trump, addressed a crowd at the Ellipse in Washington, DC. There, he reiterated false claims that "we won this election, and we won it by a landslide". He also willfully made statements that, in context, encouraged – and foreseeably resulted in – lawless action at the Capitol, such as: "if you don't fight like hell you're not going to have a country anymore". Thus incited by President Trump, members of the crowd he had addressed, in an attempt to, among other objectives, interfere with the Joint Session's solemn constitutional duty to certify the results of the 2020 Presidential election, unlawfully breached and vandalized the Capitol, injured and killed law enforcement personnel, menaced Members of Congress, the Vice President, and Congressional personnel, and engaged in other violent, deadly, destructive, and seditious acts.

President Trump's conduct on January 6, 2021, followed his prior efforts to subvert and obstruct the certification of the results of the 2020 Presidential election. Those prior efforts included a phone call on January 2, 2021, during which President Trump urged the secretary of state of Georgia, Brad Raffensperger, to "find" enough votes to overturn the Georgia Presidential election results and threatened Secretary Raffensperger if he failed to do so.

In all this, President Trump gravely endangered the security of the United States and its institutions of Government. He threatened the integrity of the democratic system, interfered with the peaceful transition of power, and imperiled a coequal branch of Government. He thereby betrayed his trust as President, to the manifest injury of the people of the United States.

Wherefore, Donald John Trump, by such conduct, has demonstrated that he will remain a threat to national security, democracy, and the Constitution if allowed to remain in office, and has acted in a manner grossly incompatible with self-governance and the rule of law. Donald John Trump thus warrants impeachment and trial, removal from office, and disqualification to hold and enjoy any office of honor, trust, or profit under the United States.'

From an article of impeachment adopted against Donald Trump in the House of Representatives on 13 January 2021.[12]

Sources

1 Amy Gardner and Paulina Firozi, 'Here's the Full Transcript and Audio of the Call Between Trump and Raffensperger', *Washington Post*, 5 January 2021, https://www.washingtonpost.com/politics/trump-raffensperger-call-transcript-georgia-vote/2021/01/03/2768e0cc-4ddd-11eb-83e3-322644d82356_story.html.

2 Ashton Carter et al., 'All 10 Living Former Defense Secretaries: Involving the Military in Election Disputes Would Cross into Dangerous Territory', *Washington Post*, 3 January 2021, https://www.washingtonpost.com/opinions/10-former-defense-secretaries-military-peaceful-transfer-of-power/2021/01/03/2a23d52e-4c4d-11eb-a9f4-0e668b9772ba_story.html.

3 Arnold Schwarzenegger, 'Arnold Schwarzenegger on Why Republicans Must Stop Trump', *The Economist*, 5 January 2021, https://www.economist.com/by-invitation/2021/01/05/arnold-schwarzenegger-on-why-republicans-must-stop-trump.

4 "Let's Have Trial by Combat" over Election – Giuliani', Reuters, 6 January 2021, https://www.reuters.com/video/watch/idOVDU2NS9R.

5 Charlie Savage, 'Incitement to Riot? What Trump Told Supporters Before Mob Stormed Capitol', *New York Times*, 10 January 2021, https://www.nytimes.com/2021/01/10/us/trump-speech-riot.html.

6 Ashley Parker et al., 'How the Rioters Who Stormed the Capitol Came Dangerously Close to Pence', *Washington Post*, 15 January 2021, https://www.washingtonpost.com/politics/pence-rioters-capitol-attack/2021/01/15/ab62e434-567c-11eb-a08b-f1381ef3d207_story.html.

7 Lauren Gambino and Daniel Strauss, 'Congress Certifies Joe Biden as President Hours After Storming of Capitol', *Guardian*, 7 January 2021, https://www.theguardian.com/us-news/2021/jan/06/congress-certify-election-biden-republicans-object.

8 CNN (@CNN), video via Twitter, 7 January 2021, https://twitter.com/cnn/status/1347014923767967744.

9 John Wagner et al., 'Pence Declares Biden Winner of the Presidential Election After Congress Finally Counts Electoral Votes', *Washington Post*, 7 January 2021, https://www.washingtonpost.com/politics/2021/01/06/congress-electoral-college-vote-live-updates/.

10 Nicholas Fandos, 'Trump Impeached for Inciting Insurrection', *New York Times*, 13 January 2021, https://www.nytimes.com/2021/01/13/us/politics/trump-impeached.html?action=click&module=Spotlight&pgtype=Homepage.

11 Jonathan Martin, Maggie Haberman and Nicholas Fandos, 'McConnell Privately Backs Impeachment as House Moves to Charge Trump', *New York Times*, 12 January 2021, https://www.nytimes.com/2021/01/12/us/politics/mcconnell-backs-trump-impeachment.html.

12 US Congress, H. Res.: Impeaching Donald Trump for High Crimes and Misdemeanors, 117th Congress, 1st Session, 10 January 2021, https://int.nyt.com/data/documenttools/articles-impeachment-trump-xml/b0422e292cebafda/full.pdf.

Community and COVID-19: Japan, Sweden and Uruguay

Amitai Etzioni

COVID-19, which spread throughout much of the world during the first half of 2020, has enabled social scientists to study the ways societies with different moral cultures and political regimes respond to the same crisis. Of particular interest is the role of communitarian values. These values stress that individuals have responsibilities to one another and the common good – for example, they are obliged to don a mask during the pandemic. Individuals are expected to make some sacrifices for society, rather than solely to seek to maximise their own utility or to assume that an aggregation of their individual choices will ensure the social welfare. Communitarian values require individuals to willingly shelter at home, even if this entails a considerable loss of income and engenders frustrations. Instead of relying on coercive government controls, communitarian societies depend on shared core values and social bonds – drawing on moral dialogues, persuasion, approbations, shaming, peer pressure and character education – in order to advance the common good.

Communitarian cultures are found in two main forms. In one, individuals are viewed basically as cells of an organic whole, and thus find significance and meaning in their contributions to the common good. This form is antithetical to liberalism, which is centred on individual rights and liberty.[1] I refer to this form of communitarianism as authoritarian communitarianism. The other incarnation views both individual rights and social

Amitai Etzioni is a University Professor and professor of international affairs at The George Washington University.

Survival | vol. 63 no. 1 | February–March 2021 | pp. 53–76   https://doi.org/10.1080/00396338.2021.1881254

responsibility as first principles, neither trumping the other; depending on changing conditions, one set of values may take precedence over the other for a time, but neither liberal nor communal values are ever to be excluded – even, say, at the height of war. This form of communitarianism seeks to incorporate liberal values into its moral culture. I refer to this type of communitarianism as liberal communitarianism.[2] Note that what is involved here is a continuum of moral cultures in which one set of values or the other has varying weight. (While collapsing liberal and libertarian thinking is likely to horrify a social philosopher, in public discourse the two often shade into each other, especially around the high standing accorded to the value of being left alone.)

Countries' responses to the first wave of COVID-19 can be evaluated in terms of how liberal–communitarian their values were, and how these values affected their approaches to dealing with the virus. Japan, Sweden and Uruguay provide three key examples of the global variation in COVID-19 responses along the communitarian continuum.

Success in Japan

In Japan, the government did not impose a lockdown to try to slow the spread of the coronavirus. It did not require businesses to close, nor did it threaten fines or other legal consequences for those who refused to comply. Instead, Abe Shinzo, who was prime minister until mid-September 2020, called for schools to be closed and later declared a state of emergency on 7 April. This state of emergency only allowed prefectural governors to request that businesses temporarily shut down or reduce their hours, and to urge people to telecommute and stay at home. Thus, changing business practices and personal behaviour in the wake of the state-of-emergency announcement was completely voluntary.[3]

Japanese researchers discovered that the highest-risk situations for COVID-19 transmission were those in which people are in closed and poorly ventilated settings, in the midst of crowds or in close physical contact with other people. These high-risk situations are known as the 'Three Cs'. In response, the government created a public-health and education campaign to raise awareness and encourage people to change their habits.[4] In

June, the *New York Times* reported, officials were 'warning people constantly to change the way they live. As some bars and clubs reopened, hostesses were told to refrain from being next to a client when singing karaoke and dancing. Nightclubs were urged to minimize music and volumes to reduce the spread of respiratory droplets. Citizens were advised to continue avoiding the "Three Cs."'[5] The *Wall Street Journal* reported: 'The rules in Japan are voluntary, a formula the country has used largely successfully in beating back COVID-19. Mask-wearing in Japan is optional, but it is nearly universal – although cases [rose in early July] in part because of infections spread by lax behavior at nightspots. During a state of emergency in April and May, when the government requested voluntary lockdown measures, new cases fell below 50 a day as most stores closed and events were canceled.'[6]

A day after Abe announced the state of emergency in seven prefectures, 86% of respondents to a telephone survey reported that they were practising more self-restraint than usual – for instance, avoiding events and outdoor activities. Responses were nearly the same for people living in the prefectures covered by the declaration of emergency and those that were not covered: 87% and 85%, respectively, changed their habits.[7] On the day after the declaration of the state of emergency, supermarkets and convenience stores announced that they were starting to implement safety precautions, such as restricting entry into their businesses to avoid overcrowding, installing partitions to separate staff and customers in checkout lines, and placing stickers and posters around stores to remind customers to maintain distance from each other.[8] A design firm created and disseminated several creative infographics encouraging social distancing.[9] In mid-April, weekday ridership on Tokyo subway lines had diminished by about 60% compared with the previous year. Fewer people occupied sidewalks, and a popular karaoke palace was closed.[10]

The Japanese government's soft approach relied in part on public shaming rather than more coercive government measures. As the *Washington Post* reported, 'in a country where fear of standing out is almost as intense as fear of the coronavirus, most people respect the guidelines: One study published in August found that the main reason people gave for wearing masks was "peer pressure," rather than preventing the virus from spreading'.[11] Some pachinko parlours initially followed the request to shut down but then reopened, while others remained open all along. On 23 April, the *Japan Times* reported that the Osaka prefectural government had received hundreds of complaints about businesses that had failed to close, pachinko parlours being the most numerous.[12] By mid-May, the governments in Tokyo, Osaka, Hyogo and Miyagi prefectures had publicised the names of open pachinko parlours to shame the owners into closing.[13] These efforts were often – though not always – successful. When shaming was not effective, the government sent teams of officials to convince owners to change their minds face to face.[14]

The soft approach gave rise to the emergence of civilian enforcers known as 'self-restraint police', who used shaming and other tactics to stop behaviour they saw as dangerous to public health. The self-restraint police are active both online and offline. Online, they monitor cars, searching for those that are on roads in a different prefecture from that of their registration. The diligence – some may say zealotry – of these volunteers is illustrated by a case study in which self-restraint police initiated the public shaming of a woman in her twenties who had tested positive for COVID-19 but nevertheless travelled across prefecture lines. In an effort to avoid facing the consequences of her actions, she seems to have lied to officials who questioned her. Online vigilantes went to work, deciding 'to try to identify her Twitter account and real name, branding her a "corona-spreading terrorist", digging up what they claimed to be photos of her and reportedly bombarding her supposed workplace with irate calls'.[15] Proprietors of a store that some believed to be her employer posted a statement on their website to say that she was not affiliated with their business and announced that they were considering filing a lawsuit because of harm to their business reputation.[16]

Offline, some self-restraint police have resorted to property destruction, abuse and threats. Someone damaged a glass door at a pachinko parlour in central Japan that was named and shamed by the government.[17] People have harassed drivers of vehicles with number plates from other prefectures, tailgated them and even vandalised the cars.[18] Families have also been mobilised. When two of the Japanese nationals evacuated at the end of January from Wuhan, China – where the pandemic outbreak began –

declined testing, the government had no recourse. But their families quickly intervened, and the two individuals soon agreed to be tested.[19]

The voluntary system was effective. On 25 May, the government lifted the last remaining state of emergency. Oshitani Hitoshi, a Tohoku University virologist and public-health expert, assessed that although Japan probably did not meet its goal of reducing interpersonal interactions by 80%, 'surprisingly, Japan's mild lockdown seemed to have a real lockdown effect'.[20] *Science* magazine reported that 'there was fairly extensive voluntary compliance'.[21] According to the *New York Times*, 'one of Japan's most visible responses has been near-universal mask wearing, seen here as a responsible thing to do to protect oneself and others, and as a small price to pay to be able to resume some semblance of normalcy'.[22]

By the time the state of emergency ended, Japan was close to its daily goal of 0.5 new cases per 100,000 people.[23] On 30 June, before a new outbreak of cases arose, Japan's rolling seven-day average of confirmed new cases of COVID-19 was 0.71 per million people. This put Japan in the company of two of the best-performing countries

The voluntary system was effective

at the time, New Zealand and South Korea, which recorded rolling seven-day averages of 0.39 and 0.88 new cases per million people, respectively. As of that date, the cumulative number of confirmed cases of COVID-19 per million people in Japan was 147.01, which was lower than the totals for both New Zealand (244.29) and South Korea (249.66). Japan, however, did have more cumulative COVID-19 deaths per one million people (7.69) than New Zealand (4.56) and South Korea (5.50).[24]

Some researchers have called into question the commonly held belief that Japanese people are more communitarian and less individualistic than Americans, and some suggest that Japanese society is becoming increasingly individualistic. But empirical and anecdotal evidence suggests that Japanese culture is still strongly communitarian, though its communitarian character is of the liberal kind.[25] Scholars have observed that Japanese people 'are more compliant with norms' than Americans and are less likely to engage in non-conformist or improper behaviour, whether that be taking extra-long breaks at work, calling in sick to work while actually healthy, engaging in petty theft, committing vandalism or driving drunk.[26] Crime rates in Japan are much lower than those in Western countries.[27] Japanese textbooks feature stories that 'teach children to be kind, considerate, an altruistic member of the group, and to recognize the importance of friendship'.[28]

In 2011, as Japan was reeling from the back-to-back-to-back wallops of an earthquake, a tsunami and a nuclear disaster, *New York Times* columnist Nicholas Kristof, who was the *Times*'s Tokyo bureau chief for five years, wrote a column hailing 'Japan's civility and selflessness'.[29] He described the community spirit that pervades public places, leading people to assume that lost wallets would be returned and allowing restaurants to loan umbrellas to customers with the full expectation that they would be returned. He recounted attempting to teach Japanese children how to play musical chairs at a birthday party for his son, only to discover that the children were horrified by the cut-throat rules of the game. Accordingly, 'what unfolded may have been the most polite, most apologetic, and least competitive game of musical chairs in the history of the world'.[30] He noted that 'gaps between rich and poor are more modest in Japan, and Japan's corporate tycoons would be embarrassed by the flamboyant pay packages that are common in America'.[31]

Since 1947, Japan has had a constitution that incorporates many of the rights that are included in those of other liberal democracies, such as freedom of speech, religion and assembly. That constitution also extends rights to women. However, these liberal values have not been fully embedded in the culture. Women in workplaces are often treated as second-class citizens.[32] There is discrimination and bullying, particularly against ethnic Koreans and the *burakumin*, that has marred Japanese culture.[33] Japan has nothing like the Americans with Disabilities Act, and having a person with a disability in one's family is considered shameful.

It is important to note that Japanese culture was predisposed towards behaviour that is beneficial to reducing the spread of COVID-19. People bow to greet one another and conduct business rather than shaking hands, and hand washing was common among the Japanese prior to the pandemic.[34] Furthermore, a culture of mask-wearing pre-dated COVID-19's arrival in Japan. Japanese people have routinely donned masks when they have colds and as precautionary measures against pollution, as well as during allergy and flu seasons. They also wore them during previous viral outbreaks, including the 1918 flu pandemic, the SARS spread of 2003 and the MERS outbreak in 2012.

Japan's response to COVID-19 suggests that a society with strong liberal–communitarian values can rely largely on social processes to lead to required behavioural adaptations. The government's main role was informative and educational, not coercive. Moreover, the fact that Japanese society is not highly liberal in some other areas did not prevent soft enforcement from working effectively even when the society faced a crisis.

Shortfall in Sweden

The Swedish government did not impose any lockdowns or ask businesses to temporarily close their doors. Instead, it issued a very limited set of restrictions, banning gatherings of over 50 people, visits to elderly care homes and crowding in restaurants. It also released guidelines that correspond with Sweden's Communicable Disease Act, which long pre-dated COVID-19 and requires people to 'take reasonable precautions to curb the spread of infectious diseases'.[35] The guidelines called for increasing hand washing, staying home if one feels sick or is high-risk, and maintaining distance from those outside one's household.[36] The law allows for the prosecution of anyone who infects others, whether knowingly or through negligence; in practice, however, people are very unlikely to face legal consequences for violating the guidelines.[37]

Enforcement of the limited government restrictions that were put in place has been spotty. For example, people have ignored the restrictions in bars, in front of police officers, with impunity.[38] In late April, when five restaurants were closed for violating the mandated social-distancing protocols, none were fined, and they were told that, after passing a new inspection, they would be permitted to reopen.[39] Photographs have shown people crowding outdoor bars.[40] The government did not promote a high level of self-restraint. After sports clubs chose to cancel youth activities, the Public Health Agency's director-general came out against such decisions, calling them 'unreasonable'.[41]

During some weeks, and in some places, self-enforcement was high. But it was inconsistent and soon declined. By late April, the BBC reported that 'usage of public transport has dropped significantly, large numbers are working from home, and most refrained from travelling over the Easter weekend'.[42] A poll found that approximately 90% of Swedes claimed that they sometimes or often maintained a metre's distance between themselves and others.[43] Yet at around the same time, a Swedish expat who travelled from the United States to Sweden to be with his elderly mother found that 'things seemed exactly normal for this time of year ... Cafés were full to the brim, and people were picnicking in parks, on the same blanket.'[44] Government officials expressed concern about nightlife crowds, and mobile-phone data indicated that the time people were spending in Stockholm's city centre had increased over the previous two weeks.[45] By the end of April, Google's mobility data showed that, of all the people of Europe, the Swedes had made the fewest alterations in their movements.[46]

In early June, Theo Vos and Katherine Leach-Kemon of the University of Washington's Institute for Health Metrics and Evaluation noted that 'even though Swedes decreased their movement in response to the govern-ment's voluntary social distancing guidelines, their mobility did not drop as steeply as it did in other places. In Norway and Denmark, for example, mobility dropped by 59 percent and 60 percent, respectively, at its lowest point, while Sweden's mobility dropped by a maximum of 33 percent.'[47]

Sweden severely limited testing through at least the end of April and still was not tracking the spread in the beginning of May.[48] In the beginning of June, Sweden's testing levels still significantly lagged behind those of its Scandinavian neighbours.[49] Sweden also refused to acknowledge the global consensus that asymptomatic people could transmit the disease until April, months after the rest of the world.[50] Even in mid-July, the Public Health Agency continued to recommend in-person attendance at work or school by people without symptoms who lived in households including someone who was sick with COVID-19, still seemingly discounting the risk of asymp-tomatic or pre-symptomatic transmission.[51] In early June, when the World Health Organization (WHO) began advising governments to encourage their citizens to wear face masks in places where it was difficult to maintain social distance, Sweden refused to follow that advice. The Public Health Agency continued to claim that people wearing face masks touch their faces more often than people not wearing them.[52]

Anders Tegnell, Sweden's state epidemiologist, argued that the WHO recommendation to promote face masks could jeopardise Sweden's overall strategy of social distancing and staying home when sick, as people might feel that, as long as they wore a mask, they no longer needed to follow the original guidelines. In fact, the Public Health Agency advised the general public not to wear face masks, even in enclosed and often crowded environments such as public transportation.[53] People who chose to wear masks faced stigmatisation by way of stares, comments and laughter, and sometimes intimidation by verbal and physical assault.[54] Hence, Sweden has had a low percentage of people wearing masks outside their homes, tying for the lowest rate among 21 countries surveyed in June 2020.[55]

Sweden refused to follow mask advice

Sweden's outbreak has been far worse and more prolonged than that of its neighbours. Most of the other countries of Europe seemed to have at least temporarily brought the spread of COVID-19 to heel by early June, but the virus was still raging across Sweden.[56] Sweden's 30 June rolling seven-day average of 123.56 new cases per million people was approximately 22 times that of Denmark (5.52 per million people) and over 42 times that of Norway (2.90 per million people). The cumulative number of confirmed COVID-19 cases per million people in Sweden was 3,674.82 as of 31 May, compared to 2,008.39 in Denmark and 1,551.49 in Norway. By 30 June, the gap had widened: Sweden had reached a cumulative 525.78 COVID-19 deaths per million people, while Denmark had 104.45 (approximately one-fifth that of Sweden) and Norway had 45.93 (approximately one-eleventh that of Sweden).[57]

PBS NewsHour special correspondent Malcolm Brabant has reported that the coronavirus situation in Sweden has been particularly dire for the elderly. In fact, 'ninety percent of Sweden's fatalities were aged over 70. Half were in nursing homes. Oxygen wasn't provided. Instead, seniors were given morphine to ease the pain of respiratory failure.'[58] A Swedish professor characterised the deaths of people in nursing homes as a form of euthanasia, and a doctor, Jon Tallinger, protested by quitting the Swedish Health Service. An instructional video for care homes told staff to administer morphine and a palliative sedative to patients in distress, while making no mention of the option to send suffering people to the hospital. According to Tallinger, this explains why Sweden's healthcare system was able to withstand the pandemic: 'The Swedish health care system wasn't overwhelmed because they didn't send anyone to the hospital. They died in their homes and care homes.'[59]

News reports and statements by Swedish public figures reflect a mixture of communitarian and libertarian values. On the communitarian side, the *New York Times* reported, 'Sweden's approach appeals to the public's self-restraint and sense of responsibility'.[60] Similarly, Reuters indicated that the country was 'relying on Swedes' sense of social responsibility'.[61] An article in *Politico* noted that Sweden's approach is 'everyone-for-the-community'.[62] Swedes tend to trust each other and express confidence in their government agencies and public institutions; the agencies and institutions, in turn, trust their citizens.[63]

Stockholm regional healthcare director Björn Eriksson made an exemplary communitarian appeal, worth quoting at length:

> Most people have made big efforts and big sacrifices … But now we are tired and we all want things to go back to normal. But they cannot. Because then, more people will be infected by COVID-19, more will need hospital care for COVID-19, and more will die of COVID-19. It is our responsibility as residents of Stockholm to absolutely not crowd in pubs, to not celebrate with friends and family, to not meet in large crowds on streets and squares, or be close to each other on beaches or parks now that the sun is shining … Unfortunately, there are some who don't follow the recommendations and to you I say one thing: you are exposing not only yourself, but everyone else around you to an unacceptable risk. Many also think that they have had COVID-19 but few of us know with certainty. Whether or not you've had it, we must follow the recommendations of the Public Health Agency, we must reduce the spread of infection and reduce

the need for hospital care. And this only works if we all help out together
and dare to tell others if they are not following them.[64]

Prime Minister Stefan Löfven stated that 'all of us as individuals must take
responsibility. We cannot legislate and ban everything. It's about common
sense.'[65] To similar effect, in a televised speech in March, Löfven said: 'The
only way to manage this crisis is to face it as a society, with everyone taking
responsibility for themselves, for each other and for our country.'[66]

State epidemiologist Tegnell offered a more libertarian spin in an interview with the *New York Times*: 'Our whole system of communicable disease
control is based on voluntary action. The immunization system is completely voluntary and there is 98% coverage.'[67] Further, Tegnell said, 'you
give them the option to do what is best in their lives. That works very well,
according to our experience.'[68] When Sweden prohibited gatherings of 500
or more people, some organisers simply decided to limit their events to
499 people. This idea lost its lustre after staff members became infected.[69]
Tegnell argued that this example illustrated his aversion to mandates, as
'people find ways around the rules'.[70] But the story also showed that people
learn from their mistakes.

In April, the *Washington Post* reported that, among people in over two
dozen countries around the world, Swedes were some of the least fearful
of the coronavirus. Italian political philosopher Adele Lebano, who lives
in Sweden, has suggested that Swedes abdicate responsibility to the state,
writing that 'with blind trust in the government, people are relieved from
the responsibility for what happens around them – even to them – to their
fellow citizens and to their family'.[71] This leads to a culture that simultaneously encourages 'radical individualism and total dependence' and 'a
model of democratic success that favors stability over freedom, dependence
on the state over interdependence among citizens'.[72]

Denmark, Norway and Sweden are often lumped together due to their
shared Scandinavian culture and commonalities in their welfare-state governments and societies. However, a team of researchers, with members from
all three nations, noted in 2008 that Sweden's economy had grown increasingly market-oriented since the 1990s. Susanne Wiborg has found that, in

the field of education, Sweden has adopted more neo-liberal policies than either of its neighbours.[73] As of 2011, Norway and Denmark had not opened their education systems to private entities, but Sweden had, and it had gone so far as to allow for-profit providers to run private schools – a significant change for a nation that previously worked hard to prevent the incursion of private schools.[74] In 1991, there were 60 private schools in Sweden; by 2010, there were 709.[75]

Sweden has stood out in Scandinavia for consistently implementing liberal immigration policies.[76] Approximately 18.8% of the population of Sweden was foreign-born in 2018, compared to approximately 15.4% in Norway and 10.3% in Denmark.[77] Sweden also promotes multiculturalism to a greater extent than its neighbours. As of 2013, Sweden differed from other Nordic countries in not requiring immigrants to attend introduction courses upon their arrival, or to learn Swedish history or the Swedish language in order to become Swedish citizens.[78] Thus, Sweden appears to have a culture and politics that are more liberal than those of its Scandinavian counterparts, at least when it comes to economics, education and immigration.

Social Democrats and their coalitions held control of the Swedish government from before the Second World War until 1976, and again from 1982 to 1991. However, over the last few decades, Swedish politics has shifted to the right. Between 1991 and 1994, a centre-right coalition led by the Moderate Party (Sweden's main conservative party) held power, quickly putting forth proposals to enact free-market policies.[79] Even though the Social Democrats took control again in 1994, this trend continued, with the central government transferring economic responsibility to provinces, municipalities and individuals rather than maintaining it within the central state.[80] A centre-right coalition led by the Moderate Party governed between 2006 and 2014 and, since taking power back, Social Democrat-led coalitions have continued to make concessions to the right to hold power.[81]

Sweden's government, which the people broadly trusted, has done relatively little to activate communitarian elements of Swedish culture. The Swedish people heeded their government's guidance, whereby little action was required in the face of a pandemic. The fact that Swedish culture is less communitarian and more liberal and libertarian than that of other Nordic states also explains its poor performance in coping with COVID-19.

Success in Uruguay

The government in Uruguay acted quickly to confront the spread of COVID-19 within the country.[82] The health system had already started making preparations for the pandemic in February 2020.[83] The new government, which took office on 1 March, has taken the virus seriously from the beginning.[84] On 13 March, the very day the first cases of COVID-19 in the country were confirmed, the government proclaimed an emergency, closed some of the borders, called off events and ordered people entering from hard-hit countries to quarantine. By the next day, the president had closed schools and large malls, and the government had rolled out a public-health and hygiene-awareness campaign. Moreover, the government brought in esteemed medical experts to lead a scientific advisory group and brought the private sector into the loop on its plans to face the crisis.[85]

The government also implemented a contact-tracing system right away.[86] In early August, MercoPress reported that the government was releasing updates every day and also keeping the public apprised about COVID-19 developments through social media, mobile apps and chatbots. Uruguayan programmers created an app, Coronavirus UY, which facilitates case monitoring and alerts users who have been in close contact with people who have tested positive for COVID-19.[87]

Rather than relying solely on contact tracing and setting up testing sites that require people to seek out tests themselves, the government has taken a proactive approach, assigning state employees to conduct tests on 'random city blocks' as well as within 'critical job sectors such as construction'.[88] As of late July, Uruguay was one of the world's leaders in per capita testing.[89]

Under a policy called *libertad responsable* (responsible liberty), the government refrained from issuing a lockdown order, instead combining closures of some public places (schools, malls and cinemas) with the promotion of public-health recommendations (face masks, social distancing and working from home).[90] According to the *Washington Post*, Uruguayans aged 65 and older had to quarantine, though it is not clear how that requirement was enforced.[91]

By 30 June, the rolling seven-day average of new confirmed COVID-19 cases in Uruguay was 2.06 per million people, less than one-twenty-sixth of the 54.80 in Argentina and less than one-eighty-fifth of the 175.90 in Brazil. Uruguay had seen a total of 268.30 cases per million people and 7.77 deaths per million people. In comparison, Argentina and Brazil had seen 1,377.45 and 6,436.77 cases per million people, respectively, by 30 June, meaning that Argentina had experienced over five times and Brazil nearly 24 times the caseload of Uruguay. Furthermore, Argentina and Brazil had recorded 28.32 and 274.34 deaths per million people, respectively, as of the same date – approximately 3.6 and over 35 times the number of deaths in Uruguay.[92]

The public-health recommendations directly contradict many cherished Uruguayan customs, from hugs and kisses in greeting to the sharing of the *mate* gourd, from which friends and family sip a tea-like brew through the same metal straw.[93] Nevertheless, compliance has been high. As MercoPress reported, 'various industry associations and labor unions reached voluntary agreements to temporarily shut down activities in sectors such as construction and retail. Even the tourism sector, through one of its main business chambers, joined and, against their own business interest, called on citizens to stay home during the traditional April week vacation.'[94]

Uruguayan radio host Horacio Abadie attributed Uruguay's strong response to the pandemic to 'mutual trust'.[95] 'The government trusts me to behave, and I trust the government to look after me', said a jogging pensioner in a face mask.[96] Daniel Chasquetti, a political scientist and professor at the Universidad de la República, noted that 'from March 13 until the end of April, the political class in Uruguay closed ranks'.[97] This political unity, coupled with the government's reliance on science, contributed to public trust and confidence.[98] Jennifer Pribble of the University of Richmond has observed that 'the country has long stood out [in Latin America] for its vibrant participatory democracy, low inequality and expansive social policies – all attributes that help explain Uruguay's relative success in the pandemic'.[99] She noted that in 2016 data showed that 65% of Uruguayans supported the country's institutions, seven percentage points higher than residents of Argentina and over 20 points higher than those of Brazil or Chile.[100] Additionally, private companies in Uruguay participated in the country's response, engaging in public–private partnerships to help Uruguayans cope with the pandemic.[101]

In Pribble's view, Uruguay's 'unique and defining characteristics likely helped' it to contain COVID-19, as 'political trust and support for democracy encourage people to follow public health recommendations, and a strong welfare state provides income support and reliable health care to help slow infection'.[102] Others have directly credited communitarian ideals for Uruguay's success. José Luis Satdjian, sub-secretary of the Uruguayan Health Ministry, said, 'we have been able to succeed thanks to the citizens who understood the urgency and importance of taking care of themselves and each other'.[103] Similarly, Dr Giovanni Escalante, country representative of the Pan American Health Organization in Uruguay, noted that mandatory lockdowns and government enforcement of restrictions were not necessary because 'for Uruguayans, the voluntary scheme was, in real action, auto-enforced'.[104] Milagros Costabel, a Uruguay-based writer, commented that 'the government has used individual freedom and civic rights as one of the main points of its strategy – and this has been generally accepted by citizens who, faced with the option to choose, chose to preserve the safety and health of their fellow citizens'.[105] Henry Cohen, a member of the government's committee of scientific advisers for the pandemic and a highly regarded Montevideo gastroenterologist, observed that 'people were asked to enjoy their freedom in a responsible way by staying at home'.[106]

*   *   *

In natural experiments, as distinct from those conducted in laboratories, variables that cannot be controlled may contribute to a given outcome. Differences in societal responses to COVID-19, and the effects of those responses (as measured by confirmed case and death rates), including those in the three countries considered here, undoubtedly turn in part on factors other than differences in countries' moral cultures and political regimes. For instance, Japan's population is older than that of either Sweden or Uruguay and hence is more vulnerable to COVID-19, which appears to make its achievements even more notable. At the same time, Japan is an island, which physically helped to curb the contagion. Sweden benefited from sharing borders with nations that are more committed to curbing the virus than it is, while Uruguay's achievement is all the more impressive insofar as its neighbours have been much less successful in dealing with the pandemic. The levels of testing among the three nations differ, affecting the recorded infection rates, though these differences presumably have had less of an impact on the confirmed death rates. Nevertheless, given the substantial differences between Sweden, on the one hand, and Japan and Uruguay, on the other, along with the divergence between the situations in the latter two nations and the situations in less communitarian ones, it seems reasonable to conclude that differences in values had significant effects.

The ideal liberal–communitarian society can be formed only if the state is abolished, because the coercive elements of the state conflict with the core values of such a society. This is the reason communal settlements, such as kibbutzim and Amish communities, seek to exclude the government. This article, however, deals with nations, defined as communities invested in the state. In that context, a society can be relatively liberal–communitarian if the state fosters rather than undermines communal bonds; it undergirds rather than seeks to curtail the observation of rights; it looks to minimise its role, relying more on activating communal processes, though it may increase its role in a crisis; and communities and their members trust the government and do not view it as violating their liberties.

States are liberal and communitarian to varying degrees. Near one end of the liberal–communitarian continuum stands the United States, which has some communitarian elements but a strong and overarching libertarian culture that is only intensifying.[107] At the opposite end is not China, in which the government plays a major role, but Japan, owing to its great reliance on communitarian values rather than the government. Sweden is the most liberal and least communitarian of the nations examined in this article, with Uruguay falling somewhere between Sweden and Japan. (The United Kingdom falls somewhere between Sweden and the US, on the right side of the spectrum, with the other Nordic countries and European Union members on the left, between Sweden and Japan.)

There is no set optimal liberal–communitarian balance; changing historical conditions should prompt adjustments to it. The COVID-19 pandemic, in particular, calls for increased commitment to public health, a common good. Nations that do not have a sufficiently communitarian moral culture, or that were unable to adopt one, have suffered. In all three countries considered here, trust in government is relatively robust, and largely prevents the kinds of pitched conflicts that can arise between communities and governments in countries with a high level of libertarian sentiment. The Swedish government simply did not provide effective guidance. The Japanese and Uruguayan governments firmly signalled what had to be done, which was sufficient to activate communitarian processes. On balance, liberal–communitarian values have acquitted themselves well during a major international crisis.

Notes

1 See generally Alasdair MacIntyre, *After Virtue: A Study in Moral Theory*, 3rd ed. (South Bend, IN: University of Notre Dame Press, 2007); Yi-Huah Jiang, 'Asian Values and Communitarian Democracy', in National Values, Chinese Values and Muslim Values in Southeast Asia (International Workshop on Deliberating the Asian Value Debate, Taipei, 1998), https://tsubouchita-kahiko.com/image24/Asian%20 values%20and%20communitarian%20 democracy.pdf; and the works of Robert Putnam.

2 See, for example, Amitai Etzioni, *The New Golden Rule: Community and Morality in a Democratic Society* (New York: Basic Books, 1997); Amitai Etzioni, *The Spirit of Community: The Reinvention of American Society* (New York: Crown, 1993); and Philip Selznick, *The Moral Commonwealth:*

Social Theory and the Promise of Community (Berkeley, CA: University of California Press, 1992). See also Shlomo Avineri and Avner de-Shalit (eds), *Communitarianism and Individualism* (Oxford: Oxford University Press, 1992); and the works of Michael Sandel and Charles Taylor.

3 See Motoko Rich, Hisako Ueno and Makiko Inoue, 'Japan Declared a Coronavirus Emergency. Is It Too Late?', *New York Times*, 7 April 2020, https://www.nytimes.com/2020/04/07/world/asia/japan-coronavirus-emergency.html.

4 See Rupert Wingfield-Hayes, 'The Puzzle of Japan's Low Virus Death Rate', BBC News, 4 July 2020, https://www.bbc.com/news/world-asia-53188847.

5 Sui-Lee Wee, Benjamin Mueller and Emma Bubola, 'From China to Germany, the World Learns to

Live with the Coronavirus', *New York Times*, 24 June 2020, https://www.nytimes.com/2020/06/24/world/europe/countries-reopening-coronavirus.html.

6 River Davis, 'Reopened Theme Parks Ban Screaming on Roller Coasters. Riders Are Howling', *Wall Street Journal*, 8 July 2020, https://www.wsj.com/articles/reopened-theme-parks-ban-screaming-on-roller-coasters-riders-are-howling-11594222278.

7 '86% of Japanese Practicing Greater Social Distancing After Emergency Declaration: Survey', *Mainichi Daily News*, 9 April 2020, https://mainichi.jp/english/articles/20200409/p2a/00m/0na/027000c.

8 See 'Stores in Japan Taking Extra "Social Distancing" Precautions Amid State of Emergency', *Mainichi Daily News*, 9 April 2020, https://mainichi.jp/english/articles/20200409/p2a/00m/0na/009000c.

9 See 'Stay One Beatles Apart: Japan Design Firm's Take on Social Distancing', *Japan Times*, 16 May 2020, https://www.japantimes.co.jp/news/2020/05/16/national/stay-one-beatles-apart-japan-design-firms-take-social-distancing/.

10 Motoko Rich and Noriko Hayashi, 'Tokyo, in a State of Emergency, yet Still Having Drinks at a Bar', *New York Times*, 19 April 2020, https://www.nytimes.com/2020/04/19/world/asia/tokyo-japan-coronavirus.html.

11 Simon Denyer, 'As Infections Ebb, Japan Hopes It Has Cracked the Covid Code on Coexisting with the Virus', *Washington Post*, 19 September 2020, https://www.washingtonpost.com/world/asia_pacific/as-infections-ebb-japan-hopes-it-has-cracked-the-covid-code-on-coexisting-with-the-virus/2020/09/17/4742e284-eea2-11ea-bd08-1b10132b458f_story.html.

12 See 'Defiant Pachinko Parlors Show Limits of Japan's Shutdown Request', *Japan Times*, 23 April 2020, https://www.japantimes.co.jp/news/2020/04/23/national/defiant-pachinko-parlors-show-limits-japans-shutdown-request/.

13 *Ibid.*

14 Simon Denyer and Akiko Kashiwagi, 'In Japan, Busy Pachinko Gambling Parlors Defy Virus Vigilantes and Country's Light-touch Lockdown', *Washington Post*, 14 August 2020, https://www.washingtonpost.com/world/asia_pacific/in-japan-busy-pachinko-gambling-parlors-defy-virus-vigilantes-and-countrys-light-touch-lockdown/2020/05/14/8ffee74e-9447-11ea-87a3-22d324235636_story.html.

15 Tomohiro Osaki, 'Japan's "Virus Vigilantes" Take on Rule-breakers and Invaders', *Japan Times*, 13 May 2020, https://www.japantimes.co.jp/news/2020/05/13/national/coronavirus-vigilantes-japan/.

16 *Ibid.*

17 See Denyer and Kashiwagi, 'In Japan, Busy Pachinko Gambling Parlors Defy Virus Vigilantes and Country's Light-touch Lockdown'.

18 See Osaki, 'Japan's "Virus Vigilantes" Take on Rule-Breakers and Invaders'.

19 See Paul De Vries, 'COVID-19 Versus Japan's Culture of Collectivism', *Japan Times*, 22 May 2020, https://www.japantimes.co.jp/opinion/2020/05/22/commentary/japan-commentary/COVID-19-

versus-japans-culture-collectivism/.

20 Dennis Normile, 'Japan Ends Its
    COVID-19 State of Emergency',
    Science, 26 May 2020, https://www.
    sciencemag.org/news/2020/05/japan-
    ends-its-COVID-19-state-emergency.

21 *Ibid*.

22 Motoko Rich, 'Is the Secret to
    Japan's Virus Success Right in
    Front of Its Face?', *New York Times*,
    6 June 2020, https://www.nytimes.
    com/2020/06/06/world/asia/japan-
    coronavirus-masks.html.

23 Normile, 'Japan Ends Its COVID-19
    State of Emergency'.

24 Max Roser et al., 'Coronavirus
    Pandemic (COVID-19)', Our World
    in Data, 20 August 2020, https://
    ourworldindata.org/coronavirus.

25 See, for example, Yuji Ogihara,
    'Temporal Changes in Individualism
    and Their Ramification in Japan:
    Rising Individualism and Conflicts
    with Persisting Collectivism',
    Frontiers in Psychology, 23 May
    2017, https://www.frontiersin.org/
    articles/10.3389/fpsyg.2017.00695/
    full; Kazumi Sugimura, 'Adolescent
    Identity Development in Japan',
    Child Development Perspectives, vol.
    14, no. 2, June 2020, pp. 71–7; and
    Yohtaro Takano and Eiko Osaka,
    'Comparing Japan and the United
    States on Individualism/Collectivism:
    A Follow-up Review', *Asian Journal
    of Social Psychology*, vol. 21, no. 4,
    December 2018, pp. 301–16.

26 Miyuki Fukushima, Susan F.
    Sharp and Emiko Kobayashi,
    'Bond to Society, Collectivism, and
    Conformity: A Comparative Study
    of Japanese and American College
    Students', *Deviant Behavior*, vol. 30,

no. 5, May 2009, pp. 455–6.

27 *Ibid.*, p. 435.

28 Toshie Imada, 'Cultural Narratives
    of Individualism and Collectivism: A
    Content Analysis of Textbook Stories
    in the United States and Japan', *Journal
    of Cross-cultural Psychology*, vol. 43, no.
    4, 2012, p. 586.

29 Nicholas Kristof, 'The Japanese
    Could Teach Us a Thing or Two', *New
    York Times*, 19 March 2011, https://
    www.nytimes.com/2011/03/20/
    opinion/20kristof.html.

30 *Ibid*.

31 *Ibid*.

32 See Council on Foreign Relations,
    'Japan's Postwar Constitution',
    17 August 2020, https://www.cfr.
    org/interactive/japan-constitution/
    japans-postwar-constitution.

33 Kristof, 'The Japanese Could Teach Us
    a Thing or Two'.

34 See Motoko Rich and Hisako Ueno,
    'Japan's Virus Success Has Puzzled
    the World. Is Its Luck Running Out?',
    New York Times, 26 March 2020,
    https://www.nytimes.com/2020/03/26/
    world/asia/japan-coronavirus.html.

35 'What Happens If You Break
    Sweden's Coronavirus Restrictions?',
    Local, 26 May 2020, https://
    www.thelocal.se/20200526/
    what-happens-if-you-break-swedens-
    coronavirus-restrictions.

36 *Ibid*.

37 *Ibid*.

38 See Thomas Erdbrink and Christina
    Anderson, '"Life Has to Go On":
    How Sweden Has Faced the Virus
    Without a Lockdown', *New York Times*,
    28 April 2020, https://www.nytimes.
    com/2020/04/28/world/europe/sweden-
    coronavirus-herd-immunity.html.

39 *Ibid.*

40 See Maddy Savage, 'Has Sweden Got Its Coronavirus Science Right?', BBC News, 25 April 2020, https://www.bbc.com/news/world-europe-52395866.

41 Nathalie Rothschild, 'Sweden Is Open for Business During Its Coronavirus Outbreak', *Foreign Policy*, 24 March 2020, https://foreignpolicy.com/2020/03/24/sweden-coronavirus-open-for-business/.

42 Savage, 'Has Sweden Got Its Coronavirus Science Right?'

43 *Ibid.*

44 Erik Augustin Palm, 'I Just Came Home to Sweden. I'm Horrified by the Coronavirus Response Here', *Slate*, 29 April 2020, https://slate.com/news-and-politics/2020/04/sweden-coronavirus-response-death-social-distancing.html.

45 See Savage, 'Has Sweden Got Its Coronavirus Science Right?'

46 See Palm, 'I Just Came Home to Sweden. I'm Horrified by the Coronavirus Response Here'.

47 Theo Vos and Katherine Leach-Kemon, 'Five Problems with the Swedish Approach to COVID-19', Think Global Health, 4 June 2020, https://www.thinkglobalhealth.org/article/five-problems-swedish-approach-COVID-19.

48 See Adele Lebano, 'Sweden's Relaxed Approach to COVID-19 Isn't Working', *Boston Review*, 7 May 2020, https://bostonreview.net/politics/adele-lebano-sweden%E2%80%99s-relaxed-approach-COVID-19-isn%E2%80%99t-working.

49 See Vos and Leach-Kemon, 'Five Problems with the Swedish Approach to COVID-19'.

50 See Palm, 'I Just Came Home to Sweden. I'm Horrified by the Coronavirus Response Here'.

51 See Mary Harris, 'How Sweden Screwed Up', *Slate*, 14 July 2020, https://slate.com/news-and-politics/2020/07/coronavirus-COVID-sweden-herd-immunity.html.

52 See Catherine Edwards, 'Why Is Sweden Still Not Asking People to Wear Face Masks?', *Local*, 8 June 2020, https://www.thelocal.se/20200608/why-isnt-sweden-asking-people-to-wear-face-masks.

53 See 'Coronavirus: Is Swedish Trust in Authorities Starting to Falter?', *Local*, 23 June 2020, https://www.thelocal.se/20200623/coronavirus-is-swedish-trust-in-authorities-starting-to-falter.

54 See, for example, Catherine Edwards, 'Coughs and Racial Slurs: Sweden's Foreign Residents Reveal Abuse for Wearing Face Masks', *Local*, 30 June 2020, https://www.thelocal.se/20200630/coughs-and-racial-slurs-swedens-foreign-residents-reveal-abuse-for-wearing-face-masks.

55 Josh Katz, Margot Sanger-Katz and Kevin Quealy, 'A Detailed Map of Who Is Wearing Masks in the U.S.', *New York Times*, 17 July 2020, https://www.nytimes.com/interactive/2020/07/17/upshot/coronavirus-face-mask-map.html.

56 See Michael Birnbaum, 'Scientist Behind Sweden's COVID-19 Strategy Suggests It Allowed Too Many Deaths', *Washington Post*, 4 June 2020, https://www.washingtonpost.com/world/europe/sweden-epidemiologist-anders-tegnell/2020/06/03/063b20e4-a5a0-11ea-b619-3f9133bbb482_story.html.

57 Roser et al., 'Coronavirus Pandemic (COVID-19)'.

58 Malcolm Brabant, 'Denmark and Sweden Responded Differently to the Pandemic. How Did They Fare?', *PBS NewsHour*, 8 September 2020, https://www.pbs.org/newshour/show/denmark-and-sweden-responded-differently-to-the-pandemic-how-did-they-fare.

59 *Ibid*.

60 Peter S. Goodman, 'Sweden Has Become the World's Cautionary Tale', *New York Times*, 7 July 2020, https://www.nytimes.com/2020/07/07/business/sweden-economy-coronavirus.html.

61 Simon Johnson, 'Sweden to Shut Bars and Restaurants that Ignore Coronavirus Restrictions', Reuters, 24 April 2020, https://www.reuters.com/article/us-health-coronavirus-sweden-stockholm-idUSKCN2262AX.

62 Elisabeth Braw, 'What Sweden Can Teach Us About Coronavirus', *Politico*, 3 July 2020, https://www.politico.eu/article/sweden-coronavirus-lessons/.

63 See Birnbaum, 'Scientist Behind Sweden's COVID-19 Strategy Suggests It Allowed Too Many Deaths'.

64 'This Is the Stark Coronavirus Warning to Stockholmers from the Region's Healthcare Chief', *Local*, 4 June 2020, https://www.thelocal.se/20200604/this-is-the-stark-coronavirus-warning-to-stockholmers-from-the-regions-healthcare-chief.

65 Sidsel Overgaard, 'Sweden Bans Groups Larger than 50 in Its First Major Coronavirus Crackdown', NPR, 27 March 2020, https://www.npr.org/sections/coronavirus-live-updates/2020/03/27/822463152/sweden-bans-groups-larger-than-50-in-its-first-major-coronavirus-crackdown.

66 Rothschild, 'Sweden Is Open for Business During Its Coronavirus Outbreak'.

67 Christina Anderson and Henrik Pryser Libell, 'In the Coronavirus Fight in Scandinavia, Sweden Stands Apart', *New York Times*, 28 March 2020, https://www.nytimes.com/2020/03/28/world/europe/sweden-coronavirus.html.

68 *Ibid*.

69 *Ibid*.

70 *Ibid*.

71 Lebano, 'Sweden's Relaxed Approach to COVID-19 Isn't Working'.

72 *Ibid*.

73 Susanne Wiborg, 'Neo-liberalism and Universal State Education: The Cases of Denmark, Norway and Sweden 1980–2011', *Comparative Education*, vol. 49, no. 4, November 2013, p. 408.

74 *Ibid*., p. 413.

75 *Ibid*., p. 419.

76 See Emily Cochran Bech, Karin Borevi and Per Mouritsen, 'A "Civic Turn" in Scandinavian Family Migration Policies? Comparing Denmark, Norway and Sweden', *Comparative Migration Studies*, vol. 5, no. 1, March 2017, p. 7.

77 'Migration: Foreign-born Population – OECD Data', Organisation for Economic Co-operation and Development, 18 August 2020, http://data.oecd.org/migration/foreign-born-population.htm.

78 See Birte Siim, 'Gender, Diversity and Migration: Challenges to Nordic Welfare, Gender Politics and Research', *Equality, Diversity and Inclusion*, vol. 32, no. 6, 2013, p. 621.

79 See Jörgen Weibull and Susan Ruth Larson, 'Sweden', *Encyclopedia*

Britannica, https://www.britannica.com/place/Sweden.

80 *Ibid.*

81 *Ibid.*

82 See 'Standing Apart: How Uruguay Has Coped with COVID-19', *The Economist*, 18 June 2020, https://www.economist.com/the-americas/2020/06/18/how-uruguay-has-coped-with-COVID-19.

83 See Milagros Costabel, 'Uruguay Emerges as a Rare Pandemic Winner in Latin America', *Foreign Policy*, 21 July 2020, https://foreignpolicy.com/2020/07/21/uruguay-coronavirus-pandemic-success-latin-america/.

84 See S. Pelin Berkmen and Natasha Che, 'Uruguay's Secret to Success in Combating COVID-19', MercoPress, 4 August 2020, https://en.mercopress.com/2020/08/04/uruguay-s-secret-to-success-in-combating-COVID-19; and Ken Parks, 'In Midst of Covid Chaos, One Latin American Nation Gets It Right', Bloomberg, 30 June 2020, https://www.bloomberg.com/news/articles/2020-06-30/in-midst-of-COVID-chaos-one-latin-american-nation-gets-it-right.

85 See Berkmen and Che, 'Uruguay's Secret to Success in Combating COVID-19'; and Parks, 'In Midst of Covid Chaos, One Latin American Nation Gets It Right'.

86 See Azam Ahmed et al., 'Virus Gains Steam Across Latin America', *New York Times*, 23 June 2020, https://www.nytimes.com/2020/06/23/world/americas/coronavirus-brazil-mexico-peru-chile-uruguay.html.

87 See Berkmen and Che, 'Uruguay's Secret to Success in Combating COVID-19'.

88 Uki Goñi and William Costa, 'Uruguay and Paraguay Buck Latin America Coronavirus Trend', *Guardian*, 25 June 2020, http://www.theguardian.com/world/2020/jun/25/uruguay-and-paraguay-buck-latin-america-coronavirus-trend.

89 See Costabel, 'Uruguay Emerges as a Rare Pandemic Winner in Latin America'.

90 See 'Standing Apart: How Uruguay Has Coped with COVID-19'.

91 Maite Fernández Simon, 'How Tiny Uruguay, Wedged Between Brazil and Argentina, Has Avoided the Worst of the Coronavirus', *Washington Post*, 21 July 2020, https://www.washingtonpost.com/world/the_americas/coronavirus-uruguay-paraguay-brazil-argentina/2020/07/20/a7894830-c57c-11ea-a99f-3bbdff-b1af38_story.html.

92 Roser et al., 'Coronavirus Pandemic (COVID-19)'.

93 See Goñi and Costa, 'Uruguay and Paraguay Buck Latin America Coronavirus Trend'.

94 Berkmen and Che, 'Uruguay's Secret to Success in Combating COVID-19'.

95 'Standing Apart: How Uruguay Has Coped with COVID-19'.

96 *Ibid.*

97 Fernández Simon, 'How Tiny Uruguay, Wedged Between Brazil and Argentina, Has Avoided the Worst of the Coronavirus'.

98 *Ibid.*

99 Jennifer Pribble, 'Uruguay Quietly Beats Coronavirus, Distinguishing Itself from Its South American Neighbors – Yet Again', *Conversation*, 15 June 2020, https://theconversation.com/

uruguay-quietly-beats-coronavirus-
distinguishing-itself-from-its-south-
american-neighbors-yet-again-140037.

100   *Ibid.*

101   See Luisa Horwitz, 'LatAm in
        Focus: How Uruguay Got It
        Right', Americas Society/Council
        of the Americas, 16 July 2020,
        https://www.as-coa.org/articles/
        latam-focus-how-uruguay-got-it-right.

102   Pribble, 'Uruguay Quietly Beats
        Coronavirus, Distinguishing Itself
        from Its South American Neighbors –
        Yet Again'.

103   Ahmed et al., 'Virus Gains Steam
        Across Latin America'.

104   Horwitz, 'LatAm in Focus'.

105   Costabel, 'Uruguay Emerges as a
        Rare Pandemic Winner in Latin
        America'.

106   Fernández Simon, 'How Tiny
        Uruguay, Wedged Between Brazil and
        Argentina, Has Avoided the Worst of
        the Coronavirus'.

107   See E.J. Dionne, Jr, *Our Divided
        Political Heart: The Battle for the
        American Idea in an Age of Discontent*
        (New York: Bloomsbury USA, 2013).

The Coronavirus Pandemic and the Future of International Order

Hanns W. Maull

The global pandemic caused by the SARS-CoV-2 coronavirus is at its core a crisis of globalisation, encompassing three key areas: global public health, the world economy and the international political order. That order, which comprises national political structures as well as international arrangements for governance – be it for regions, issue areas or the world as a whole – is becoming increasingly incapable of meeting the demand for effective governance. Such demand has grown rapidly as the ties between economies and societies have become denser and more intricate. The deepening and widening of regional and global interdependencies have brought enormous opportunities, but also new risks and vulnerabilities that need to be managed. The institutions and policies of the international political order are meant to do so, but have not been able to keep up. The pandemic has revealed deficiencies of global governance in transnational public-health procurement, in managing the global economy and in world politics. At the same time, the crisis has introduced major new challenges in each of these areas. The interdependence of the three facets of the crisis means that whatever happens in one area will have repercussions, for better or for worse, in the other two as well.

Hanns W. Maull is Senior Distinguished Fellow, German Institute for International and Security Affairs (SWP), and Adjunct Professor for International Relations and Strategic Studies, Johns Hopkins University, School of Advanced International Studies (SAIS) Europe. He is co-author (with Alexandra Sakaki, Kerstin Lukner and Thomas Berger) of *Reluctant Warriors: Germany, Japan, and Their U.S. Alliance Dilemma* (Brookings Institution Press, 2019).

Survival | vol. 63 no. 1 | February–March 2021 | pp. 77–100   https://doi.org/10.1080/00396338.2021.1881255

The approval and roll-out of vaccines for SARS-CoV-2, while presenting a huge logistical challenge, at least holds the promise that the global public-health crisis will be contained in the months to come. Yet the economic and social disruptions caused by the pandemic, and the political changes these have triggered, both nationally and internationally, are likely to be more durable. A need by governments to address disruptions in economic activity, on both the supply and demand sides, has brought about a massive expansion of the state's role in national economic activity, and thus a transformation of politics at the national and international levels. The crisis produced a surge in state activism, empowering governments at the national/federal, state and local levels to take the lead in crisis management, but it also exposed the limitations of and constraints on government efforts. These shortcomings, which in many countries suggest a crisis of governance, have been particularly acute in international affairs, where there has been lamentably little effective international cooperation and coordination, and, in particular, a near-complete absence of American leadership. The US government under Donald Trump not only failed to adequately prepare the country for the pandemic and manage its onslaught, but also undermined international cooperation, blaming others, particularly China and the World Health Organization, for America's and the world's travails.[1] Tensions predictably increased between the US and China, while the reputation and capacity of both to exercise leadership suffered. As Kevin Rudd, the former prime minister of Australia, aptly put it: 'with a damaged United States and a damaged China, there is no "system manager," to borrow Joseph Nye's phrase, to keep the international system in functioning order'.[2] A system that was already showing signs of decay before the pandemic appeared to enter a tailspin once the virus took hold.[3]

The economic fallout

The pandemic has had a pervasive impact on global economic activity and socio-economic development.[4] Disruption caused by measures such as government-mandated shutdowns spread far and wide, tearing up not only supply chains, but all kinds of intricate arrangements that once created prosperity through the division of labour, both within and between countries.[5] The disruption of supply chains alone, according to calculations by the International Trade Center, was likely to reduce global exports of manufacturing inputs by at least $228 billion in 2020.[6] Production facilities faced the prospect of closing as workers fell ill, as in the case of Smithfield Foods, a meat-processing firm in the US that normally produces about 5% of American pork.[7] Whole industries have seen demand evaporate, as in the case of airlines and tour operators. Shutdowns affected key sectors such as agriculture, manufacturing and many service industries. Millions of migrant workers have lost their jobs, with a major impact on the remittances that are by far the most important source of support for poor people worldwide.[8] The pandemic also severely harmed the informal sector, which in India and Pakistan accounts for about 70% of the total workforce.[9] As people and firms struggled to find alternative sources of supply or demand, new connections, both within and across borders, were forged; patterns of production and consumption shifted; and lifestyles underwent major changes.[10]

Economic crisis management in most economies involved massive state interventions on both the supply and the demand side of the economy. These interventions injected a huge dose of money into national economies – as well as the global economy – that were already awash with it following the international financial crisis in 2008–09, but struggling to translate the influx of money into economic growth. This produced a vastly enlarged global supply of money.[11] Since the risk of inflation seems remote at present, cheap money may last for quite some time, and national governments may find themselves largely in control of national economies as certain economic activities come to depend on government loans, transfers and subsidies.[12] As a result, states will also hold – and will have to service, though for the time being at very low or even negative interest rates – vastly expanded levels of public debt.

It seems reasonable to expect national economies and the world economy to bounce back in 2021, as China's economy has already begun to do. Yet beyond this short-term return of growth, huge uncertainties persist about the longer-term economic trajectory. Moreover, serious questions should be asked about the massive expansion of the state's role in national economies. Will government intervention be able to secure a return to economic growth, beyond the short-term rebound that will likely take place in 2021? Will central banks and financial markets oblige? Will interest and inflation rates remain low? There are signs that the stimulus effect of cheap money has already weakened significantly,[13] and some believe that the world will soon enter another great depression.[14]

Governments will have to find a way of balancing between the conservation of existing economic structures and their 'creative destruction' through innovation, and between social fairness and policies that favour the top 1%. Given the massive scope of state interventions, established interests and activities are likely to benefit disproportionately, at least initially. Yet the highly disruptive nature of the pandemic seems likely to favour the creation of new businesses. Indeed, the crisis might well trigger significant changes in nations' underlying socio-economic models and assumptions, producing, for example, a shift away from export-led growth, or even 'de-growth'. This, in turn, would imply major changes in demand patterns. The fallout from the pandemic will thus interact with ongoing debates about the merits and deficiencies of economic globalisation, and probably reshape them significantly. This can be expected to modify, but not reverse, globalisation: the forces driving it are too powerful, and its impact too broad and deep, for a complete reversal. Indeed, both the rapid worldwide spread of SARS-CoV-2 and the impressive speed with which vaccines were developed testify to the enduring, and still growing, power of globalisation.

The ways in which governments and societies balance between conservation and innovation, and the concentration and redistribution of private wealth, are also likely to have consequences for countries' relative position in the world economy. Yet that economy itself seems likely to undergo significant changes. The markers of 'international competitiveness' may come to be determined by factors that differ from those that were decisive in the past. Thus, geographic proximity and political affinity might become more important, and efficiency less important, in establishing international economic cooperation. Supply chains may be rearranged to reduce or eliminate dependence on a single supplier. Inventories may make a comeback while 'just-in-time' systems are scaled back. Regional cooperation will, as indicated by the launch of Asia's Regional Comprehensive Economic

Partnership on 1 December 2020, probably gain in importance, though it will be shaped, more than in the past, by geopolitical and geo-economic considerations.[15] 'Competitive connectivity' will lead to multiple frameworks for regional and trans-regional cooperation that in some cases are overlapping and mutually compatible, and in others competitive and constraining. Considerations of efficient resource allocation that have dominated the organisation of globalised networks over the last decades will henceforth be mitigated (though not entirely replaced) by concerns about security of supply and sustainability.

The second fundamental choice faced by governments concerns the implications for social fairness of the economic- and fiscal-policy decisions they will make. Government interventions have been justified by a need to protect public health and overall economic activity, which at first glance may seem to be egalitarian concerns. Yet the impact of the pandemic has been anything but egalitarian.[16] In principle, the expansion of the state's role in national economies would seem to argue for more attention to issues of social equity and fairness, as the state in theory represents all citizens. In practice, the characteristics of national political economies will shape governmental choices and their implications. Will governments find the strength to address the pervasive social inequalities that undermine economic growth and fuel populism, or will they rather allow cheap money to continue to drive asset prices that mostly benefit the very rich, and permit government transfer payments to be captured by well-connected vested interests? It remains to be seen whether the present era of government activism will usher in another progressive age, or more plutocracy.[17]

The political fallout

The surge in state activism reflected a heightened demand for governance as the pandemic threatened what is considered a core responsibility of the modern state: public health.[18] Governments responded by imposing extensive reductions in a broad range of economic and social activities, which tended to enhance their domestic political legitimacy: people generally appeared inclined to accept the need for such drastic steps, at least in the initial phase of the crisis. A surge in support for the state was observed in both authoritarian and democratic systems, in the West and in the East, but actual performance diverged widely, with countries in Asia-Pacific coping best.[19] During the second and third waves of the pandemic in autumn and winter 2020–21, these differences persisted, and even widened: while some countries, such as New Zealand, Taiwan and Vietnam, continued to effectively contain the pandemic, others, such as the United States and many Latin American and European countries, suffered from weaknesses in governance and a lack of collective social discipline. When governments lose their capacity to persuade citizens to trust them, many fall back on repression, yet even in states where this strategy is highly developed, such as China, it is unclear whether control can be effectively maintained without the legitimacy derived from significant levels of popular approval.[20] On the other hand, it is also far from clear whether poor government performance necessarily undermines public trust and legitimacy. Governments may be able successfully to convince people that their approach is working by blaming scapegoats, cultivating a 'rally around the flag' effect or projecting 'determined leadership' in the 'battle' against the foe, as both Donald Trump in the United States and Xi Jinping in China tried to do in their virus-related communications.[21]

Still, it seems reasonable to predict that governments which consistently fail to deliver progress in containing the pandemic and neglect social fairness will eventually find themselves in trouble.[22] As the consequences of the pandemic are likely to be disproportionately borne by the lower strata of society, perceptions of fairness may be critical to governments' survival. Yet this also raises the issue of what constitutes a 'fair' policy: who should receive and who should be excluded from any benefits provided, and how should burdens be allocated? It is easy to see how divisive and politically explosive these questions could be.

Most of the increase in governance demands driven by the SARS-CoV-2 pandemic has been met at the national level, with the exception of the European Union. Of course, national governments play an indispensable role in combatting pandemics: even within the EU, authority for public health, as well as most of the relevant resources, reside with states. At the same time, the overall response to the pandemic will depend on the coordination of national efforts and the deployment of national capabilities and resources on an international scale. Ideally, governance in a pandemic would imply a seamless web of coordinated national efforts that direct resources to where they are needed most in the most efficient way.

Two states are of particular importance, given their position at the centre of the international order: China and the United States. Already, the successes and failures of these countries' responses to the pandemic have reverberated around the globe. China's initial failure to contain the virus caused it to spread. Later, Beijing tried to use its eventual success in containing the outbreak and its offer of support to other countries as a means of projecting its influence abroad.[23] That effort largely backfired, though Beijing's ability to overcome its early blunders meant that China's economy rebounded quickly and is still on track to overcome the United States', possibly as early as 2028.[24] Still, the test for China's political resilience is far from complete, as the leadership itself seems to understand.[25]

Washington refused to assume a leadership role

America's failure to manage the pandemic has been more damaging as the virus has ravaged the country and Washington has refused to assume a global leadership role.[26] The administration of newly elected president Joseph Biden faces the immense task of repairing and rehabilitating not just the United States but also an international order that has been badly damaged by the impact of the pandemic and four years of mismanagement by the Trump administration. The US will need years, if not decades, to revitalise its democracy, heal its social ills and reclaim its leadership in world affairs.

Even beyond these two countries, defective state responses to the pandemic risk not only national political upheavals but also negative international ramifications – most obviously through new outbreaks of infection, but also through migratory pressures and the spread of terrorist violence. Under some circumstances, it may be possible to substitute deficient state capacities with international efforts, but experience with such interventions in the past has been mixed at best, suggesting the great difficulties such efforts face.[27] The ability of states in general, and of states with large populations and special geopolitical or geo-economic significance in particular, to cope with the pandemic is thus a key factor in determining the future of international order and global governance.

The sorry state of international cooperation

Both the global health emergency and the economic crisis it unleashed cried out for international policy coordination.[28] The actual response was, to put it mildly, underwhelming. Only the European Union has begun to take important steps towards an effective collective response, nudged forward by a joint Franco-German initiative for a massive EU recovery fund.[29] Beyond the EU, however, the record of international cooperation has been poor. This is in contrast with the management of the international financial crisis that began in August 2007 and reached its first climax with the demise of the US investment bank Lehman Brothers on 15 September 2008. That crisis was managed, by and large successfully, firstly through closely coordinated action by central banks and then through a series of G20 summit meetings.[30] At the first such meeting in Washington on 14–15 November 2008, the attending leaders, staring into the abyss of another great depression, agreed on a host of commitments and an action plan with specific measures, including targets that were to be met by 31 March 2009.[31] Four more G20 summits were to follow, two in 2009 and two in 2010. After that, the summits continued on an annual basis.

In 2020, the G20 chair was held by Saudi Arabia, while the United States chaired the G7.[32] Neither grouping contributed in a meaningful way to the management of the pandemic, nor its economic repercussions. The G7 issued a first statement on SARS-CoV-2 on 3 March and organised a virtual leaders' meeting on 16 March. This meeting produced a rather anodyne statement that contained well-intentioned language, if few specifics – for example, it strongly endorsed and pledged support for the work of the World Health Organization, which Trump later decided the US would leave.[33] On 25 March, the G7 foreign ministers' virtual conference produced no communiqué, apparently because the US insisted on referring to SARS-CoV-2 as the 'Wuhan virus'.[34] On 16 April, Washington organised another virtual meeting, but the participants once again failed to agree on a communiqué.[35] By that time, Trump had already decided to replace the G7 summit scheduled to take place in the United States with another virtual gathering. Thus, while US leadership produced no meaningful cooperation, it did generate considerable irritation.

The G20, with Saudi Arabia in the chair, did little better. Ironically, in 2019, when Japan held the chair, it had organised a conference focused on global health that had considered, among other topics, outbreaks of infectious diseases.[36] Despite this and other warnings, international cooperation to tackle the pandemic in 2020 was perfunctory at best.[37] Saudi Arabia organised two virtual summits of G20 leaders, the only significant result of which was a decision, taken at the behest of the International Monetary Fund and the World Bank, to freeze governmental loan repayments from low-income countries to G20 members, and calls on private creditors to do the same.[38] The payment freeze was a welcome but merely a first, small step to address the plight of developing countries in the pandemic.

Otherwise, crisis management was driven by national responses that were rarely coordinated with other countries. This was perhaps to be expected given that the world order had been deteriorating since the mid-2000s, with tensions rising between China, Russia and the West well before the outbreak of the pandemic. Indeed, China and the US seemed to be wading into a new cold war – a systemic contest to establish which country had the superior political order. The first round in this contest had occurred in 2008–09 when the financial crisis provided an opportunity to debate the relative merits and shortcomings of the 'Washington consensus' versus the 'Beijing consensus'. The present round is pitting an authoritarian (or neo-totalitarian) China and a (sometimes falteringly) liberal-democratic West – consisting of the US, the UK, the other Anglo-Saxon countries, Japan (and perhaps the other East Asian democracies), and the core member states of the European Union – against each other as each side tries to prove its worth in managing the pandemic.[39] China's seemingly successful approach in containing the virus rests on the Communist Party's total control over society and the flow of information, including international narratives about the pandemic and its causes.

A European exception?

Compared to the dismal record of international cooperation overall, the European Union did achieve significant results – though whether this was enough to fully meet the challenge is a separate issue. As elsewhere, the crisis initially overwhelmed the capacity of European institutions to cope, an unsurprising outcome given that the EU has been notoriously bad at crisis management. National governments imposed border controls without any serious effort at cooperation or coordination. This contradicted the spirit, and sometimes also the letter, of the Schengen agreement on document-free travel within the EU.[40] National measures, such as Germany's ill-considered (and short-lived) export ban on medical equipment, also affected the movement of goods across borders in ways that contravened the principle of a European common market.

The crisis initially overwhelmed European institutions

Initially, European cooperation focused on the eurozone. After some early missteps, Christine Lagarde of the European Central Bank (ECB) quickly found her feet, and the bank moved forcefully to pump additional liquidity into financial markets. This helped to dampen a spike in interest rates for France, Italy and Spain. On 9 April, the Eurogroup decided on a number of measures to provide financial support to member states that had been hit hardest by the pandemic, including loans of up to €200bn by the European Investment Bank to the private sector, a €100bn fund to support the unemployed, and borrowing facilities provided by the European Stability Mechanism to strengthen pandemic-affected national health systems with sums of up to 2% of GDP. On average, member states mobilised national financial resources to combat the pandemic and its economic consequences to the tune of about 3% of GDP; in total, about €1,900bn of public money was allocated to various European programmes and facilities.[41] This was roughly comparable to the US government's $2,000bn CARES programme, both in terms of its absolute value and its relative importance in relation to overall economic activity. The support of the US Federal Reserve Board in the form of monetary-policy measures to provide liquidity for the US economy was, however, significantly larger than that of the ECB.

In July 2020, EU leaders, at the initiative of France and Germany, agreed a European recovery fund (officially called 'Next Generation EU') that promised roughly to double the size of the EU's budget for the seven years to 2027 and to make transfer payments equivalent to up to 8% of GDP to those countries most seriously affected by the pandemic.[42] Perhaps even more importantly, in what some described as the EU's 'Hamiltonian moment', the leaders also agreed to issue jointly guaranteed bonds, thus opening the door to a mutualisation of EU debts and the issuance of European bonds as an important new financial instrument and investment vehicle. Overall, Brussels was expected to issue as much as €200bn-worth of bonds in 2021.[43] The recovery package survived blackmailing efforts by the governments of Hungary and Poland, which wanted to have the rule-of-law conditionality clauses removed from the regular budget, but they eventually had to settle for postponement of those clauses at a decisive four-day summit in December 2020.[44] On 27 December 2020, vaccinations against the SARS-CoV-2 virus began in all EU member states.

As so often in the past, the EU faltered in crisis management initially, but eventually saw the need for members to work together and arrive at common solutions.[45] Yet the pandemic hit at a time when the EU was already badly shaken by a series of earlier shocks – the euro crisis from 2010 onward, the Ukraine crisis of 2014, the migration crisis of 2015, the rise of populism in many member states and Brexit.[46] It remains unclear how this cascade of crises will ultimately affect the Union. Plausible scenarios range from a Potemkin-village EU in which the treaties and institutions still exist but have largely ceased to be relevant, to a revitalised Europe that holds its own as a major global player through its skilful use of regulatory power.[47]

Underlying the effects of the pandemic and other crises are problems of political decay – erosion of the legitimacy and effectiveness of political leaders and institutions; corrupt and unresponsive elites; a lack of practical commitment to the normative foundations of the EU order; and the resultant cynicism and low levels of participation.[48] These problems are apparent both at the European and at the member-state level. In some ways, the EU has been a victim of its own success: institutions that were designed for the original six member states of the European Community have struggled to keep up with successive enlargements. Moreover, the EU so far has failed to become a state; it continues to be a *sui generis* arrangement of close cooperation and some integration between nation-states that fulfils some of, but not all, the criteria of a state.[49] It is a community of law (*Rechtsgemeinschaft*), but it does not have a sovereign people, creating problems of democratic legitimacy. Its European identity is feeble, and the Union on its own is unable to control and defend its borders.

If Europe wants to overcome the challenges it faces, it will need to address the roots of this political decay. This will require innovation in Europe's economies, societies and political institutions. This will mostly be a national challenge for member states, though the European level is in need of an overhaul as well.

The EU needs to be decisive about its principles

Redesigning Europe should involve both more and less integration. More integration and more supranationalism will be needed to transform the European Union into a global player: it is no coincidence that the EU is at its most powerful and influential where it has a capacity for collective action, as in trade (with the EU Commission) and, to some extent, in international finance (with the euro and the ECB).[50] New European capacities for collective action are required for the Common Foreign and Security Policy, the Common Security and Defence Policy and in cyberspace, to name just a few examples.[51] At the same time, the EU needs to prioritise its work much more carefully and to pull out of areas where it provides little or no real benefit.[52] There is no reason, for example, why the EU needs a Common Agricultural Policy that has become a byword for corrupt practices and mostly benefits big agribusiness, rather than smaller European farms. Subsidies and policies should be managed nationally.

To regain its poise and move forward, the Union also needs to be much more decisive about its normative foundations and principles. The membership of countries governed by illiberal regimes bent on cementing their hold on societies, as in Hungary and Poland, is profoundly corrosive of the European project, starting with the scandalous subsidisation of these regimes and their cronies with European taxpayer money.[53] While the EU eventually agreed on a rule-of-law mechanism that could limit the flow of

EU money to countries in violation of certain basic principles, the implementation of this mechanism was successfully delayed by the governments of Poland and Hungary, and its effectiveness remains to be tested. As *The Economist* has pointed out, the earlier Maastricht criteria for eurozone member states were mostly honoured in the breach.[54]

The way out of the present conundrum will require reviving European integration through smaller groupings with larger ambitions, possibly through a 'treaty within the treaty' that could begin shifting resources away from old activities towards new ones.[55] The eurozone could represent such a core, but that would require strengthened institutional arrangements.[56]

European institutions also need to be fortified against their manipulation or even destruction from within by non-democratic, illiberal or authoritarian forces that might gain control over governments even in the founding members of the European Community. They further need to be reoriented towards socio-economic innovation and revitalisation within Europe.[57] The notion of a European Marshall Plan may be useful in that sense – provided it is understood that the key to the success of the Marshall Plan was its innovative institutional design, rather than the money it provided per se.[58] One great risk for the future of the European project is the prospect of the huge economic stimulus that has been mobilised against the pandemic being absorbed by powerful vested interests and networks associated with the past decay of the continent's political order, at the national as well as the European level.

Three countries will be particularly critical in the struggle for Europe's future: Italy, France and Germany. Italy is the weakest of the major European economies, and consequently has the deepest need for institutional reforms; its persistent problem has been low growth, which has prevented it from bringing its public debt under control.[59] France's position is stronger, yet its economy, society and political institutions also desperately need innovation and change. Emmanuel Macron may well represent France's last chance for reform in a liberal-democratic mould; if his presidency fails, he might be followed by a president from the extreme right. His early initiatives were impressive, but the momentum of his presidency has since stalled, firstly because of the protests of the *gilets jaunes* and then due to the pandemic.[60] Macron has tried to mobilise German support for his ambitious domestic- and foreign-policy agenda, but so far with little success. Yet the joint French–German initiative to launch a €500bn (later €750bn) rescue programme for the countries most badly affected by the pandemic, in which Berlin for the first time accepted mutualised European debt issuance and thus fundamentally changed its policy towards Southern European countries, might herald a revival of Franco-German joint leadership in Europe. That would be a welcome change: German leadership in European affairs has for too long been dangerously lacklustre. Before agreeing to the rescue programme, Berlin had stalled on Macron's proposals for reforming the European Union, without devising any alternative ideas or projects.

This neglect of its European responsibilities could turn out to be very costly for Germany. Angela Merkel, who as a political leader initially had a remarkably good pandemic, seems to have recognised this: she has begun to emphasise that the European Union will need to change in response to the challenges posed by the pandemic, and signalled Germany's willingness to assume a larger financial burden than in the past.

*   *   *

Rather than changing the trajectory of world politics, the SARS-CoV-2 pandemic has accelerated earlier tendencies towards the erosion of international cooperation and a return of power politics.[61] These trends can be traced to two principal causes: a crisis of political order and the revival of nationalism and populism.

It may seem paradoxical to discuss a crisis of political order at a time when the role of the state in the economy has greatly expanded, but political leaders have still encountered difficulties in meeting demands for regulation and in their management of conflicting interests within and between nation-states. While some governments, notably in Asia-Pacific, have been able to contain the pandemic effectively, many others have failed to do so. Success or failure has been unrelated to the type of government: there are democracies and authoritarian governments that have done well, and others that have done badly.[62] Trust in government, social discipline, astute political leadership and administrative competency seemed to be key in the successful governance of the public-health emergency.

Governments have addressed the socio-economic fallout of the crisis by printing huge amounts of additional money, pushing up debt levels dramatically and thus deferring adjustment and postponing difficult decisions. The impact of this solution on social inequality has so far been discouraging, and there are few signs that the monetary and fiscal stimuli adopted by governments and central banks will address this concern effectively in the future. Moreover, the vast expansion of the role of governments has done little to enhance governance capacity or effectiveness beyond the national level, with the possible exception of the European Union. This may have fed the other major cause of the governance crisis: the revival of nationalism and populism.

Nationalist and populist ideologies encourage the illusionary and destructive assumption that problems such as the SARS-CoV-2 pandemic, economic shocks and even social inequality can be solved at a national level. While the nation-state remains the most significant actor in the contemporary political order, in cases where governance at the national level falls short of demand, this can lead to a spillover of problems into other domains, heightening the demand for governance in other places and at other levels. Yet a preoccupation with nationalism and sovereignty makes it difficult to maintain an effective international order capable of supplying this governance. Thus, while problems of political order may develop at the national level, their most serious effect is to cause deficiencies in international governance.

The leadership of China's Communist Party has probably been the most astute at recognising that a widening gap between demand for and supply of governance is creating problems. The party's response has been to concentrate power at the very top, in the hands of one man, Xi Jinping, the 'chairman of everything'; and to exploit the potential of technological innovation to facilitate effective governance and social control. China's performance in the pandemic illustrates both the weaknesses and the strengths of its top-down model: a failure by local officials to convey the seriousness to the party hierarchy of the initial outbreak allowed the disease to spread, but once the seriousness had been grasped the party had the ability to enforce strict lockdown measures and exercise stringent control of social behaviour. To the extent that China wishes to expand its influence and impose its governance model beyond its own borders – on states, regional and even global institutions – the logic of its foreign policy could be described as imperial.[63] The American model of governance has had its imperial features too, though in Europe and East Asia it has been what Geir Lundestad has called an 'empire by invitation',[64] and its hegemony has been moderated by a capacity for self-correction provided for by US democracy. Yet the American model is today in deep trouble, both at home and abroad. Not only has it been discredited by the four years of the Trump administration, but its structural flaws have been painfully exposed. Some of those flaws go back to the very foundation of the United States as a partly slave-based society, and it remains to be seen whether American democracy will be able to overcome this legacy. If the Gilded Age, a period in American history with remarkable similarities to the present, provides any useful guidance, it will take decades of determined effort to revitalise American politics in a liberal mould.[65]

A more plausible alternative to the Chinese governance model is provided by European integration. Based on the principles of liberal democracy and social fairness, its peculiar strength is that the model integrates, at least to some extent, national and regional/supranational governance through a liberal-democratic form of multilateralism. Yet the European model also suffers from political and institutional decay, and its ability to live up to the demands of national, regional and global governance remains uncertain. As the American, Chinese and European models compete with each other politically and (for America and China) even militarily, they each face a broader evolutionary contest of cultural adaptation to the rising demand for global governance and an effective international order. It is entirely conceivable that none of them will survive, not least because they may try to work against, rather than with, each other. This risks further undermining not only the global capacity for effective governance, but also their own governance at home.

Acknowledgements

I would like to thank Fabio Basagni, Sven Biscop, Achim von Heynitz, Midori Tanaka and James Tawney for helpful comments and suggestions.

Notes

[1]   Examples of decisions that under-mined cooperation include the president's imposition of travel bans on European allies without prior information, the withdrawal of financial support from the World Health Organization and a failure by the US to propose any transnational initiatives. China did contribute to the pandemic through its initial mis-management of and suppression of information about the outbreak, and then launched a rather ham-fisted pro-paganda offensive to spread its own narrative about how it had handled the crisis. See European Think-tank Network on China, 'Covid-19 and Europe–China Relations: A Country-level Analysis', Special Report, 29 April 2020.

[2]   Kevin Rudd, 'The Coming Post-COVID Anarchy: The Pandemic Bodes Ill for Both American and Chinese Power – and for the Global Order', *Foreign Affairs*, 6 May 2020, https://www.foreignaffairs.com/ articles/united-states/2020-05-06/ coming-post-covid-anarchy.

[3]   See Hanns W. Maull (ed.), *The Rise and Decline of the Post-Cold War International Order* (Oxford: Oxford University Press, 2018); and Richard Haass, *World in Disarray: American Foreign Policy and the Crisis of the Old Order* (New York: Penguin Books, 2017).

[4]   See Gita Gopinah, 'The Great Lockdown: Worst Economic Downturn Since the Great Depression', IMF Blog, 14 April 2020, https://blogs.imf.org/2020/04/14/ the-great-lockdown-worst-economic-downturn-since-the-great-depression/; Gita Gopinah, 'A Long, Uneven and Uncertain Ascent', IMF Blog, 7 October 2020, https://blogs.imf. org/2020/10/13/a-long-uneven-and-uncertain-ascent/; Adam Tooze, 'The Normal Economy Is Never Coming Back', *Foreign Policy*, 9 April 2020, https://foreignpolicy. com/2020/04/09/unemployment-coronavirus-pandemic-normal-economy-is-never-coming-back/?mc_cid=48174c48ec&mc_eid=f33365e64e; and Martin Wolf, 'Ten Ways Coronavirus Crisis Will Shape World in Long Term', *Financial Times*, 3 November 2020, https://www.ft.com/ content/9b0318d3-8e5b-4293-ad50-c5250e894b07.

[5]   Survey data suggests about 75% of US companies experienced COVID-19-related supply-chain disruption. Kaj Malden and Suzanna Stephens, 'Cascading Economic Impacts of the COVID-19 Outbreak in China', U.S.–China Economic and Security Review Commission, Staff Research Report, 21 April 2020, available at https:// www.uscc.gov.

[6]   Olga Solleder and Mauricio Torres Velasquez, 'The Great Shutdown:

How COVID-19 Disrupts Supply Chains', International Trade Center, 5 May 2020, http://www.intracen.org/covid19/Blog/The-Great-Shutdown-How-COVID19-disrupts-supply-chains/.

7   'The Spread of Covid Has Caused a Surge in American Meat Prices', *The Economist*, 13 May 2020, https://www.economist.com/graphic-detail/2020/05/13/the-spread-of-covid-has-caused-a-surge-in-american-meat-prices.

8   International remittances flowing to low- and middle-income countries before the pandemic amounted to about three times all official development assistance. Remittances declined by about 20% during the pandemic, according to World Bank estimates, though they may recover somewhat in 2021. See Sophie Eisentraut et al., 'Polypandemic: Special Edition of the Munich Security Report', Munich Security Conference, November 2020, https://doi.org/10.47342/CJAO3231. Much of the remitted money benefits the poorer citizens of developing countries. See 'Lockdowns in Asia Have Sparked a Stampede Home', *The Economist*, 4 April 2020, https://www.economist.com/asia/2020/04/02/lockdowns-in-asia-have-sparked-a-stampede-home.

9   'India and Pakistan Try to Keep a Fifth of Humanity at Home', *The Economist*, 26 March 2020, https://www.economist.com/asia/2020/03/26/india-and-pakistan-try-to-keep-a-fifth-of-humanity-at-home.

10 See Matt Craven et al., 'COVID-19: Implications for Business', McKinsey & Company, executive briefing, 13 April 2020, available at https://www.mckinsey.com/business-functions/risk/our-insights/covid-19-implications-for-business.

11 The mobilisation of public funds worldwide vastly exceeded the total volume of supportive financial actions taken by governments and central banks during the financial crisis of 2008–09. See Tooze, 'The Normal Economy Is Never Coming Back'; and Martin Wolf, 'Five Forces that Will Define Our Post-Covid Future', *Financial Times*, 16 December 2020, https://www.ft.com/content/dd359338-6200-40d3-8427-901bad134e21. The balance sheet of the Federal Reserve increased from about $0.870 trillion in July 2007 to about $2.5trn in early 2010, about $4.5trn in mid-2016 and almost $7.4trn in December 2020, an increase of about 850%; by December 2020, this was equivalent to about 30% of US GDP. See Board of Governors of the Federal Reserve System, 'Total Assets of the Federal Reserve', https://www.federalreserve.gov/monetarypolicy/bst_recenttrends.htm. Between March and April 2020, the balance sheet of the European Central Bank jumped by about 13% and of the Federal Reserve by about 57%. See 'Euro Area Central Bank Balance Sheet', Trading Economics, https://tradingeconomics.com/euro-area/central-bank-balance-sheet; and Board of Governors of the Federal Reserve System, 'Credit and Liquidity Programs and the Balance Sheet', https://www.federalreserve.gov/monetarypolicy/bst_recenttrends.htm.

12 For an assessment of how inflation might still revive, see 'A Surge in

Inflation Looks Unlikely, but Is Still Worth Keeping an Eye On', *The Economist*, 12 December 2020, https://www.economist.com/briefing/2020/12/12/a-surge-in-inflation-looks-unlikely.

[13] See Sebastian Mallaby, 'The Age of Magic Money: Can Endless Spending Prevent Economic Calamity?', *Foreign Affairs*, July–August 2020, https://www.foreignaffairs.com/articles/united-states/2020-05-29/pandemic-financial-crisis; and Raphaële Chappe and Mark Blyth, 'Hocus-Pocus: Debating the Age of Magic Money', *Foreign Affairs*, November–December 2020, https://www.foreignaffairs.com/articles/2020-10-13/hocus-pocus.

[14] See, for example, George Friedman, 'Recession and Depression', Other News, 21 April 2020, https://www.other-news.info/2020/04/recession-and-depression; Tooze, 'The Normal Economy Is Never Coming Back'; and Martin Wolf, 'The World Economy Is Now Collapsing', *Financial Times*, 14 April 2020, https://www.ft.com/content/d5f05b5c-7db8-11ea-8fdb-7ec06edeef84.

[15] See Heribert Dieter, 'Die asiatische Freihandelszone RCEP', *SWP Aktuell*, no. 97, December 2020, https://www.swp-berlin.org/fileadmin/contents/products/aktuell/2020A97_AsiatischeFreihandelszoneRCEP.pdf.

[16] See Wolf, 'Five Forces that Will Define Our Post-Covid Future'.

[17] See Michael Lee, 'Populism or Embedded Plutocracy? The Emerging World Order', *Survival*, vol. 61, no. 2, April–May 2019, pp. 53–82.

[18] The reduction in mortality rates and the extension of average life expec-tancy beginning in the nineteenth century reflected advances in public-health policies, notably through the widespread implementation of clean-water procurement and sanitation in urban areas. See Albrecht Ritschl, 'Von Herdenimmunität und Lockdown', FAZ, 3 April 2020.

[19] One important factor explaining the crisis-management successes of Hong Kong, Singapore, South Korea and Taiwan during the pandemic was that they had suffered through the earlier SARS pandemic and drawn lessons for how to effectively prepare for similar situations. When the pandemic started, these countries were able to draw on carefully prepared contingency plans. See Francis Fukuyama, 'The Pandemic and Political Order', *Foreign Affairs*, July–August 2020, https://www.foreignaffairs.com/articles/united-states/2020-04-07/pandemic-will-accelerate-history-rather-reshape-it; Daniel Kaufman, 'What the Pandemic Reveals About Governance, State Capture, and Resources', Brookings Institution, 7 July 2020, https://www.brookings.edu/blog/future-development/2020/07/10/what-the-pandemic-reveals-about-governance-state-capture-and-natural-resources/; and Ian Bremmer, 'The Best Global Responses to COVID-19 Pandemic', *Time*, 12 June 2020, https://time.com/5851633/best-global-responses-covid-19/.

[20] We cannot exclude the possibility that advanced technologies of social control are capable of delivering total control. China is certainly working towards this, and the situation in Xinjiang

demonstrates how far the Communist Party has advanced in this direction. It is clear, however, that this level of control would be possible only through techniques of mind control that are completely incompatible with any notion of human dignity and freedom.

[21] This did not work particularly well for Donald Trump, however: see 'Americans Are Not Rallying Around Donald Trump During the Pandemic', *The Economist*, 15 April 2020, https://www.economist.com/graphic-detail/2020/04/15/americans-are-not-rallying-around-donald-trump-during-the-pandemic.

[22] This certainly is the view taken by former Australian prime minister and China scholar Kevin Rudd; he sees the position of both America and China suffering serious damage as a result of their governance performance during the pandemic. See Rudd, 'The Coming Post-COVID Anarchy'.

[23] See Michael D. Swaine, 'Chinese Crisis Decision Making: Managing the COVID-19 Pandemic, Part Two: The International Dimension', China Leadership Monitor, 1 September 2020, https://www.prcleader.org/swaine-1.

[24] According to a report by Reuters, an internal document prepared for the Communist Party leadership warned that China's international reputation was at its lowest point since 1989. See 'Internal Chinese Report Warns Beijing Faces Tiananmen-like Global Backlash over Virus', Reuters, 4 May 2020, https://www.reuters.com/article/us-health-coronavirus-china-sentiment-ex-idUSKBN22G19C. On the Chinese economy, see David Dollar, 'China's Economy Bounces Back, but to Which Growth Path?', China Leadership Monitor, 1 September 2020, https://www.prcleader.org/dollar.

[25] See Minxin Pei, 'China's Coming Upheaval', *Foreign Affairs*, May–June 2020, https://www.foreignaffairs.com/articles/united-states/2020-04-03/chinas-coming-upheaval; and Tai Ming Cheung, 'The Chinese National Security State Emerges from the Shadows to Center Stage', China Leadership Monitor, 1 September 2020, https://www.prcleader.org/cheung.

[26] See Rudd, 'The Coming Post-COVID Anarchy'; George Packer, 'We Are Living in a Failed State', *Atlantic*, June 2020, https://www.theatlantic.com/magazine/archive/2020/06/underlying-conditions/610261/; and Pew Research Center, 'U.S. Image Plummets Internationally as Most Say Country Has Handled Coronavirus Badly', 15 September 2020, https://www.pewresearch.org/global/2020/09/15/us-image-plummets-internationally-as-most-say-country-has-handled-coronavirus-badly/. The one exception to this harsh assessment is the role played by the Federal Reserve, which once more played a critical role in providing international liquidity.

[27] See Predrag Jurecović and Walter Feichtinger (eds), *Erfolg oder Misserfolg von internationalen Interventionen: Innovative Messmethoden und Fallstudien* (Vienna: Bundesministerium für Landesverteidigung, 2019); and Roland Paris and Timothy D. Siks (eds), *The Dilemmas of Statebuilding: Confronting the Contradictions of Postwar Peace Operations* (London: Routledge, 2009).

28 See Ngozi Okonji-Iweala, 'Finding
a Vaccine Is Only the First Step: No
One Will Be Safe Until the Whole
World Is Safe', *Foreign Affairs*, 30 April
2020, https://www.foreignaffairs.
com/articles/world/2020-04-30/
finding-vaccine-only-first-step;
and Philip H. Gordon, '"America
First" Is a Dangerous Fantasy in a
Pandemic: Foreign Aid and Global
Leadership Will Be Integral to Any
Solution', *Foreign Affairs*, 4 April
2020, https://www.foreignaffairs.
com/articles/2020-04-04/america-first-
dangerous-fantasy-pandemic.

29 See Victor Mallet, Guy Chazan and
Sam Fleming, 'The Chain of Events
that Led to Germany's Change over
the Recovery Fund', *Financial Times*,
22 May 2020, https://www.ft.com/
content/1d8853f4-726d-4c06-a905-
ed2f37d25eee.

30 This was hitherto a rather obscure
framework for international
economic-policy coordination that
was set up in the wake of the Asian
financial crisis in 1997–98. The first
G20 meeting took place in Berlin in
1999 at the level of finance ministers.

31 'Declaration of the Summit
on Financial Markets and the
World Economy', Washington
DC, 15 November 2008, available at http://www.g20.utoronto.
ca/2008/2008declaration1115.html.

32 After the suspension of Russia's membership (which had turned the G7 into
the G8) in 2014 in response to Moscow's
annexation of Crimea, the group had
reverted to its original format bringing together the seven largest Western
industrial democracies, plus the presi-
dents of the European Council and the
European Commission.

33 See 'The World Health Organisation
Is Under Fire from America's
President', *The Economist*, 16 April
2020, https://www.economist.com/
science-and-technology/2020/04/16/
the-world-health-organisation-is-
under-fire-from-americas-president;
and Katie Rogers and Apoorva
Mandavilli, 'Trump Administration
Signals Formal Withdrawal
from W.H.O.', *New York Times*, 7
July 2020, https://www.nytimes.
com/2020/07/07/us/politics/
coronavirus-trump-who.html.

34 See Patrick Wintour, 'G7 Backing
for WHO Leaves Trump Isolated
at Virtual Summit', *Guardian*,
17 April 2020, https://www.
theguardian.com/world/2020/apr/16/
g7-backing-for-who-leaves-trump-
isolated-at-virtual-summit.

35 See *ibid*.

36 See 'Okayama Declaration of the
G20 Health Ministers', Okayama,
Japan, 19–20 October 2020, available
at http://www.g20.utoronto.ca/2019/
G20Okayama_HM_EN.pdf.

37 See David E. Sanger et al., 'Before
Virus Outbreak, A Cascade of
Warnings Went Unheeded', *New York
Times*, 19 March 2020, https://www.
nytimes.com/2020/03/19/us/politics/
trump-coronavirus-outbreak.html.

38 See 'Leaders' Declaration', G20
Riyadh Summit, 21–22 November
2020, https://www.g20riyadhsummit.
org/wp-content/uploads/2020/11/
G20-Riyadh-Summit-Leaders-
Declaration_EN.pdf; Okonji-Iweala,
'Finding a Vaccine Is Only the
First Step'; and Delphine Strauss
and Jonathan Wheatley, 'Global

Lenders Seek Debt Relief for Poorest Countries', *Financial Times*, 5 March 2020, https://www.ft.com/content/6eca167c-6ec0-11ea-9bca-bf503995cd6f.

39   See Michael McFaul, 'Cold War Lessons and Fallacies for US–China Relations Today', *Washington Quarterly*, vol. 43, no. 4, 2020, pp. 7–39.

40   Schengen had already been badly damaged by migration flows into the EU and, in particular, by the migration crisis of 2015; six of the agreement's 26 member countries never fully abolished the supposedly temporary border-control measures they had put in place at that time. See 'Why Europe's New Border Controls Won't Help Much', *The Economist*, 21 March 2020, https://www.economist.com/europe/2020/03/19/why-europes-new-border-controls-wont-help-much.

41   See Sam Fleming and Mereen Khan, 'Eurozone Strikes Emergency Deal on Coronavirus Rescue', *Financial Times*, 10 April 2020, https://www.ft.com/content/b984101a-42b8-40db-9a92-6786aec2ba5cv.

42   See Martin Sandbu, 'EU Crosses the Rubicon with Its Emergency Recovery Fund', *Financial Times*, 22 July 2020, https://www.ft.com/content/bd570dde-3095-4074-bd37-18003f2bd3c2; and Peter Becker, 'A European Economic Policy in the Making: Success with Modest Means', SWP Research Paper, October 2020, https://www.swp-berlin.org/fileadmin/contents/products/research_papers/2020RP13_EuropeanEconomicPolicy.pdf.

43   See 'The EU's €750bn Recovery Plan Comes One Step Closer', *The Economist*, 14 November 2020, https://www.economist.com/europe/2020/11/14/the-eus-eu750bn-recovery-plan-comes-one-step-closer; and Tommy Stubbington, 'EU Hires Banks to Start Breakthrough Joint Bond Programme', *Financial Times*, 19 October 2020, https://www.ft.com/content/4ec5d621-1135-48a7-b912-de915d2de515.

44   See 'The EU At Last Agrees on Its Covid-19 Fund and Seven-year Budget', *The Economist*, 11 December 2020, https://www.economist.com/europe/2020/12/11/the-eu-at-last-agrees-on-its-covid-19-fund-and-seven-year-budget.

45   See Douglas Webber, *European Disintegration? The Politics of Crisis in the European Union* (London: Macmillan International, 2019), pp. 3–13.

46   See *ibid*.

47   See Michael Leigh, 'Relaunch or Disintegration? What Covid-19 Means for the Future of Europe', LSE, 14 December 2020, https://blogs.lse.ac.uk/europpblog/2020/12/14/relaunch-or-disintegration-what-covid-19-means-for-the-future-of-europe/.

48   The notion of decay in political order is ably explored in Francis Fukuyama's magisterial *Political Order and Political Decay: From the Industrial Revolution to the Globalization of Democracy* (New York: Farrar, Straus & Giroux, 2015).

49   This issue is central in the tussle between Germany's Constitutional Court and the European Court of Justice over the policies of the European Central Bank. See 'Germany's Highest Court Takes Issue with the European Central Bank', *The Economist*, 7 May 2020, https://www.

economist.com/europe/2020/05/07/
germanys-highest-court-takes-issue-
with-the-european-central-bank.

50   See Anu Bradford, *The Brussels Effect:
How the European Union Rules the
World* (Oxford: Oxford University
Press, 2020).

51   See Annegret Bendiek, Minna
Ålander and Paul Bochtler, 'CFSP:
The Capability–Expectation Gap
Revisited', *SWP Comment*, no. 58,
November 2020, https://www.
swp-berlin.org/fileadmin/contents/
products/comments/2020C58_
CFSPOutput.pdf.

52   See Vivien A. Schmidt, *Europe's Crisis
of Legitimacy: Governing by Rules and
Ruling by Numbers in the Eurozone*
(Oxford: Oxford University Press,
2020), pp. 294–302.

53   See Selam Gebrekidan, Matt Apuzzo
and Benjamin Novak, 'The Money
Farmers: How Oligarchs and Populists
Milk the E.U. for Millions', *New York
Times*, 11 March 2019, https://www.
nytimes.com/2019/11/03/world/europe/
eu-farm-subsidy-hungary.html.

54   Charlemagne, 'Poland and
Hungary Enjoy a Physics Lesson
Courtesy of the EU', *The Economist*,
26 November 2020, https://www.
economist.com/europe/2020/11/26/
poland-and-hungary-enjoy-a-physics-
lesson-courtesy-of-the-eu.

55   Ronja Kempin and Hanns W. Maull,
'Weniger und besser ist mehr,
Plädoyer für eine grunderneuerte EU',
Internationale Politik, 2016, pp. 80–7,
https://internationalepolitik.de/de/
weniger-und-besser-ist-mehr.

56   See Schmidt, *Europe's Crisis of Legitimacy*.

57   See Becker, 'A European Economic
Policy in the Making'.

58   See Tony Judt, 'Introduction', in
Martin Schain (ed.), *The Marshall Plan:
Fifty Years After* (London & New York:
Palgrave Macmillan, 2001).

59   It is instructive to compare the evolution of public debt in Belgium and
Italy. Both countries were seriously
over-indebted at the time of the
creation of the common European
currency. Despite its many political
problems, Belgium has managed to
reduce its public-debt burden over
the last two decades, while Italy has
failed to do so. The reasons for this
lie in their different macroeconomic
trajectories, which in turn reflect
deficiencies in Italian governance.
See Gerald Braunberger, 'Gerald: Das
italienische Dilemma', FAZ, 23 April
2020. My assessment of the Italian
situation relies on Andrea Lorenzo
Capussela, *The Political Economy
of Italy's Decline* (Oxford: Oxford
University Press, 2018).

60   See William Drozdiak, *The Last
President of Europe: Emmanuel Macron's
Race to Revive France and Save the World*
(New York: PublicAffairs, 2020).

61   See Richard Haass, 'The Pandemic
Will Accelerate History Rather than
Reshape It', *Foreign Affairs*, 7 April
2020, https://www.foreignaffairs.
com/articles/united-states/2020-04-07/
pandemic-will-accelerate-history-
rather-reshape-it.

62   See Fukuyama, 'The Pandemic and
Political Order'.

63   See Christine Lee and Alexander
Sullivan, *People's Republic of the United
Nations: China's Emerging Revisionism
in International Organizations*
(Washington DC: Center for a New
American Security, 2019), https://

www.cnas.org/publications/reports/
peoples-republic-of-the-united-nations.

64 Geir Lundestad, 'Empire by Invitation?
The United States and Western Europe,
1945–1952', *Journal of Peace Research*,
vol. 23, no. 3, 1986, pp. 263–77.

65 See Richard White, *The Republic
for Which It Stands: The United
States During Reconstruction and
the Gilded Age, 1865–1896* (Oxford:
Oxford University Press, 2017);
Thomas Picketty, *Capital in the
Twenty-first Century* (Cambridge,
MA: The Belknap Press of Harvard
University Press, 2014); Sarah
Chayes, *On Corruption in America
and What Is At Stake* (New York:
Alfred A. Knopf, 2020); and Robert
G. Kaiser, 'Corruption and Greed
in America's New Gilded Age',
Washington Post, 23 October 2020,
https://www.washingtonpost.
com/outlook/corruption-and-
greed-in-americas-new-gilded-
age/2020/10/22/8d0ba280-11b4-11eb-
ba42-ec6a580836ed_story.html.

War and Peace: Reaffirming the Distinction

Chiara Libiseller and Lukas Milevski

In recent years, the idea that the boundaries between war and peace are blurring has gained favour in the field of strategic studies. Concepts such as 'hybrid warfare' and the 'grey zone' have captured the perceived ambiguity. According to their champions, Western strategic thought has been constrained by a flawed binary distinction between war and peace, while other actors – mainly Russia and China – have become more flexible in their strategic thinking and intentionally exploit the limitations of the Western conception. These commentators contend that the West needs to replace the artificial dichotomy of war and peace with a continuum of war and peace to meet new challenges.[1]

Certainly, concepts and categories are arbitrary. Reality does not dictate them; they are intellectual constructs of our choice.[2] They cannot be definitively true or false but only more or less useful.[3] After reviewing the criticism of the traditional distinction between war and peace that these two recent concepts have prompted, we argue that they have blurred the boundaries between the two. In fact, the traditional understanding of war and peace based on Carl von Clausewitz's theory – in particular, its emphasis on the role of agency and intentions – leads to a clear and policy-relevant understanding of war and its boundaries, and offers a more useful approach to confronting the myriad means and effects that are currently subsumed

Chiara Libiseller is a PhD candidate in the War Studies Department of King's College London. **Lukas Milevski** is an assistant professor at the Institute for History at Leiden University, and author of *The Evolution of Modern Grand Strategic Thought* (Oxford University Press, 2016).

Survival | vol. 63 no. 1 | February–March 2021 | pp. 101–112   https://doi.org/10.1080/00396338.2021.1881256

under the concepts of hybrid war and grey-zone conflict, as well as a more systematic approach to understanding war.

Unsettling war

There is a tendency in Western strategic thought to over-classify. Every novel form of war seems to give rise to a new classification. Conventional war, which tends to be seen as the prototype of war, has been joined by unconventional or irregular war, hybrid war and many smaller-scope categories such as asymmetric warfare, grey-zone warfare, information warfare, cyber warfare and ambiguous warfare.[4] Two weaknesses are inherent in this proliferation of new conceptions of war and warfare. Firstly, the emphasis on form is unhelpful, not least because current Western understanding is often fatalistic about the present and future character of war, as if the West were a passive actor that can only accept and try to adapt to whatever version of warfare the enemy conjures. This disposition ignores the fact that wars take shape as a result of the interaction of adversaries.[5] If the West consistently finds itself stymied by the character of any particular war, it is simply not practising strategy well enough to control the interaction and succeed. Secondly, the ad hoc introduction of new concepts can ill serve strategic theory itself by blithely overriding it.[6]

The concept of hybrid warfare incorporates a number of diverse, and to some extent logically unrelated, elements of both war and peacetime competition into a single concept, thus blurring the line between the two situations. In its original conception, proposed by Frank Hoffman in 2007, the term referred primarily to the domain of war.[7] Generalising from an analysis of Hizbullah's approach in its 2006 war against Israel, Hoffman maintained that 'hybrid wars incorporate a range of different modes of warfare, including conventional capabilities, irregular tactics and formations, terrorist acts including indiscriminate violence and coercion, and criminal disorder'. He expected future adversaries to use a mixture of conventional and irregular means that were 'operationally and tactically directed and coordinated within the main battlespace to achieve synergistic effects'.[8]

As the concept was more widely adopted, the relatively tight focus on battlefield integration was increasingly ignored, such that most scholars today understand hybrid warfare to be simply the mixture of conventional and irregular means used by an actor in its overall war effort. Murat Caliskan has described the concept as the rediscovery of grand strategy.[9] The primary stimulus for this mutation of the hybrid-warfare concept is Russia's invasion of Crimea in 2014 and its subsequent instigation of civil war in eastern Ukraine. Some commentators consider both campaigns to be of the same nature, representative of Russia's new way of war, but only one of them actually turned into a war. Yet the term hybrid warfare is applied to both campaigns to capture non-violent as well as violent means, spanning both times of peace (but not friendly cooperation) and war.

This redefinition paved the way for a further mutation of the concept: after 2014, hybrid warfare increasingly turned into *Russian* hybrid warfare, tightly connecting the term and the particular case. The term is now commonly applied to Russian foreign policy in general.[10] Russia's use of disinformation campaigns and cyber attacks increasingly shifted the focus of scholars investigating hybrid warfare to these non-military means, side-lining the crucial role that the Russian threat of and actual use of force played in both Crimea and Donbas.[11] As part of this discursive shift, the object of the hybrid-warfare concept changed: while Russia has been engaged in actual war in Ukraine, some Western commentators interpret this war simply as an element of hybrid war directed against the West. While Russia's actions might indeed be intended as a hostile signal to the West, to suggest that Russia is engaged in war against the West 'is a dangerous misuse of the word "war"'.[12] In fact, it is mainly Russia's non-military campaigns that have extended to countries beyond Ukraine. Thus, over the years, hybrid warfare has changed from an operational concept to, as Ofer Fridman puts it, a 'catch-all description for the new Russian threat to European security'.[13]

More recent interpretations of the term imply an overlapping of war and peace in which non-military action by itself is interpreted as an act of war. In a world of hybrid wars, there is less and less space for a concept of peace. And if hybrid warfare is understood to be simply the mixture of conventional and unconventional means in war, it would be difficult to find a war that was not hybrid. In its broadest definition – referring to Russia's disinformation campaigns in the West, with no threat or use of force – the term completely redefines both war and peace: it suggests that war can exist not only with no use of force, but even with no threat of it. The concept thus erodes the traditional analytical separation between war and peace that turns on the distinction between mass military violence and non-military forms of power without providing a clear alternative delineation. It lumps together elements found in both situations into a single category, highlighting means while ignoring context or aims. For these reasons, the concept of hybrid war limits our ability to understand the dynamics of conflict.

The related idea of grey-zone challenges blurs the distinction between peace and war by creating an undefined middle ground 'that is neither fully war nor fully peace', 'a landscape churning with political, economic, and security competitions that require constant attention' or competition 'primarily below the threshold of armed conflict'.[14] The concept is usually employed to analyse recent Russian and Chinese actions, or the behaviour of revisionist states more generally.[15] Ambiguity is central to this approach: David Barno and Nora Bensahel argue that grey-zone conflicts 'involve some aggression or use of force, but in many ways their defining characteristic is ambiguity – about the ultimate objectives, the participants, whether international treaties and norms have been violated, and the role that military forces should play in response'.[16] As with hybrid warfare, the assumption is that while it does not quite look like war, it certainly cannot be peace either.

The concept itself may create more ambiguity than the phenomenon it aims to describe. As with the hybrid-warfare concept, its promoters remain vague about how it can actually be differentiated from war and peace, or how the two concepts should be redefined to make room for an in-between category. If the grey zone is merely defined as competition, the difference between it and the regular conduct of international politics is unclear. Moreover, definitions of the concept seem mainly to stem from flawed perceptions of war and peace rather than changes in reality: Hal Brands says grey-zone activity is 'deliberately designed to remain below the threshold of conventional military conflict and open interstate war', Michael Mazarr that it moves 'gradually toward its objectives rather than seeking conclusive results in a specific period of time'.[17] Conflict in the grey zone is thus contrasted not with the Clausewitzian characterisation of war, but with an ideal version of war as conventional war – battles between state militaries – that has dominated Western strategic thought for decades.[18] Formulations of the grey-zone concept also rely on a positive notion of peace, defined as 'the integration of human society'.[19] In strategic studies, however, the understanding of war has usually relied on a negative notion of peace, namely 'the absence of violence'.[20]

Thus, promoters of the grey-zone idea have opened conceptual space that they are unable to fill. By claiming that grey-zone challenges are neither fully peace nor fully war, they redefine those concepts without clarifying how they are to be understood. One response is that because reality is murky and ambiguous, the concepts used to capture it must be too. But concepts can never fully capture reality. The question is whether these particular ones are more helpful in guiding analysis and action than traditional concepts of war and peace.

Resettling war

As the idea of conventional war has come to dominate our understanding of war in general, even good Clausewitzians sometimes struggle with the concept of war. Hew Strachan notes that it 'involves the use of force', but acknowledges that a 'state of war can exist between opponents without there being any active fighting'. He identifies contention as a key element of war and suggests that 'war assumes a degree of intensity and duration to the fighting', although this runs counter to his earlier observation that states of war may exist without fighting. He proposes that those involved in waging war do so in a public rather than a private capacity, but feels stymied by the phenomenon of mercenaries participating in war. Finally, he recognises that war always has a political aim, but acknowledges that often wars are waged beyond political sense.[21] Strachan's critical elements of war stem from Clausewitzian considerations, but are mixed with other elements. Clausewitz's foundational definition of war is *'an act of force to compel our enemy to do our will'*.[22] This has encouraged others to focus exclusively on the use of violence. The level of violence, for instance, is the defining factor in the Correlates of War dataset project, which sets the baseline for war as the occurrence of 1,000 battle deaths in a year.[23]

By focusing almost exclusively on violence, Western thinking on war misses the nuance of Clausewitz's definition, which specifies not only (1) violence (an act of force) but also (2) the imposition of will (3) by an adversary for war to arise. Unless all three criteria are satisfied, the phenomenon in question is not war, even if it breaks peace. Accordingly, peace and war are not strict opposites; mass violence can take different forms, of which war is only one.

Underlying Clausewitz's three criteria is an appreciation of political and strategic agency and intent. He also famously stated that 'war is simply a continuation of political intercourse, with the addition of other means'.[24]

Peace and war are not strict opposites

A mutual acknowledgement emerges that violence has become the primary means of achieving political goals. Mutual recourse to violence reflects shared recognition of the inadequacy of regular non-violent political means to achieve desired outcomes. This state of affairs is likely to change over time, in response to strategic successes or failures; indeed, the very point of strategy is to force the enemy to change its mind.[25] But it reflects the particular intentions and agency of parties involved in a war at its outset.

Forms of war are a conceptual dead end because intentions may endure even as forms change. Intensity of warfare lacks definitional relevance because, even though new conditions set in, reciprocal political and strategic intentions, which give instrumental primacy to military force over all other political means, endure. Thomas Hobbes understood this in discussing war in his *Leviathan*: 'the nature of war, consisteth not in actual fighting; but in the known *disposition* thereto'.[26] Jan Almäng, writing about the vagueness of war, emphasised the strategic actors' representations of their mutual interaction by citing the phony war between the Allies and Germany in late 1939 and early 1940 as an example of a situation in which war existed although warfare hardly occurred.[27] Yet what is representation, if not a direct enunciation of agency and intention? The phony war is considered war because the adversarial intentions of the Allies on one side and Germany on the other elevated military force to instrumental primacy. The lack of intense fighting during the phony war does not change the basic mutual recognition of the importance of violence to gain the desired political goals at that time. During the interregnum in which warfare did not arise, it was just because no side was ready to act on its intentions until campaigning season began.

Maintaining the instrumental primacy of military force reflects a political decision and underlying attitude. During the Cold War, after Michael Howard and Peter Paret's 1976 translation of *On War* increased Clausewitz's popularity and currency, the liberal West interpreted his characterisation of war as politics by other means predominantly as a normative statement about civil–military relations and war's instrumental nature, firmly subordinated to policy direction. This raises the question of whether the Cold War would fit the Clausewitzian definition of war. It would not. Despite intense and extensive concern about nuclear weapons and strategy, neither side ever seriously intended to settle the rivalry directly with nuclear (or conventional) weapons unless the other side crossed certain very fundamental red lines. Instead, they relied on deterrence. But deterrence is not war, because the intention to use force is conditional for the former but not the latter.

As Strachan notes, 'today we too often use [Clausewitz's] normative statement about war's relationship to policy as though it applied to the causes of war, and so fail to recognize how often states go to war not to continue policy but to change it. The declaration of war, and more immediately the use of violence, alters everything.'[28] Strachan thus suggests that Clausewitz focused on the relationship between policy and the conduct of war, rather than the causes of war. Even this eminently reasonable interpretation may be reading too much into Clausewitz's words. Like strategy, politics is fundamentally concerned with shaping the future, albeit a much broader future than that with which strategy is concerned. Intentions therefore underlie policy, and are hostile when they involve harming the opposite party for whatever political purpose. Hostile intention must exist in a political relationship between future belligerents before manifesting itself as violence in war; otherwise, recourse to war would be unnecessary. The failure to appreciate that hostile intentions are part of politics but not yet necessarily war has given rise to the concepts hybrid warfare and the grey zone.

Clausewitzian definitions provide a simple and clear-cut categorisation of war and peace that is useful for making policy. Naturally, aggressors do conduct attacks cognisant of the possibility of resistance. But unless violence is reciprocated, there is no state of war. If there is reciprocal violence and an intention to continue relying on it to achieve political goals, then war exists. If not, it doesn't. Only if one of the political agents involved has not yet made up its mind about whether to resort to force does the distinction become blurry. Thus, war begins in earnest with defence. Attack alone is not sufficient, as the Germans demonstrated with their invasion of Austria in 1938; the Soviets with their invasions of the Baltic states in 1939–40, Hungary (which resisted to a degree) in 1956 and Czechoslovakia in 1968; and the Russians with their invasion of Crimea in 2014.

*   *   *

The claim that concepts such as hybrid warfare or the grey zone better reflect the real world, and therefore provide a stronger basis for policy and strategy in practice than the old distinction between war and peace, does not easily survive scrutiny.

The concepts emerged from Russia's conduct in Ukraine and China's in the South China Sea. Impressed with their apparent success, Western commentators have argued that the Western reaction should mirror the threat – that is, that it should take hybrid form or be conducted in the grey zone.[29] This way of thinking presages a tit-for-tat approach: the Chinese build islands, the United States and its partners sail through the South China Sea on freedom-of-navigation voyages; the Russians disseminate fake news, NATO allies try to refute it. Such responses are inherently reactive, and merely delay a full reckoning with China's and Russia's intentions to shape their respective strategic environments. The attractiveness of the tit-for-tat approach lies in its capacity to prevent escalation to outright war: if the West assumes its opponents operate by the rules they themselves have established, their actions too will remain hybrid or in the grey zone.

Yet there is a risk here of a kind of mirror-imaging. If the Russians or Chinese do not view Western activity through the hybrid or grey-zone lens, they may construe Western responses as escalation towards war and react accordingly. And in fact, the concepts of hybrid warfare and the grey zone are products of a broadly Western, and especially American, strategic culture. The Russians do not think about hybrid war in the same way that the West does. Their term for it is a direct transliteration of the Western term and is only used in referring to the Western concept.[30] Indeed, the West's hybrid and grey-zone concepts bolster Russian narratives about insidious Western aggression insofar as they can be used to characterise Western support for pro-democratic revolutions in Russia's sphere of influence and in the Middle East, as well as Russian actions in Ukraine.

The crucial difference between the new concepts and the old war–peace distinction lies in political awareness and determination. If everything is conceived in diluted hybrid or grey terms, then the political costs of inadequate action are presumptively low, and a given political leader can afford to kick the can down the road. Challenges cast as hybrid or grey-zone can also be treated as non-strategic and handled in a merely technocratic manner. This has been a flaw of modern strategic thinking since the early Cold War: concerns about surprise attack and accidental war ignored longer-term historical factors in political relations in favour of technical issues which could presumably be solved without mobilising the political will that would be required to support a fighting war.[31] By contrast, the Clausewitzian war–peace distinction is premised on the importance of understanding what geopolitical outcome an opponent is attempting to achieve and what it would mean. That knowledge can facilitate an honest, thorough and clear strategic assessment of whether a country should seek peace or prepare for war.

Acknowledgements

We would like to thank Joe Maiolo and Jeff Michaels for comments on an earlier draft of this article.

Notes

[1] See, for example, Geraint Hughes, 'War in the Grey Zone: Historical Reflections and Contemporary Implications', *Survival*, vol. 62, no. 3, June–July 2020, p. 133; and Michael C. McCarthy, Matthew A. Moyer and Brett H. Venable, *Deterring Russia in the Gray Zone* (Carlisle, PA: Strategic Studies Institute, US Army War College, 2019), p. 9, https://publications.

armywarcollege.edu/pubs/3687.pdf.

2   See Colin S. Gray, *Categorical Confusion? The Strategic Implications of Recognizing Challenges Either as Irregular or Traditional* (Carlisle, PA: Strategic Studies Institute, US Army War College, 2012), p. vii, https://publications.armywarcollege.edu/pubs/2171.pdf.

3   See Colin S. Gray, *Strategy for Chaos: Revolutions in Military Affairs and the Evidence of History* (Abingdon: Routledge, 2002), p. 17; and Jeffrey H. Michaels, *The Discourse Trap and the US Military: From the War on Terror to the Surge* (London: Palgrave Macmillan, 2013).

4   See, for example, Frank G. Hoffman, *Conflict in the 21st Century: The Rise of Hybrid Wars* (Washington DC: Potomac Institute, 2007); McCarthy, Moyer and Venable, *Deterring Russia in the Gray Zone*; and Lyle J. Morris et al., *Gaining Competitive Advantage in the Gray Zone: Response Options for Coercive Aggression Below the Threshold of Major War* (Santa Monica, CA: RAND Corporation, 2019).

5   See Lukas Milevski, 'The Nature of Strategy versus the Character of War', *Comparative Strategy*, vol. 35, no. 5, December 2016, pp. 438–46.

6   See John Gerring, 'What Makes a Concept Good? A Criterial Framework for Understanding Concept Formation in the Social Sciences', *Polity*, vol. 31, no. 3, 1999, pp. 357–93, 382; and Donald Stoker and Craig Whiteside, 'Blurred Lines: Gray-zone Conflict and Hybrid War – Two Failures of American Strategic Thinking', *Naval War College Review*, vol. 73, no. 1, Winter 2020, pp. 12–48.

7   Hoffman, while not the first, was the most influential definer of 'hybrid warfare'. See Hoffman, *Conflict in the 21st Century*.

8   Ibid., p. 29.

9   Murat Caliskan, 'Hybrid Warfare Through the Lens of Strategic Theory', *Defense & Security Analysis*, vol. 35, no. 1, January 2019, pp. 40–58.

10 See Bettina Renz, 'Russia and Hybrid Warfare', *Contemporary Politics*, vol. 22, no. 3, June 2016, p. 293.

11 See Ofer Fridman, *Russian Hybrid Warfare: Resurgence and Politicization* (Oxford: Oxford University Press, 2018), p. 115.

12 Ibid., p. 52.

13 See Samuel Charap, 'The Ghost of Hybrid War', *Survival*, vol. 57, no. 6, December 2015–January 2016, p. 51.

14 Quoting, respectively, US Department of Defense, 'Quadrennial Defense Review', February 2010, p. 73, https://archive.defense.gov/qdr/QDR%20as%20of%2029JAN10%201600.pdf; Nadia Schadlow, 'Peace and War: The Space Between', *War on the Rocks*, 18 August 2014, https://warontherocks.com/2014/08/peace-and-war-the-space-between/; and Morris et al., *Gaining Competitive Advantage in the Gray Zone*, p. iii.

15 See, for example, Hal Brands, 'Paradoxes of the Gray Zone', *E-Note*, Foreign Policy Research Institute, 5 February 2016, https://www.fpri.org/article/2016/02/paradoxes-gray-zone/; Michael J. Mazarr, *Mastering the Gray Zone: Understanding a Changing Era of Conflict* (Carlisle, PA: Strategic Studies Institute, US Army War College, 2015), https://publications.armywarcollege.edu/pubs/2372.pdf; Schadlow, 'Peace and War'; and James J. Wirtz, 'Life in

the "Gray Zone": Observations for Contemporary Strategists', *Defense & Security Analysis*, vol. 33, no. 2, April 2017, pp. 106–14.

16   David Barno and Nora Bensahel, 'Fighting and Winning in the "Gray Zone"', *War on the Rocks*, 19 May 2015, https://warontherocks.com/2015/05/fighting-and-winning-in-the-gray-zone/.

17   Quoting, respectively, Brands, 'Paradoxes of the Gray Zone', p. 1; and Mazarr, *Mastering the Gray Zone*, p. 58.

18   See, for example, Hughes, 'War in the Grey Zone', p. 133.

19   Johan Galtung, 'An Editorial', *Journal of Peace Research*, vol. 1, no. 1, March 1964, p. 2.

20   *Ibid*.

21   Hew Strachan, 'Introductory Essay: The Changing Character of War', in Karl Erik Haug and Ole Jørgen Maaø (eds), *Conceptualising Modern War* (London: Hurst & Co., 2011), pp. 8–9.

22   Carl von Clausewitz, *On War*, translated and edited by Michael Howard and Peter Paret (Princeton, NJ: Princeton University Press, 1984), p. 75 (emphasis in original).

23   See Meredith Reid Sarkees, 'The COW Typology of War: Defining and Categorizing Wars (Version 4 of the Data)', Correlates of War Project, p. 1, https://correlatesofwar.org/data-sets/

COW-war/the-cow-typology-of-war-defining-and-categorizing-wars/@@download/file/COW%20Website%20-%20Typology%20of%20war.pdf.

24   Clausewitz, *On War*, p. 605.

25   Lukas Milevski, 'Choosing Strategy: Meaning, Significance, Context', *Infinity Journal*, vol. 6, no. 2, Summer 2018, pp. 15–18.

26   Thomas Hobbes, *Leviathan* (Oxford: Oxford University Press, 1998), p. 84 (emphasis added).

27   Jan Almäng, 'War, Vagueness and Hybrid War', *Defence Studies*, vol. 19, no. 2, April 2019, p. 195.

28   Hew Strachan, 'Strategy in the Twenty-First Century', in Hew Strachan and Sibylle Scheipers (eds), *The Changing Character of War* (Oxford: Oxford University Press, 2011), p. 508.

29   See, for example, Kathleen H. Hicks et al., 'By Other Means, Part I: Campaigning in the Gray Zone', Report of the CSIS International Security Program, July 2019, https://csis-website-prod.s3.amazonaws.com/s3fs-public/publication/Hicks_GrayZone_interior_v4_FULL_WEB_0.pdf.

30   See Fridman, *Russian Hybrid Warfare*.

31   See Bruce Kuklick, *Blind Oracles: Intellectuals and War from Kennan to Kissinger* (Princeton, NJ: Princeton University Press, 2006), p. 58.

Towards a Quantum Internet: Post-pandemic Cyber Security in a Post-digital World

David C. Gompert and Martin Libicki

As the internet and other data networks have grown, reliable and economical cyber security has proved elusive. Even as massive funding is shovelled into cyber security, the costs of cyber crime are escalating. Russian hackers' success in penetrating supposedly protected US government systems reveals that today's approaches to cyber security cannot keep up with today's threats, let alone future ones. Network attacks are rising at roughly the pace of network use, doubling every few years. Because data networks are meant to enable access, sharing and teaming, protecting them without diminishing their utility has, on the whole, been frustrating if not futile. Insecurity is especially severe for individuals, societies and nations that rely on political freedom, free markets and free speech – notably, the United States and its allies.

The situation could get worse due to the dramatic expansion of remote work. The COVID-19 pandemic has sharply increased the number of jobs being done remotely, which has proven so efficient and popular that it is sure to persist after the pandemic. As a result, the growing reliance of economies, societies and governments on the integrity, confidentiality and availability of digitally transmitted information will expose them to cyber threats as never before.

David C. Gompert is presently on the faculty of the US Naval Academy and is a special advisor to Ultratech Capital Partners. He has served as US acting director of national intelligence. **Martin Libicki** is the Maryellen and Richard L. Keyser Distinguished Visiting Professor in Cyber Security Studies at the US Naval Academy.

Survival | vol. 63 no. 1 | February–March 2021 | pp. 113–124   https://doi.org/10.1080/00396338.2021.1881257

The most sophisticated of these threats come from adversaries of the West. For President Vladimir Putin's Russia, cyber war is a uniquely cost-effective asymmetric weapon owing to the country's own comparatively low reliance on networks and weakness in conventional military power. Russia is likely to wage cyber war more aggressively as Western workers, societies, economies and governments present more inviting targets. Indeed, the National Security Agency has warned that the dispersal of US government work presents 'countless opportunities' for hacking, especially by Russian agents.[1] Russia's massive SolarWinds cyber-intelligence operation – a prolonged, undetected and pervasive cyber penetration of US government networks – showed that not just '.com' and '.org' were vulnerable, but '.gov' too. It was especially alarming that Russian hackers were able to smuggle malicious code into US government networks via regular system-software updates.

China is much stronger technologically than Russia though less likely to wage cyber war, in part inhibited because of its own vulnerabilities.[2] But China is also engaged in a high-tech race with the United States. Its leaders grasp the economic and military importance of advanced information technologies. If China becomes more capable and less vulnerable than the United States in cyber security, it could imperil US interests.

The promise of quantum information technology

A long-term solution to the cyber-security problem may lie in quantum physics. Quantum transmissions can instantly reveal interference and thus ensure safe network key distribution. This raises the prospect of an un-hackable 'quantum internet' – not as new infrastructure in place of the digital internet, but as an expanding constellation of secure quantum links within it. The cost of a quantum internet would be borne mostly by market demand for cyber security. It could provide an effective response to private cyber crime, Russian cyber war and Chinese efforts to gain information dominance.

The theory of quantum mechanics, devised to explain the smallest forms of matter and energy, has been around for more than a century and continues to progress. Yet the world it describes is so unlike our observable world that even scientists can still find it bewilderingly counter-intuitive.

According to quantum mechanics, energy is not continuous but instead comes in little packets, or quanta. These quanta, such as those that make up light photons, can behave like waves, yet, when observed, they are more like particles. Because it is impossible to know at any moment both the location and the speed of any such particles, they must be thought of as indefinite or probabilistic.[3] Thus, electrons are hazy clouds, not points. Any particle can be in multiple quantum states at any moment, which is called being in superposition. A pair of particles in a joined quantum state can, when separated, exhibit identical behaviour simultaneously regardless of how far apart they are. Albert Einstein famously called this phenomenon 'spooky action at a distance'. It is generally known as entanglement.

One upshot of these features of quantum mechanics is that information need not be limited to ones and zeros, as digital bits are, but may take on numerous values between one and zero, called quantum bits or 'qubits'. By virtue of this property, quantum computers can crunch far more numbers in dramatically less time than digital ones can.[4] At this stage, stacks of super-computers are unable to crack robust encryption algorithms. More powerful quantum computers, once they are available, may be up to the task.[5] That could precipitate a revolution in codebreaking. Even quantum enthusiasts admit that practical quantum computers are at least a decade away.

The day of quantum communications is at hand, however, thanks to recent progress in generating, storing and transmitting qubits – for instance, via 'entangled' photons across fibre-optic cables. Importantly, quantum communications can link digital computers, albeit across limited ranges and bandwidths.

Given the prospect of worsening cyber crime and cyber war, the most immediate benefit of quantum communications seems to lie in cyber security. While smart hackers can read and copy bits in transit without leaving a trace, the hacking of qubits is instantly revealed. 'The beauty of qubits from a cybersecurity perspective', explains Martin Giles, 'is that if a hacker tries to observe qubits in transit, their super-fragile state causes them to collapse into 1 or 0 digital bits'.[6] This would unavoidably reveal interference with the transmission. Hence, a secret message that has not been interfered will still be secret upon arrival.

In addition, the distribution of digital keys to encryption algorithms is vulnerable to undetected interception. Quantum key distribution has been mooted as a substitute. Key distribution occurs in the first few bytes of a transmission and provides security for the remainder. Quantum communications systems engineered by both the Chinese and the Americans can show proof that key distribution has not been compromised, allowing encrypted messaging to proceed securely.

The way people work

Computing has progressed over the last half-century – evolving from mainframes to minicomputers to personal computers and distributed processing – in response to the changing way people work. Digital technologies have enabled, driven and exploited the integration of computers and telecommunications and the construction of an immense broadband infrastructure. This has transformed work by boosting the ability of individuals, teams and organisations to get and share information and to cooperate. Among the results of data networking so far are the internet itself, email, texting, social media, online news and streaming entertainment.

The advantages of data networking are profound: global economic integration, the open flow of competing ideas, support for democratisation and productive organisational devolution. There are certainly some disadvantages. They include autocratic manipulation, information overload, the spread of conspiratorial and debasing information, cyber crime and cyber war. Owing to intense competition and insatiable user demand, innovations come rapid-fire. Important recent ones are the cloud, artificial intelligence and quantum technology.

While most endeavours experience diminishing economic returns on investment, networks tend to yield increasing returns as they are expanded.[7] (Indeed, according to Metcalfe's law, the value of a network increases in proportion to the square of its number of users.) Because of this, whole economies now depend vitally on networks. While classified networks supporting military and intelligence activities are secured by partitioning and need-to-know barriers, the utility of most other domains – .org, .com, .edu and much of .gov – turns on accessibility. Most public data networks, including the internet itself, are highly vulnerable to disruption or corruption.

Internet use – for email, video chat, online news, social media, shopping and entertainment, among other things – has soared during the COVID-19 pandemic. More than half of locked-down Americans polled say the internet has been essential.[8] Its use is up by 50% or more.[9] Broadband providers confirm a corresponding 50% increase in traffic.[10] This is partly because people seek more information during a crisis. But most of the increase results from more work being done remotely.

Working at home has been both economic and popular. One chief financial officer said his company went from '16,000 people in 60 offices to 16,000 people in 16,000 offices' without losing efficiency.[11] Remote work is being baked into professional life, altering where people need to live, the demand for office buildings and commuting. While these ramifications will take time to play out, reversing the dispersal of work will only get harder. The expansion of distributed work has not been limited to the private sector. Virtually all of the 13,000 employees of the US Patent and Trademark Office have gone online, and it is anticipated that most will remain off-site when the COVID-19 crisis has passed.[12] The daily average of persons working physically in the Pentagon decreased from over 24,000 to 5,300.[13]

As network use rises, economic, societal and national-security benefits will depend increasingly on better security. Cyber attacks are increasing at about the rate of increase in use, both doubling every four years or so.[14] Worldwide costs of cyber crime have been escalating, up from $3 trillion a year in 2015 to a pre-pandemic projection of $6trn a year in 2021 – larger than Japan's GDP.[15] The FBI reports that cyber crime has increased by 300% during the pandemic.[16] Other estimates are much higher.[17] Some of the upsurge – for instance, in cure scams – is attributable specifically to the pandemic. Also, crises tend to bring out hackers, as the 2008–09 global financial collapse demonstrated. But of the three categories of factors contributing to the increase – COVID-related, crisis in general and remote work – remote work is the largest. The number of unsecured remote desktop machines rose by an estimated 40% as the pandemic took hold.[18] To a significant degree, the increase will outlast the pandemic.[19]

Worsening cyber security

Because remote work and network use will remain high, and because there is a strong correlation between network use and cyber crime, it is fair to expect a large and sustained increase in the latter. If just half the increase in remote work during the pandemic were to remain after it had passed, network use would still be up about 25% over the pre-pandemic trend line, and the cost of cyber crime could increase by that much. The problem extends beyond routine, at-home work. Valuable intellectual property, such as chip designs and drug formulae, may be found online. A growing volume of official government business, much of it sensitive, will be performed remotely. For instance, the amount of patent information online has skyrocketed, and cyber-security professionals have had to scramble out of fear that adversaries will exploit vulnerabilities. Likewise, government personnel records have become easy prey.

Even before the pandemic, the economics of cyber security were discouraging. Investment in cyber security has been rising fast – from $3 billion in 2004 to $124bn in 2019 – and could be as much as $1trn cumulatively over the next five years.[20] This steepening investment, however, has not slowed growth in the costs of cyber crime, which proceeds in proportion to network use. Cyberspace is thus an 'offence-dominant' domain, in which returns on investment in cyber security sharply diminish.[21] In time and money spent, lines of code written and people employed, the effort required to protect, detect, patch, work around and recover from attacks far exceeds that of hacking. Organisations typically experience a flattening of the curve that relates cyber security achieved to cyber-security investment.[22] The dispersal of work makes hacking cheaper and security dearer. Adequate security for distributed work could break corporate and government budgets unless a new approach is developed.[23]

Analysis of cyber threats usually dwells on malware, ransomware, phishing, service disruptions and the like. But national and global cyber security are also at risk, especially when critical networks are in danger and foreign powers are involved. Potential perpetrators of cyber attacks range from singleton hackers to great powers. In turn, there are three basic categories of cyber threat: rampant cyber crime, sophisticated nation-state interference and strategic rivalry. The consequences of the first type for the US and other Western societies need no belabouring: reduced availability of and faith in information, degraded collaboration, loss of privacy, loss of confidence in government and other institutions, unreliable utility services and outright theft. While cyber crime might not rise to the level of cyber war, it cumulatively harms the targets' national security. Cyber security is one of the Department of Homeland Security's most critical missions.

Of the myriad foreign sources of cyber threats, Russia is in a league of its own. With its economy sputtering because of low energy prices, Russia is relatively weak in more expensive sorts of power, such as conventional military forces. Yet it has an aggressive external strategy, and sees cyber attacks – along with manipulation of social media – as an effective tool for undermining the confidence of Western publics in government information and institutions. Russia's relatively modest reliance on networked data makes it hard to deter by the threat of retaliation.[24] Fear of reprisal clearly did not dissuade Putin from approving a large-scale attack on US government systems. Furthermore, the cost to Russia of the SolarWinds large-scale espionage operation is unknown, but surely a tiny fraction of the roughly $15bn that the US government spends annually to secure its networks.

Meanwhile, the United States and its chief strategic rival, China, are competing to develop advanced information technology, including artificial intelligence and quantum computing. The prize is economic advantage and a military edge. The significance of the former is mitigated by the linkage between the Chinese and US economies. With tensions in the Western Pacific running high, however, Chinese technological advantages in the military realm could have grave implications.

Artificial intelligence has more immediate potential than quantum computing to reshape military capabilities. Accordingly, the US armed forces are acquiring and applying it creatively and energetically. In the long haul, though, quantum technology could have comparable strategic significance. Quantum computing can offer unprecedented intelligence advantages to the side that masters decryption first, and a lead in quantum technology would translate readily into superiority in cyber security.

The Chinese government and associated technology companies are making quantum communications a high priority. As Google and IBM race to produce useful quantum machines, so are China's Alibaba and Huawei. China is said to be leading in quantum communications, which spells trouble for the United States in cyber security.[25] As matters now stand, both China and the United States are vulnerable to cyber attack by virtue of their economic reliance on data networks, so mutual deterrence is in place.[26] But if one side combines superior offensive and superior defensive capabilities – which having an advantage in quantum technology could enable it to do – the current stability of mutual cyber deterrence could collapse.

Towards a quantum internet

In due course, technology may progress to the point at which quantum cyber security and its advantages transcend quantum key distribution. American and Canadian scientists have successfully teleported qubits of photons across 44 kilometres of fibre-optic cable.[27] China has achieved long-range line-of-sight transmission through space via its Micius quantum-communication satellite. The Chinese are also working on drones as quantum-communication nodes.[28] But obstacles remain. Terrestrial range, even for key distribution, will remain limited to tens of kilometres until quantum repeaters are invented. Researchers have shown that these are theoretically possible.[29]

Quantum links that transmit entangled photons require additional high-quality fibre-optic links. This does not dictate the need for wholesale overhaul of the existing broadband infrastructure, and COVID-19 has been driving the most rapid internet upgrade in years.[30] Still, in the near term, technologies cannot offer enough bandwidth efficiency to support wide use of quantum communications. Until they can, the impact of quantum communications in thwarting cyber crime against ordinary at-home work activities will be slight. And even when quantum communications can palpably improve cyber security, it will be important to avoid the panacea paradox, whereby whole networks are treated as secure when in fact only some of their links are. Even if networked by quantum communications, digital platforms may still be vulnerable at other poorly secured points of entry, including poor access controls, ill-advised protocols, malware-laden computers, clients, servers, routers and compromised supply chains. Although total cyber security will remain unattainable, the promise of quantum communications justifies its vigorous development.

For now, only certain sensitive channels that rely on encryption – such as those involving military, intelligence, homeland security, other critical government functions and financial markets – could acquire the enhanced cyber security that quantum links provide.

*   *   *

As Brad Smith, the president of Microsoft, has put it, the wholesale Russian attack has provided a 'moment of reckoning' that calls for 'more effective and collaborative leadership by the US Government and the tech sector to spearhead a strong and coordinated global cybersecurity response'.[31] A concerted drive towards a quantum internet could become the centrepiece. The potential benefits include greater security for financial and commercial assets and transactions; intellectual property and other sensitive information; communications between and within governments; military systems, operations and support; and intelligence domains. Economically, the benefits of distributed work could be more fully realised. Strategically, a determined US-led push could yield an edge in quantum technology and cyber security over adversary powers.

The US government, leading information-technology and information-services companies, and top universities in quantum science should collectively articulate the need for and commitment to develop, deploy and use quantum communications. Concerted, yet competitive, efforts should be made to overcome range and bandwidth obstacles. Priorities for national security should be established. Government research and development is crucial, but the security benefits of quantum communications warrant larger and directed corporate investment. In the US, practical private–public partnerships should be adopted whereby quantum ventures have access to government as well as commercial markets and may retain their intellectual-property rights. The Department of Defense, Department of

Homeland Security and Department of Energy (in particular, the national laboratories) have complementary roles to play, as does the intelligence community. While governments cannot dictate that some private tech firms work with others who may compete with them, it can remove obstacles and fund teamwork.

The challenges of advancing quantum communications and developing a quantum internet also call for a dedicated partnership of US allies. Canadian and European quantum work is world-class. NATO has a proven capacity for facilitating cooperation in sensitive defence and intelligence affairs, and its key missions already include cyber security. With provisions for including Japan, Australia and other close and capable partners, NATO would be a suitable organisation to guide a joint endeavour. Indeed, the incoming US administration, led by strong advocates of the Atlantic Alliance, is sure to champion joint efforts to counter both Russia's cyber threat and China's attempts to gain technological supremacy.

Notes

[1] Lily Hay Newman, 'The NSA Warns that Russia Is Attacking Remote Work Platforms', *Wired*, 7 December 2020, https://www.wired.com/story/nsa-warns-russia-attacking-vmware-remote-work-platforms/.

[2] See, for example, Greg Austin, 'The Strategic Implications of China's Weak Cyber Defences', *Survival*, vol. 62, no. 5, October–November 2020, pp. 119–38.

[3] This concept, introduced by German physicist Werner Heisenberg in 1927, is known as 'Heisenberg's uncertainty principle'.

[4] Google has reported that its Sycamore quantum computer solved a 'chore' in 200 seconds that would have taken IBM's Summit supercomputer – one of the fastest supercomputers in the world – 10,000 years. See Neil Savage, 'Google Quantum Computer Achieves Chemistry Milestone', *Scientific American*, 4 September 2020, https://www.scientificamerican.com/article/googles-quantum-computer-achieves-chemistry-milestone/.

[5] Researchers at the Princeton Quantum Initiative believe that codebreaking with quantum computing will not be feasible anytime soon. Exchange with author, May 2020.

[6] Martin Giles, 'Explainer: What Is Quantum Communication?', *MIT Technology Review*, 14 February 2019, https://www.technologyreview.com/2019/02/14/103409/what-is-quantum-communications/.

[7] See W. Brian Arthur, 'Increasing Returns and the New World of Business', *Harvard Business Review*, vol. 74, no. 4, July–August 1996,

pp. 100–9, https://hbr.org/1996/07/increasing-returns-and-the-new-world-of-business.

8   See Pew Research Center, '53% of Americans Say the Internet Has Been Essential During the COVID-19 Outbreak', 30 April 2020, https://www.pewresearch.org/internet/2020/04/30/53-of-americans-say-the-internet-has-been-essential-during-the-covid-19-outbreak/.

9   See Mark Beech, 'COVID-19 Pushes Up Internet Use 70% and Streaming More than 12%, First Figures Reveal', *Forbes*, 25 March 2020, https://www.forbes.com/sites/markbeech/2020/03/25/covid-19-pushes-up-internet-use-70-streaming-more-than-12-first-figures-reveal/?sh=661bc2ac3104; Jason Cohen, 'Data Usage Has Increased 47 Percent During COVID-19 Quarantine', *PCMag*, 5 June 2020, https://uk.pcmag.com/why-axis/127260/data-usage-has-increased-47-percent-during-covid-19-quarantine; and OECD, 'Keeping the Internet Up and Running in Times of Crisis', 4 May 2020, https://www.oecd.org/coronavirus/policy-responses/keeping-the-internet-up-and-running-in-times-of-crisis-4017c4c9.

10 Beech, 'COVID-19 Pushes Up Internet Use 70% and Streaming More than 12%, First Figures Reveal'.

11 BlackRock chief financial officer Gary Shedlin, quoted in Sam Ro, 'One CEO Sees Blessings amid the Horror: Morning Brief', Yahoo, 14 October 2020, https://www.yahoo.com/now/blackrock-ceo-larry-fink-remote-work-blessings-morning-brief-100013589.html.

12 Author communication with USTPO Public Affairs Office, October 2020.

13 David Vergun, 'DOD Personnel Prove Productive, Resilient During Pandemic', *DOD News*, US Department of Defense, 21 September 2020, https://www.defense.gov/Explore/News/Article/Article/2355591/dod-personnel-prove-productive-resilient-during-pandemic/#:~:text=12%2C%202020%2C.&text=In%20the%20early%20days%20of,percent%20occupancy%20rate%2C%20she%20said.

14 See Kelly Bissell, Ryan M. LaSalle and Paolo Dal Cin, 'Innovate for Cyber Resilience: Lessons from Leaders to Master Cybersecurity Execution', Accenture, 2020, https://www.accenture.com/_acnmedia/PDF-116/Accenture-Cybersecurity-Report-2020.pdf.

15 See Steve Morgan, 'Cybercrime to Cost the World $10.5 Trillion Annually by 2025', *Cybercrime Magazine*, 13 November 2020, https://cybersecurityventures.com/annual-cybercrime-report-2019/.

16 'FBI: 300% Increase in Cyber Crimes since COVID-19', Compulink, 31 July 2020, https://www.compu-link.com/fbi-300-increase-in-cyber-crimes-since-covid-19/.

17 See, for example, '2020 Cyber Security Statistics: The Ultimate List of Stats, Data & Trends', PurpleSec, 2020, https://purplesec.us/resources/cyber security-statistics/.

18 See, for instance, Edward Gately, '10 Destructive COVID-19 Data Breaches', Channel Futures, 20 July 2020, https://www.channelfutures.com/mssp-insider/10-seriously-destructive-covid-19-data-breaches.

19 See, for example, Katherine Guyot and Isabel V. Sawhill, 'Telecommuting Will Likely Continue Long After the Pandemic', Brookings Institution, 6 April 2020, https://www.brookings.edu/blog/up-front/2020/04/06/telecommuting-will-likely-continue-long-after-the-pandemic/.

20 Steve Morgan, 'Global Cybersecurity Spending Predicted to Exceed $1 Trillion from 2017–2021', *Cybercrime Magazine*, 10 June 2019, https://cybersecurityventures.com/cybersecurity-market-report/.

21 See 'A New Kind of Insanity: The Risk of Diminishing Returns in Cybersecurity', Lumen, 29 March 2018, https://blog.lumen.com/a-new-kind-of-insanity-the-risk-of-diminishing-returns-in-cybersecurity/.

22 See Lawrence A. Gordon and Martin P. Loeb, 'The Economics of Information Security Investment', *ACM Transactions on Information and System Security*, vol. 5, no. 4, November 2002, pp. 438–57.

23 Some products, of course, are specifically needed and do work, at least temporarily. Furthermore, while organisations have trouble estimating threats, risks and effects of attacks, nervous boards tend to respond generously to cyber-security budget requests. Given the possibility of catastrophic consequences, investment in cyber security is like an insurance policy with hefty premiums. In addition, cyber-security marketing is ubiquitous, aggressive and slick, continually offering something new and improved.

24 Russia has 15% as many internet users per capita as the United States and 13% as many as China.

25 See David C. Gompert, 'Spin-on: How the US Can Meet China's Technological Challenge', *Survival*, vol. 62, no. 3, June–July 2020, pp. 115–30.

26 See David C. Gompert and Phillip C. Saunders, *The Paradox of Power: Sino-American Strategic Restraint in an Age of Vulnerability* (Washington DC: National Defense University, 2011).

27 See 'Fermilab and Partners Achieve Sustained, High-fidelity Quantum Teleportation', Fermilab, 15 December 2020, https://news.fnal.gov/2020/12/fermilab-and-partners-achieve-sustained-high-fidelity-quantum-teleportation/.

28 See Anil Ananthaswamy, 'The Quantum Internet Is Emerging, One Experiment at a Time', *Scientific American*, 19 June 2019, https://www.scientificamerican.com/article/the-quantum-internet-is-emerging-one-experiment-at-a-time/.

29 *Ibid.*

30 See Will Douglas Heaven, 'Why the Coronavirus Lockdown Is Making the Internet Stronger than Ever', *MIT Technology Review*, 7 April 2020, https://www.technologyreview.com/2020/04/07/998552/why-the-coronavirus-lockdown-is-making-the-internet-better-than-ever/.

31 Brad Smith, 'A Moment of Reckoning: The Need for a Strong and Global Cybersecurity Response', Official Microsoft Blog, 17 December 2020, https://blogs.microsoft.com/on-the-issues/2020/12/17/cyberattacks-cybersecurity-solarwinds-fireeye/.

Japan's Grand Strategy: The Abe Era and Its Aftermath

Christopher W. Hughes, Alessio Patalano and Robert Ward

On 28 August 2020, Abe Shinzo formally announced that he was stepping down as Japan's longest-serving prime minister since the Second World War.[1] Facing a relapse in the medical condition that had forced him to step down as prime minister for the first time in 2007 after just one year in office, he admitted that his health had deteriorated to the point that he was at risk of making errors. With public frustration about the government's response to the COVID-19 pandemic translating into plummeting approval rates, and continued media rumblings over political-funding scandals, Abe seemed to understand that he needed to make way for new leadership.[2] An iconoclastic politician who had set out to re-energise a sluggish economy, revise Japan's constitution and change the country's role in international affairs, Abe was departing the scene having advanced his agenda, but – by his own admission – before he could fully deliver results on several issues of importance to him.[3]

How should we assess the significance and success of Abe's second stint in power? Opinions are divided.[4] Positive assessments have identified successes in three areas. Domestically, Abe fully capitalised on reforms

Christopher W. Hughes is Professor of International Politics and Japanese Studies and Pro-Vice-Chancellor (Education) at the University of Warwick. He has held visiting professorships at Harvard University, the University of Tokyo and Waseda University, and is author of *Japan's Foreign and Security Policy Under the 'Abe Doctrine'* (Palgrave Macmillan, 2015). **Alessio Patalano** is Reader in East Asian Warfare and Security, and Director of the King's Japan Programme at King's College London. **Robert Ward** is IISS Japan Chair and Director of Geo-economics and Strategy.

Survival | vol. 63 no. 1 | February–March 2021 | pp. 125–160   https://doi.org/10.1080/00396338.2021.1881258

that have given the Prime Minister's Office greater capacity to implement policy.[5] In security matters, although he did not achieve his signature goal of revising Article 9 – the 'peace clause' – of the Japanese constitution, Abe expanded the potential boundaries of Japan's participation in international activities and partnerships.[6] Diplomatically, Abe re-engineered Japan's international outlook and leadership role. Significantly, Abe achieved all this under the shadow of systemic challenges including an ageing population, tight domestic fiscal constraints, a more mercurial United States and an increasingly assertive China.[7]

Critics have taken a different view. On the one hand, the poor performance of Japan's economy has raised questions over the long-term significance of his premiership. In August 2020, for example, second-quarter GDP data indicated that Japan had recorded its worst quarterly economic contraction since the end of the Second World War.[8] This was largely owing to the impact of the COVID-19 pandemic, but was aggravated by the negative consequences of Abe's decision in October 2019 to again raise the consumption tax. By the time Abe stepped down, his vaunted 'Abenomics', with its 'three arrows' for economic reform (monetary, fiscal and structural), had failed to lift inflation, rehabilitate Japan's public finances or noticeably improve the country's economic-growth trajectory.[9] Other critics have focused on the security reforms that Abe introduced. These have altered Japan's traditional approach to internationalism and weakened significantly its post-war identity as a 'pacifist' or 'anti-militaristic' country.[10] From this perspective, Japan is back as an international actor, but not necessarily for the better, its pacifist profile having been damaged and questions raised about the longer-term sustainability and efficacy of Abe's strategy.

We take the view that the Abe era has indeed brought about significant changes in Japan, and that these changes are likely to endure. Abe's premiership was successful in attaining many of its self-declared objectives. After Abe returned to power in 2012, he charted a new grand strategy – the 'Abe Doctrine' – that broke with the past and continues to determine the frameworks, practices and tools employed by Japan as an international actor. For the first time in Japan's post-war history, military and non-military levers of power were proactively mobilised to preserve and enhance the prime minister's vision of Japan's long-term interests. In articulating these interests and the means of attaining them, the Abe Doctrine satisfies understandings of the term 'grand strategy' as used in the field of international relations.[11]

Criticisms of Abe's reforms can sometimes serve to obscure the two most potentially significant developments of the Abe years: an increase in Japan's perceived capacity to influence international affairs and shape their outcome, and the concomitant enhancement of its 'convening' ambitions and power to influence its international environment. This is what sets Abe's Japan apart, and the country will not revert to a more reactive or passive role in the foreseeable future. Instead, Suga Yoshihide is likely to build on his predecessor's framework, though he may well shift emphasis away from certain key foreign-policy issues that proved insurmountable and costly for Abe.

The Abe Doctrine

The policy choices made between 2012 and 2020 under the Abe Doctrine represented a significant departure from the so-called 'Yoshida Doctrine' – named after Yoshida Shigeru, Japanese prime minister in 1946–47 and 1948–54 – that had set Japan's post-war strategic trajectory.[12] For Abe, personal political revival was not the only objective; his dramatic return to power in 2012 was intended to signal that 'Japan Is Back' as a significant international player and that the pledge by the revisionist factions of the governing Liberal Democratic Party (LDP) to domestically 'take back Japan' would facilitate the restoration of Japanese foreign policy.[13]

The Abe Doctrine was constructed by Abe himself and embraced by many of the key revisionist and establishment figures around him in the LDP. These senior elites included Suga, a close adviser to Abe since his first administration and his chief cabinet secretary throughout his second mandate – making Suga the longest holder of his government role in Japanese history. Abe's doctrine was driven by a belief that as an advanced industrial democracy, Japan should recover its place as a 'tier-one country' among the great powers.[14] This doctrine posited a Japan that could help to shape international affairs, not merely react to them. Indeed, this renewed status, propelled by reinvigorated economic and military capabilities, was seen as vital for Japan to successfully navigate the ever more severe regional and global challenges that it faced.

For Japan to restore its national power and throw off its past malaise, it needed to 'escape from the post-war regime' that was seen as having effectively imposed upon Japan the identity of a defeated power.[15] The Abe Doctrine thus sought to displace the Yoshida Doctrine, which was blamed for perpetuating a regime of defeat and producing a 'small' Japan on the international stage.[16] Abe hoped that Japan would instead move towards becoming a proud and 'beautiful country', empowered with a wide set of tools, from the country's economic might as the world's third-largest economy to its far-from-negligible military capabilities, and with a voice on how the international system was to be organised.[17]

Dismantling the Yoshida Doctrine

In this respect, the Abe Doctrine was designed to systematically dismantle three key tenets of the Yoshida Doctrine. Firstly, Abe aimed to move away from a minimalist and reactive defence posture by upgrading key capabilities of the Japan Self-Defense Forces (JSDF), removing constitutional constraints on the use of military power for international security and enabling Japan to participate in what it characterises as regimes of 'collective self-defence'. Secondly, Japan was to move away from a similarly minimalist level of commitment towards the US–Japan security treaty and function as a more fully fledged and integrated alliance partner, rather than constantly hedging against alliance dilemmas of entrapment or abandonment.[18] Thirdly, Japan was to exercise more overt leadership in East Asia and beyond, refusing to accede to a rising China's dominance in the region, and shifting from default engagement with Beijing to a more pronounced counterbalancing role.

Abe's doctrine was also meant to tackle what he perceived as the domestic roots of Japan's international underperformance by addressing two long-standing legacies. The first were what he thought of as 'masochistic' interpretations of Japan as a wartime aggressor.[19] These were to be overcome through what was at times overt, revisionist denial and the relativisation of history.[20] For Abe, existing narratives hindered domestic appetite for a wider range of political possibilities and were being used by other states to limit Japan's international presence.[21] Secondly, the Abe Doctrine envisaged removing mechanisms introduced in the immediate post-war period to demilitarise and democratise Japan. Notably, this meant reinterpreting and revising the 1947 constitution, particularly Article 9. These mechanisms, which limited Japan's ability to integrate the use of military power with other tools of statecraft in the pursuit of national security, were thought to undermine Japan's national identity and sense of patriotism, as well as its status as a truly sovereign state.[22]

The signature approach of the Abe Doctrine was defined, therefore, by an attempt to shake loose from past constraints and to demonstrate greater autonomy and agency. Japan would now present itself as a proactive power with strong economic and military capabilities, and the ability both to work with partners and to convene and organise international frameworks itself to further its own interests.[23] To that end, Abe's doctrine also sought to propound, if with some inconsistencies, a values-oriented diplomacy focusing on the rule of law, free markets, human rights and democracy.[24] Japan aspired to present itself as a rule-setter and bastion of the liberal economic order, in contradistinction to competitors such as China.[25] The essence of Abe's grand strategy was aptly summed up in Japan's first National Security Strategy (NSS) as a vision aimed at moving Japan away from passive pacifism towards making 'a proactive contribution to peace'.[26]

Re-engineering the machinery of domestic and foreign policy

For his new grand strategy to be fully implemented, Abe needed to ensure that the Prime Minister's Office (Kantei) would be in a position to set policies and see that they were implemented across government. Hence, a key element of his vision was the pursuit of greater centralisation of Japan's traditionally fragmented foreign-policy apparatus. Abe, in large part supported by Suga, looked to exploit administrative reforms already in train to consolidate the Kantei's control over the devising and implementing of foreign and security policy, and to enhance its ability to bypass other ministries where necessary.[27] The creation, under Abe, of Japan's first National Security Council (NSC) in December 2013, and the government's adoption of the NSS that same year, were designed to significantly increase the Kantei's ability to centrally coordinate foreign policy in a way not previously seen in post-war Japan.[28]

The fragmentation of domestic policymaking weighed on Abe's mind because of the need for Japan to have greater control over its foreign-policy practice in the face of challenging international circumstances. The Abe Doctrine was calculated to equip Japan to respond to and manage the developing security and foreign-policy landscape, especially the challenges presented by the US–Japan alliance and the rise of China. For Abe, as for all previous Japanese administrations, the overriding priority was the strengthening of the US–Japan relationship so as to maintain the US-centred liberal-economic and regional-security orders from which Japan had benefited so greatly in the post-war period. Abe knew that for Japan to act as a rule-setter, the existing international system needed to be maintained.

Yet Abe's administration was also aware that US–Japan ties were becoming problematic, and that the government would need to go further in committing to the relationship than any of its predecessors. Abe and his advisers were all too aware of the United States' ongoing relative decline as a global hegemon, and its concomitantly diminishing ability – and willingness – to provide public economic goods and defend its allies without condition. The Trump presidency compounded these concerns with its disregard for upholding the United States' own liberal-international trading and democratic order, and its capricious and transactional approach to dealing with security-treaty partners. The Trump approach included demands for greater financial contributions to the costs of US regional bases and deployments, including those in Japan, and the president even openly mused about the future necessity of the US–Japan alliance.[29]

The conclusion drawn by Abe in dealing with Washington was that Japan could only mitigate the risks of US decline by deepening its investment in US hegemony and the American presence in the East Asia region, which was seen as clearly preferable to any abdication of the regional order to Chinese control. In practice, this meant simultaneous attempts to upgrade Japan's capabilities and agency in organising the region, and the tightening of US–Japan military cooperation and integration.[30] Abe's objective was to demonstrate Japan's indispensability to the US and thus its status as a more equal alliance partner; to exert influence on US strategic choices; and where necessary to step into any gaps in US diplomatic and economic leadership in the region.[31]

The Abe Doctrine was also concerned with managing China's rise. Abe recognised the need to coexist and cooperate with China economically, but also believed that Japan should be prepared to compete with China's diplomatic influence in the region and, if necessary, to counterbalance militarily Chinese threats to Japan's territorial- and maritime-security interests.[32] The Abe Doctrine posited that the only position China would respect was one of Japanese strength. Achieving such a position would allow for selective engagement and competition, and working with a range of partners to constrain China and shepherd it to the negotiating table.[33] In this way, it was also hoped that Japan, in being able to influence both US and Chinese international behaviour, could avoid becoming caught in the midst of a looming Sino-US confrontation.

Agency through convening power

Japan under Abe sought to exercise renewed agency and buttress the country's approach to the US and China by taking the initiative in relations with a range of other regional states. Indeed, it was an inherent part of the Abe Doctrine to vigorously pursue bilateral relations with other key US allies and partners in the region – not to hedge against the US–Japan alliance, but to strengthen the traditional US hub-and-spokes security architecture. In so doing, Japan led the way in transforming this architecture into a more synergic network of alliances.[34] Abe's government, like those before him, viewed the Association of Southeast Asian Nations (ASEAN) as a crucial diplomatic arena and source of partners to counter China's rising influence. Abe assiduously visited every ASEAN state in the first 18 months of his second premiership, seeking to make common cause over issues related to the United Nations Convention on the Law of the Sea (UNCLOS) and maritime security in the South China Sea. Japan also viewed closer economic links with Southeast Asian states as an alternative to China's development model and a way of helping reduce Japan's own risk of increasingly asymmetric economic interdependence with China.[35]

Although Abe's personal attitude towards South Korea was often perceived as ambivalent, he nevertheless expressed hopes for enhanced Japan–South Korea security cooperation against North Korea's missile and nuclear threats. He made some progress towards this goal. The second Abe government further vowed to pick up where it left off in courting India as an economic and security partner to check Chinese influence, and from early on it emphasised Australia as an emerging military partner.[36]

New regional frameworks and coalitions

The Abe Doctrine also set out to foster and convene new regional frameworks to complement those centred on the US. From the beginning of his second premiership, Abe sought to revive the Quadrilateral Security Dialogue (known as 'the Quad') bringing together Australia, India, Japan and the US. The Abe Doctrine's emphasis on seeking like-minded liberal partners meant reaching for security partnerships with out-of-region states, including major European actors such as the United Kingdom and France, the NATO Alliance and, towards the end of Abe's mandate, the European Union.[37]

In the economic sphere, Abe rapidly perceived the possibilities of joining with the Obama administration's sponsorship of the Trans-Pacific Partnership (TPP). After the US withdrew from the deal in 2017, Japan became a leader of the TPP's successor, the Comprehensive and Progressive Agreement for Trans-Pacific Partnership (CPTPP), with the goal of setting the rules of the game in trade and, importantly, creating a coalition of the like-minded as a means of containing China.[38] In 2016, in what was partly an effort to promote an alternative regional vision to China's Belt and Road Initiative (BRI), Japan articulated its concept of a 'Free and Open Indo-Pacific' (FOIP). The concept was deliberately designed to be flexibly and broadly defined in order to attract a diverse range of state participants. FOIP purports to be based on maintaining a rules-based regional order, and incorporates both economic aspects in terms of providing investment for quality infrastructure projects and promoting free trade, and security aspects centred on maritime security. FOIP was initially termed a 'strategy' but later came to be more commonly referred to as a 'vision', given that Japan wanted to avoid the impression that it was a containment strategy vis-à-vis China. The latter interpretation might have deterred many states in East and South Asia, and further afield in Africa, from taking part and being seen as having overtly taken sides with Japan. FOIP's appeal as a vision for Asia that reinforced the stability of the existing order influenced the Trump administration's thinking as it developed its own Indo-Pacific Strategy in 2019, although this was cast in more military terms.[39]

Post-war legacies

Abe's strategy called for the diplomatic legacies of the post-war period to be dealt with in what he frequently described as a 'general settlement of post-war accounts'. After his visit to the Yasukuni Shrine in December 2013 drew international criticism, Abe was determined that Japan's history would no longer be used against it for diplomatic leverage. His 2015 statement on the 70th anniversary of the end of the Second World War was crafted to walk a fine line in not giving ground on his revisionist view of history while offering enough standard expressions of Japanese remorse for the war to close off the need for further Japanese apologies.[40] Barack Obama's visit to Hiroshima in May 2016 and Abe's own visit to Pearl Harbor in December that same year were meant to draw a line under any historical issues in the US–Japan relationship.

Other elements of Abe's bid to release Japan from historical legacies included a possible peace treaty with President Vladimir Putin's Russia and the return of the four islands that were occupied by the Soviet Union in 1945 (which Japan calls the Northern Territories and Russia calls the Southern Kurils), as well as a resolution to the problem of North Korea's abduction of Japanese citizens – a cause that had expedited his rise in national politics.[41] Abe initially supported Obama's 'strategic patience' towards and containment of North Korea, allowing Japan some diplomatic space to seek a solution with Pyongyang. Tokyo then lined up behind Donald Trump's policy of 'maximum pressure' in the hope of coercing North Korea to cooperate.

Abe's realpolitik

By the end of 2015, Abe had already managed to introduce a series of measures designed to underpin a new and more effective role for Japan within the US–

Japan alliance. He had enacted a law on designated state secrets to reinforce Japan's ability to swap key military intelligence and defence-industrial data with the US; secured a reinterpretation of Article 9 of the constitution to allow Japanese military participation in forms of collective self-defence; and passed new security legislation that would enable Japan to more 'seamlessly' work alongside the US and other partners under specific circumstances.[42]

Broader guidelines for US–Japan defence cooperation

In April 2015, the two governments also agreed to revise the guidelines for defence cooperation, the first such revision of their bilateral agreement since 1997. One of the most remarkable aspects of the revised defence guidelines concerned a critical shift in emphasis: the rigid distinction in previous guidelines between bilateral cooperation on 'Japan' and 'regional' contingencies was removed to emphasise that bilateral cooperation should now be global, and not necessarily restricted geographically to Japan itself or to the surrounding region. Moreover, cooperation could now encompass the full gamut, from peacetime operations to wartime contingencies. Another key objective was to establish mechanisms – the Alliance Coordination Mechanism (ACM) and the upgraded Bilateral Planning Mechanism (BPM) – through which the partners could work together operationally on a daily basis through seamless responses. The ACM in particular could draw on recent experience, including operations during the Great East Japan Earthquake in March 2011, which had exposed limits in the capacity for operational cooperation within the alliance.[43] A focus on peacetime operations helped to widen the scope of the alliance to new domains, such as cyber and space. These changes enhanced integration with the US and offered a boost to Abe's vision of a more proactive Japan beyond the boundaries of Northeast Asia. At the same time, it planted the seeds for Japan's greater strategic and operational dependency on the United States' military machinery.

When Abe returned to power in 2012, his desire to upgrade the US–Japan alliance had taken on a sense of urgency because of Tokyo's deteriorating relationship with Beijing, especially in relation to the Senkaku Islands, which China claims and calls the Diaoyu.[44] Notwithstanding the Obama administration's initial reticence when Beijing escalated tensions in 2012 by deploying law-enforcement cutters inside the islands' territorial waters, Obama himself eventually confirmed in 2014 that Article 5 of the US–Japan security treaty encompassed the defence of the islands.[45] This did not mean that the United States would automatically become involved in the military defence of the islands, but Obama's position that 'our treaty commitment to Japan's security is absolute, and Article 5 covers all territories under Japan's administration, including the Senkaku Islands' satisfied the Japanese government at a time of increasing Chinese pressure. (In December 2013, Beijing adopted an East China Sea Air Defence Identification Zone (ADIZ) that included the islands.[46]) Obama similarly continued to support plans to relocate the US military base at Futenma in Okinawa, and his visit to the Hiroshima memorial was seen in Japan as implicit agreement from the US that acts of remembrance, rather than repeated apologies by Japan, were now sufficient, and that historical matters could be removed from Japan's diplomatic agenda.[47]

Despite the Trump administration's frequent references to the uneven nature of the US–Japan alliance, rumoured requests to double or even quadruple Host Nation Support (HNS) spending for the maintenance of US bases in Japan, and pressure on Japanese automakers to increase production in the US,[48] Abe managed to have his signature FOIP framework endorsed and adopted by the White House.[49] Abe also asked Trump to reconsider the decision not to join the CPTPP agreement, but Trump declined to do so. Japanese leadership in the CPTPP now represents a significant strategic asset that new US President Joe Biden should not undervalue, particularly given the conclusion of the China-centred, 15-country Regional Comprehensive Economic Partnership (RCEP) trade deal in November 2020.[50] When Japan assumes the chair of the CPTPP in 2021 it will be in a position to ensure that the bloc continues to develop, even if the US does not return in the short term.

Strength and adaptability with regard to China

The primary goal of Abe's China policy was to engage Beijing from a position of strength, keeping the door open for economic engagement where possible, while preventing bilateral issues from becoming chronically debilitating.

Most importantly, Tokyo sought to prevent changes to the status quo in the territorial and maritime-boundary disputes in the East China Sea. Chinese President Xi Jinping's aim to consolidate his power at home and expand Chinese influence overseas made early interactions with Beijing testy and required a degree of firmness from Japan.[51] By 2017, once Xi and Abe had both consolidated their domestic power bases, Abe could more easily de-emphasise areas of disagreement with Beijing, especially given that the Trump administration was increasing trade pressure on China and Japan, providing the countries with some grounds for common cause. Sino-US tensions allowed Abe, for example, to focus on the complementarity of his FOIP initiative with Beijing's BRI.[52] To mark the 40th anniversary of the Sino-Japanese Treaty of Peace and Friendship, Abe became in October 2018 the first Japanese prime minister to visit China in seven years, signing some 52 memoranda of cooperation across a wide range of areas. (Abe also secured an agreement for Xi to visit Japan, a visit originally scheduled for spring 2020 but postponed due to the COVID-19 crisis.) In May of that same year, Tokyo and Beijing agreed to a maritime- and air-communication mechanism aimed at enhancing crisis prevention in the East China Sea.[53] No timeline was specified for its implementation, however, and it did not extend to the countries' coastguards, which account for the majority of front-line encounters.

Abe's operational response to the situation in the Senkaku Islands com-bined tactical pushbacks against intrusions in the islands' territorial waters with clear 'red lines', including the option of initiating maritime-security operations (MSO) as provided for in Article 82 of the JSDF Act in cases where the capabilities of the Japan Coast Guard were insufficient.[54] The Abe cabinet also allocated financial resources for acquiring relevant mili-tary and law-enforcement capabilities for dealing with 'offshore islands' scenarios.[55] At the diplomatic level, the Abe government sought to draw international attention to Chinese behaviour in several ways. Japan's official publications, most notably the 2020 edition of the country's defence White Paper, highlighted the 'relentless' nature of Chinese assertiveness;[56] and in international forums such as G7 summits, the Japanese government secured support for the principle of respecting the 'rule of law' in the management of maritime disputes.[57] Abe's decision to regularly deploy the Japan Maritime Self-Defense Force (JMSDF) to Southeast Asia on missions in support of capacity-building for good governance at sea, such as the 'Ship Riders' initiatives, further reinforced and amplified his government's message.

Abe's approach proved that his government was willing to stand up to China by combining direct actions to counter Chinese behaviour in the East China Sea with more tailored military and diplomatic activities to draw international attention to, if not pressure on, Chinese actions. However, this strategy had its limits. In July 2020, Beijing intensified its activity around the Senkaku Islands, seeking not merely to showcase its presence around the disputed territory, but also to exercise control and, as a result, to directly challenge Japanese administration of the islands. The chasing of Japanese fishing vessels inside the islands' territorial waters would suggest an intention to challenge control by asserting law-enforcement rights.[58] Similarly, Beijing has more recently signalled an interest in regaining a degree of leadership through stronger trade links with regional countries, as showcased by the conclusion of the RCEP, and its declared intention to explore a trilateral trade agreement with Japan and South Korea.[59]

A new doctrine of defence engagement

Japan's defence policy and posture were the areas in which the Abe Doctrine departed the most from Yoshida's. On matters of policy, Abe abolished Japan's long-standing, self-imposed defence-spending cap of 1% of GDP and reversed previous trends by increasing the defence budget on a yearly basis.[60] This change was complemented by the replacement, beginning in 2014, of the bans on arms exports enacted in 1967 and 1976 with the 'Three Principles on Transfer of Defense Equipment and Technology'. Japanese defence spending was still dwarfed by that of China, but the changes allowed Japan to announce from 2018 the conversion of two helicopter destroyers into fixed-wing-aircraft carriers, plans to acquire the largest inventory of F-35 combat aircraft after the US, the development of hypersonic missiles to be deployed in the second half of the 2020s, and the development of a new cyber force and investments in dual-use technologies for the military use of space, among other significant procurements.[61] Larger budgets were coupled with a greater contribution by uniformed officers to the policy-making process, notably through the assignment of military personnel to senior positions within the National Security Secretariat.[62] On matters of posture, the Abe administration produced two defence-review documents, or National Defense Program Guidelines (NDPG), that outlined a transition towards improved capabilities for operating across multiple domains.[63]

Japan's important contribution to the disaster-relief operations in the aftermath of the 2013 typhoon in the Philippines had presented Abe with a clear example of the potential rewards of a more robust agenda of defence engagement.[64] The 2014 NDPG contained the first indications of a desire to enhance Japan's presence, building primarily on long-standing naval-diplomatic initiatives across Southeast Asia and the Indian Ocean. In 2018, a new NDPG confirmed and further expanded this approach. In particular, Abe's decision to focus on engagement in the troubled waters of the South China Sea, and on an enhanced leadership role in counter-piracy operations in the Indian Ocean, were key elements of Japan's commitment to Indo-Pacific security.[65]

Abe played to Japan's strengths

Aware that Japan's material capabilities were limited, the Abe government sought to play to Japan's strengths by investing in maritime capacity-building and by demonstrating commitment through naval presence. The expansion of China's military might – especially its capacity to project power at sea in the Indian and Pacific oceans – had heightened regional awareness of the centrality of sea lanes and sea cables to regional stability, connectivity and prosperity. Concern had only grown as maritime disputes worsened and challenges to the established US-led maritime order multiplied, even though the 2016 ruling on the South China Sea by the Permanent Court of Arbitration highlighted the legal flimsiness of Chinese claims.[66] Hence, the Abe government focused its efforts on naval activities that enhanced Japan's desired image as an engaging and proactive security actor committed to maintaining the international status quo. Port calls, diplomatic visits and military exercises were the means of building new, or reinforcing existing, partnerships with countries such as Australia, the Philippines and Vietnam.[67]

Japan also worked to enhance cooperation with NATO and the EU in counter-piracy efforts in the Gulf of Aden, and raised its leadership profile in maritime security by taking command of CTF-151, the multinational task group based at Combined Maritime Forces in Bahrain. Abe became the only Japanese prime minister to twice address NATO's decision-making body, the North Atlantic Council (NAC), doing so in 2007 and 2014. In 2019, he also concluded a milestone trade agreement with the EU, the EU–Japan Economic Partnership Agreement (EPA), which helped boost the liberal-economic order in the absence of US leadership.[68] Equally significant, Abe worked with considerable success to strengthen bilateral partnerships with major European powers, notably France and the UK. In both cases, the Japanese government and its European counterparts set up regular meetings among defence and foreign ministers, created regular opportunities for joint exercises and explored opportunities for defence-industrial cooperation.[69]

Of no less significance, the maritime focus allowed Japan to maximise the positive impact of capacity-building programmes with countries such as Sri Lanka. This enhanced Japan's influence among key emerging states. Japanese activities were pursued in coordination with close allies, notably the US, which was advantageous for both countries. For example, the JMSDF's historic first visit to Cam Ranh Base in Vietnam in 2016 facilitated a subsequent and equally significant visit by the US Navy. To ensure that defence engagement of this kind produced maximum effect, the Japanese government increased the number of its defence attachés, from 49 in 36 embassies in 2012, to 58 in 40 embassies and two government missions by 2015.[70]

Other important successes came in the development of ties with India, which has emerged as a key defence-engagement partner, particularly in terms of maritime cooperation. In December 2013, the two countries conducted their second bilateral exercise (covering basic manoeuvre and security training), with subsequent opportunities for training only growing in frequency and scope. The following year, Japan joined India's *Malabar* exercise (conducted with the US), and became a permanent member of the exercise in 2015.[71] This is India's prime military exercise covering missions from high-end warfare to maritime security and interdictions operations.[72]

By 2016, India and Japan had added regular counter-piracy bilateral exercises, allowing them to compare practices and command structures. Visits to India by Japanese uniformed chiefs became a regular occurrence. Increased defence engagement also contributed to the development of other formats, such as trilateral cooperation with the US and the Quad initiative.

Unfinished business

Abe's vigorous approach and degree of success in raising Japan's profile as an international security actor stands in contrast with the much less satisfactory results of Japan's diplomacy in its immediate neighbourhood. The Russian, South Korean and North Korean cases were particularly disappointing. In each case, the Abe Doctrine failed to resolve the legacies of the past. Abe's repeated efforts to establish a rapport with President Putin – involving no fewer than 27 bilateral summits – did not advance Japanese goals. During these encounters, Abe set forth proposals for joint economic activities to create an opening for a bilateral peace treaty and the return to Japan by Russia of two of the four islands of the Northern Territories/Southern Kurils. Russia was non-committal on Japanese proposals and added conditions for the islands' return, including the stipulation that they not host any US bases.[73]

Abe's approach failed to gain support either at home or abroad. In Japan, conservatives decried Abe's suggested willingness to give up territory to Russia. Internationally, Japan's effort to court Russia translated into restrained Japanese support for international sanctions on Moscow; especially in the aftermath of the chemical attack in Salisbury, UK, this raised questions about the credibility of Abe's avowed commitment to a rules-based order.[74]

The deterioration of Japan's ties with South Korea was even more damaging to Abe's broader ambitions. In August 2015, on the occasion of the 70th anniversary of the end of the Second World War, Abe had reaffirmed his country's 'deep remorse and heartfelt apology' for the wartime suffering inflicted on the people of Asia. Yet Japan's wartime behaviour remained a highly emotional issue in South Korea. In December 2015, Abe and Park Geun-hye, then South Korea's president, signed an agreement intended to resolve the dispute over the Imperial Japanese Army's practice of forcing Korean women, referred to as 'comfort women', into sexual slavery. The Japanese government committed ¥1 billion ($8 million) to a private foundation established in South Korea to provide care for surviving women in an agreement intended to represent a 'final and irreversible solution'.[75] With the signing of the agreement, the Japanese government expected that the South Korean government would work to bring about a sense of resolution among its citizens and cease to raise the comfort-women issue in bilateral settings. After Park's fall from power in 2017, however, the limits of this approach became clear. Abe was seen by South Koreans to have conceded little in offering only a limited apology for Japanese behaviour, with most of the concessions coming from the Korean side. The deal proved domestically unworkable for new President Moon Jae-in, leading to the dissolution of the private foundation. The fact that the Obama administration had helped to broker the deal to prevent the further deterioration of ties between its two allies added to the sense that the agreement had been made under duress without adequately addressing the underlying issues, and raised doubts about Japan's ability to deal with its closest neighbour on its own.

The critical blow to Japan–South Korea relations arrived in 2018, when South Korea's Supreme Court upheld compensation awards against Japanese companies for their wartime conduct, with each complainant awarded around $100,000. The verdict caused consternation in Japan, with the government pointing out that the judgment violated the 1965 Treaty on Basic Relations between the two countries that had settled all outstanding claims arising from the colonial era.[76] Tensions intensified to the point that Japan, in mid-2019, imposed export controls on the transfer of key substances and parts for use in the manufacture of South Korean semiconductors. The episode underlined how, despite decades of diplomatic efforts, a shared solution to Japan's wartime legacy remained elusive.

For the Abe government, the court ruling was symptomatic of a deeper impasse in relations for which it felt South Korea was to blame. Despite the fact that the governments had made steady progress in defence and security cooperation through the General Security of Military Information Agreement (GSOMIA), a bilateral intelligence-sharing pact, as well as joint exercises and regular talks by senior military officials, spats had arisen. In 2018, a South Korean military exercise near a set of disputed islets in the Sea of Japan, which South Korea controls and calls Dokdo, and which Japan claims and calls Takeshima, heightened tensions. This was later followed by a request from South Korea that the JMSDF not hoist its 'Rising Sun' naval ensign during an international fleet review, and an alleged fire-control-radar lock-on by a South Korean naval vessel against a Japanese maritime-patrol aircraft.[77]

On North Korea too, Abe's doctrine failed to deliver the intended results. The prime minister's interest in the issue of the Japanese citizens abducted by North Korean Special Forces dated to Koizumi Junichiro's premiership in 2001–06, and Abe was personally committed to resolving it. However, Abe's efforts to establish communication with North Korean leader Kim Jong-un had to be carried out in parallel with two very different American diplomatic approaches. Neither Obama's 'strategic patience' policy, nor Trump's 'maximum pressure' approach, were well suited to the achievement of Abe's goals. Abe managed to obtain some assurance from Trump and Moon that they would raise the question of the Japanese abductees with Kim, but to little effect. Abe also failed to gain support for his stance on North Korean missile programmes and the special threat they posed to Japan (particularly North Korea's short- and medium-range missiles), which Trump did not discuss with Kim.[78] Japanese policymakers feared that Trump had abandoned Japan in favour of headline-making diplomacy with North Korea. Meanwhile, Moon, Putin and Xi all conducted separate summits with Kim.[79]

Finally, Abe was to remain frustrated in his ultimate ideological goal of constitutional revision. Even though he had recalibrated his ambitions in the face of domestic opposition towards a seemingly moderate proposal to revise paragraphs one and two of Article 9 to recognise that the 'JSDF is maintained as an armed organisation to take necessary self-defence measures', he still ran out of time to achieve any revision by his original deadline of 2020. Arguably, Abe's reinterpretation of Article 9 to allow for 'collective self-defence' was in substance a more significant change to Japan's defence posture, but Abe's inability to revise the constitution as the last vestige of the post-war order was perhaps his main personal regret.

Suga and the Abe Doctrine

Abe's resignation speech in August 2020 gave a clear assessment of what remained to be accomplished, giving the impression that he was listing his expectations for his successor. Certainly, as chief cabinet secretary throughout Abe's second premiership and a member of Abe's cabinet in 2006–07, Suga was both close to Abe politically and instrumental in implementing his policy agenda. Moves by Suga soon after taking office pointed to a government of continuity. Suga's new cabinet, announced in September 2020, inherited many key figures from the Abe administration. Eight of the 20 portfolios were reappointments, including the foreign minister, Motegi Toshimitsu, and the economy, trade and industry minister, Kajiyama Hiroshi. Kono Taro, a key figure in the second Abe administration who had served first as foreign minister and then as defence minister, remained in the cabinet, albeit with new responsibility for the administrative-reform portfolio.

Upholding key policies

An October meeting of Quad foreign ministers in Tokyo and the (virtual) Mekong–Japan Summit in November allowed Suga to affirm key elements of Abe's FOIP initiative, including maritime-domain awareness and upholding the rule of law.[80] Suga's first overseas visits, to Vietnam and Indonesia in October, were also symbolically important. The choice of countries echoed the first foreign visits by Abe in January 2013 after the start of his second administration, and served to affirm the centrality of the Abe-era 'Indo-Pacific' concept in the Suga administration's thinking. Indeed, en route to Vietnam, Suga described Japan as an 'Indo-Pacific nation'.[81] Suga's tweak of the Abe-era 'free and open', values-based Indo-Pacific formulation at the November 2020 ASEAN summit, where he called for a 'peaceful and prosperous' Indo-Pacific, caused some concern that the concept might be weakened in order to smooth relations with China, but Suga is unlikely to change the substance of Japan's original FOIP policy in the region.[82]

Suga's call at the November meeting of the Asia-Pacific Economic Cooperation (APEC) forum to expand the CPTPP also suggested continuity in Abe's coalition-building diplomacy.[83] The CPTPP, of which China is not a member, has taken on greater importance as a channel for Japan's regional influence since the signing of the RCEP, which, once it enters into force, will become the world's largest trade bloc and include China. Japan, as the largest economy in the CPTPP and the second-largest economy in the RCEP, as well as by virtue of its free-trade and economic-partnership arrangements with a number of ASEAN countries and Australia, lies at the centre of Asia's spaghetti bowl of trade deals. Tokyo is thus well placed to build and sustain coalitions within the RCEP to balance China's influence. Suga can also be expected to continue building relations with India and Australia. National and economic security will remain important areas for Suga: witness the Japan–Australia Reciprocal Access Agreement, announced during Australian Prime Minister Scott Morrison's visit to Tokyo in November, which provides for reciprocal visits by personnel and assets from both countries' armed forces; and the continued efforts by Japan, Australia and India to develop supply-chain alternatives to China in the region.[84]

Changes of priority and nuance

Although Suga's perceptions of Japan's international position resemble Abe's, important shifts in priorities and nuance are already under way. In part, this reflects the dramatic changes wrought by the COVID-19 pandemic on the domestic economy in 2020. Suga inherited an economy in the midst of its worst recession since the end of the Second World War. Prospects for recovery in 2021 are so uncertain that Japan's GDP may not regain its 2019 level until 2023, or even 2024. Fiscal stimulus to counteract the economic damage of the pandemic will leave Japan with a public-debt-stock-to-GDP ratio of nearly 270% by the end of 2020, with little prospect of substantial improvement into the middle of the current decade.[85] This compares with Abe who, when he took office for the second time in December 2012, could look forward to buoyant economic growth in 2013, partly on the back of the monetary-policy loosening mandated by Abenomics. The debt-to-GDP ratio at that time was a still high but broadly stable 230%.

Suga's immediate priority will therefore be economic recovery. A tight electoral calendar will increase the urgency of this goal. The next lower-house election must be held by late October 2021. Assuming the election is held before then, and that the LDP retains at least a large majority (even if reduced from Abe's landslide of 2017), Suga will also have to face an LDP leadership election in September 2021; he is currently serving out the remainder of Abe's final three-year term. The next upper-house election will take place in mid-2022. Personal diplomacy was a hallmark of Abe's second premiership; he made some 80 visits abroad in this period. Economic priorities and elections suggest that Suga is unlikely to have the time to repeat this feat, even once the worst of the COVID-19 pandemic has passed.

Suga has also been quick to make subtle institutional changes that will alter the balance of Japan's domestic- and foreign-policy formation. Under Abe's second premiership, the Ministry of Economy, Trade and Industry (METI) enjoyed significant influence in policymaking, and its personnel were well represented in key advisory roles to the prime minister. Suga carried out a reshuffle of these positions soon after taking office and disbanded the Council on Investments for the Future (Mirai Toshi Kaigi).[86] Abe used to chair meetings of the council as an important driver of Abenomics and a conduit for METI influence on policy. Suga's move thus marked an important change. Although Suga has set up a replacement body to deliberate policy, the Growth Strategy Council (Seicho Senryaku Kaigi), this is chaired by the chief cabinet secretary and not the prime minister. Hence, it has been downgraded in terms of institutional status compared with its predecessor. Also striking is Suga's solicitation of advice from non-political experts: in the first month of his premiership he had more than 70 meetings with private-sector figures, compared with just 24 for Abe at the start of his second premiership.[87] Suga's preference therefore seems to be for a more diverse policymaking environment than was the case under Abe, with no one policy group able to dominate.

Other ministries, such as the Ministry of Foreign Affairs or the Ministry of Finance, may see their influence rise as a result of these changes. A bigger role for the foreign ministry might suggest a de-emphasising of economic issues in some areas of foreign policy. Policy towards China may take a harder edge. Imai Takaya, a key foreign-policy adviser to Abe and formerly with METI, was a driver of the moderate thawing of Abe's attitude towards China's BRI and his willingness to cooperate with the BRI where projects met Japanese standards. But with Imai's stepping down as special adviser to the prime minister upon Abe's departure, the foreign ministry may exert greater influence on security concerns. Imai encouraged Abe's persistent courting of President Putin, ostensibly to achieve a solution to the bilateral dispute over the Northern Territories/Southern Kurils but also with a view to building economic relations with Russia. Given the lack of reciprocity from Moscow and the cost to Abe's political capital as a result, Suga may well prefer to park efforts to improve relations with Russia. Similarly, Suga, while signalling his ongoing support for some of Abe's other initiatives, may devote less energy to them given their inherent difficulty. He will surely wish to continue to press North Korea on the abductions issue, but will see it as less of a personal badge of honour, or shame; and while constitutional revision is a common goal of all LDP leaders, it may not be at the top of Suga's list.

Challenges of a new US administration

A change of president in the US will also bring challenges. The Trump challenge catalysed some of Abe's most important policy successes, including the CPTPP and the EU–Japan Economic and Strategic Partnership agreements (the EPA and SPA, launched in 2018). Trump's undermining of the rules-based international order had spurred Abe to shore it up, and the US president's focus on China had opened up policy space for Japan, allowing it to harden its China policy (albeit to a lesser degree than Trump's), while periodically incentivising China to reach out to Japan to offset US pressure. The bipartisan consensus in Washington over the strategic threat China poses to the US augurs against a complete volte-face on China by the Biden administration, but greater nuance is likely, particularly if President Biden seeks to co-opt Chinese support in areas such as climate change and global health security. Japan will thus fear grand-bargain accommodation between Washington and Beijing that leaves Tokyo's policy positions towards China exposed.[88]

Although Suga will undoubtedly prioritise US–Japan relations over everything else, pressures around the countries' security alliance will remain.[89] Biden can be expected to focus more than Trump did on managing the alliance, but Washington will continue to push Japan to do more to support the relationship. The burden-sharing discussion may broaden from a focus on Japanese financial support for the US military presence in Japan to allowing for greater American use of bases and facilities, or even joint research and development (R&D) on military technology, such as space-based and uninhabited systems. Tokyo may also come under pressure from Washington to improve its toxic relations with South Korea. Biden played a key personal role in 2013–14 in easing tensions between Seoul and Tokyo, not least because of US concerns over the costs of these tensions for the countries' ability to counter China and North Korea.

Other goals for the US–Japan alliance could include an active role for Japan in the Taiwan Strait, but the Suga administration's level of defence activism remains to be seen. In June 2020, the Abe government decided to scrap the *Aegis* Ashore (land-based) ballistic-missile-defence system, ostensibly for reasons of cost and concern about the system's technical flaws. The decision had the potential to widen the scope of discussion on Japan's future missile and defence capabilities, including a shift for the first time to limited strike potential against enemy missile bases, which remains problematic under Japan's defence-oriented security policy. At the time this issue went to press, however, the Suga administration looked set to approve replacement of the *Aegis* Ashore system with two new destroyers fitted with *Aegis* missile interceptors – this despite the pressure that this would place on Japan's maritime forces, which are already facing personnel shortages.

Suga also is unlikely to take early steps for shifting the country's defence posture towards the adoption of policies for an offensive use of strike capabilities. While the practice to review the NDPG every five years suggests that the document may be soon updated, Japan's defence posture is likely to continue to emphasise the procurement of 'counter-strike' capabilities. This will entail the integration of stand-off capabilities within the country's force structure, but without as yet the necessary intelligence and command-and-control structures to conduct effective strikes against imminent missile threats. Moreover, despite the increasing demand to enhance the security of Japan's defence-industrial base, Suga has not yet articulated plans to protect technologies or to boost R&D in dual-use emerging technologies to respond to Beijing's rapid advancement of its civil–military fusion strategy.

Suga's digital-reform push

While circumstances may militate against the deployment by the Suga administration of a grand strategy to the same extent as his predecessor, the prime minister's domestic focus on digital reforms points to a clear effort to build on Abe's legacy. Suga's digital push is not new – in January 2020, Nishimura Yasutoshi, Japan's minister for the economy and fiscal policy, outlined a 'digital new deal' for Japan that included the digitisation of the country's bureaucracy, as well as the development of post-5G systems and quantum and artificial-intelligence (AI) technologies.[90] Some ¥1.7 trillion ($16.3bn) was earmarked for digital-related funding in 2020/21.[91] The COVID-19 crisis has only increased the urgency of such reforms, exposing the shortcomings in Japan's administrative digital infrastructure. The delays in disbursing pandemic-related financial support in mid-2020, for example, were directly attributable to the still small percentage of administrative tasks that are transacted online: less than 12% of the total, according to the Japan Research Institute.[92]

Suga plans to create a new 'Digital Agency' to coordinate Japan's digital policy, which is now split between METI and the Ministry of Internal Affairs and Communications, with predictable consequences for the efficiency of policy formation. This focus on digital reforms dovetails with other domestic priorities for Suga, including reforming Japan's large but inefficient small- and medium-sized-enterprise (SME) sector and raising the productivity of the economy to boost growth. The digital-reform push also sits alongside Suga's broader desire to effect institutional change by breaking down barriers between Japan's siloed and turf-conscious government agencies.[93]

Suga's digital reforms are still in their early stages, and focused on digitising government paperwork and integrating the government's information-technology systems. Japan has fallen behind its rich-country peers in terms of its digital capabilities – witness its slippage in terms of global cross-border data-flow volumes from fifth in 2001 to 11th in 2019, according to the International Telecommunication Union.[94] This reflects both Japan's institutional fragmentation and the largely domestic focus of Rakuten, LINE, Yahoo! Japan and other Japanese internet companies. Japan is similarly lagging in areas such as cloud computing and 5G. NEC, for example, which is Japan's largest telecommunications-equipment and -systems supplier, has only a 0.7% share of global 5G base stations.[95] The possession of advanced digital and technological resources affects national competitiveness and gives a country credibility and leverage in digital rule-making and cooperation. The latter is especially important for medium powers such as Japan given the trend towards great-power techno-nationalism and the resulting fragmentation of technological ecosystems.

Sustaining Abe's 'connectivity' legacy

Although the need to secure 'connectivity' animated FOIP and other areas of Abe's economic statecraft, digital policy for much of his second administration was largely focused on digital rule-making. The e-commerce chapters of the CPTPP and EPA, or the 'Osaka Track', which Abe launched at the Osaka G20 meeting in 2019 in order to secure a regime of 'data free flow with trust', are good examples of this.[96] Abe was concerned with Japan's strategic need to secure access to other countries' data for its own development of emerging technologies, and with the lack of rules in what is still a new area. Domestic digital and technological development under Suga will be critical to sustaining the connectivity within Abe's foreign-policy structures. ASEAN, a fulcrum of FOIP, is an important test bed in this regard. Notwithstanding Japan's existing digital-transformation programmes in the region, competition from China, which dominates the region's e-commerce and thus its distribution networks and payments systems, is already fierce. Parts of the region even lead Japan in terms of the volume of cross-border data flows.

Abe's legacy and Suga's plans

Suga inherits from Abe a different Japan from the country that Abe inherited in 2012. Under Abe's leadership, Japan has re-emerged as a primary actor in international affairs. It stands at the centre of many of the Asia-Pacific region's main economic, political and security mechanisms. It has assumed greater leadership in key processes such as the CPTPP, and cultivated key relationships beyond its alliance with the US, including with ASEAN, Australia, India, and partners in Europe and NATO. Suga has inherited a

Japan with a renewed sense of agency that is capable of convening larger groups of states and of potentially resorting to the use of military power in support of stability. It is perhaps symptomatic of this change that in 2013, when Abe visited Vietnam in his first overseas trip, he announced the 'strategic' nature of the bilateral relationship. In October 2020, when Suga visited Vietnam, he described how the relationship had taken on a strategic character through an agenda of cooperation that encompassed digital-economy initiatives, cyber-security cooperation and even the possibility of arms export.[97]

We have argued that Japan, having embraced the Abe Doctrine, is no longer the country that the Yoshida Doctrine had significantly influenced. It no longer merely benefits from the 'warm' embrace of its alliance with the US, but has pursued its own agency in security matters. The US alliance remains a pillar of Japan's foreign and security policy, but Tokyo has sought to evolve into a more equal partner, and certainly a more proactive one – crucially strengthening links with other bilateral partners of the US, notably Australia and India. Abe's agenda also included the development of new networks with actors in Southeast Asia and the Indian Ocean, including Indonesia, the Philippines, Sri Lanka and Vietnam, who share Japan's concerns about Chinese ambitions. Within this context, the Abe Doctrine has rejected a passive approach to security and developed an unprecedented defence-engagement activism that has underwritten the country's credibility. One key question yet to be answered about Suga is how he will draw upon Abe's legacy to consolidate Japan's new-found convening power. Suga has an opportunity to do so with the CPTPP and through the connectivity agenda outlined by Abe's grand strategy and enshrined in FOIP.

A significant contributor to Abe's success in operationalising his strategy was his ability and willingness to adapt to evolving circumstances. Given the ongoing uncertainty about the future of the Japanese economy, Suga will have to be similarly flexible. In this respect, it will be interesting to observe how Suga relates to South Korea's newly announced Southern Policy, Seoul's own take on the Indo-Pacific, and how a post-Brexit tilting of the UK towards the Indo-Pacific might add to an already growing bilateral relationship between London and Tokyo. Under Abe, maritime security led the way in Japan's security activism because of its investment in the stability of the Indo-Pacific's main economic arteries and its need to sustain a rules-based order. Under Suga, maritime-security cooperation is likely to retain its importance in Japan's defence agenda, but digital connectivity, cyber-security cooperation and the resilience of supply chains might well gain greater primacy. If so, this might lead Suga to adapt FOIP.

Ultimately, Suga's success in advancing the grand strategy laid out by Abe will depend on the new Biden administration's approach to the Indo-Pacific. While the consensus in Washington over competition with China is unlikely to change, how the next administration will tackle the Indo-Pacific and its wide array of economic and security issues is uncertain. The Biden team has thus far made clear that it intends to mend alliances and relationships that had been undermined by Trump, but it is unclear what this means for the Indo-Pacific. It may be that Biden will tend to focus on transatlantic relations, where ties seem more fractured. Domestically, Suga's priorities will be a stronger economy, an end to the COVID-19 pandemic and a renewal of Japan's technological capabilities, with foreign and security initiatives perhaps requiring more collaboration with partners. That may be easier to achieve for a Japan that changed in important ways under Abe.

Notes

[1] Prime Minister's Office of Japan, 'Abe Naikaku Sōri Daijin Kisha Kaiken', 28 August 2020, https://www.kantei.go.jp/jp/98_abe/statement/2020/0828kaiken.html; and Robin Harding and Christian Shepherd, 'Shinzo Abe to Step Down as Japan's Prime Minister', *Financial Times*, 28 August 2020, https://www.ft.com/content/201aa32b-5e72-4e48-aa4e-1901b66d505d.

[2] See Michael J. Green, 'Shinzo Abe's Decision to Step Down', Center for Strategic and International Studies, 28 August 2020, https://www.csis.org/analysis/ shinzo-abes-decision-step-down.

[3] See 'What's at Stake for Shinzo Abe's Successor?', *New York Times*, 2 September 2020, https://www.nytimes.com/2020/09/02/opinion/shinzo-abe-japan.html; Tobias Harris, 'Shinzo Abe Will Be a Tough Act to Follow', *Foreign Affairs*, 22 September 2020, https://www.foreignaffairs.com/articles/japan/2020-09-22/shinzo-abe-will-be-tough-act-follow; and Tobias Harris, *The Iconoclast: Shinzō Abe and the New Japan* (London: Hurst, 2020).

[4] See, for example, Michael Auslin, 'The Abe Era Ends, Cheering China, Concerning Washington', *Foreign*

Policy, 28 August 2020, https://foreignpolicy.com/2020/08/28/abe-japan-resignation-united-states-ally/; Zack Cooper and Jeffrey W. Hornung, 'Abe's Resignation Could Leave Japan Less Secure – and Destabilize Its U.S. Alliance', RAND Blog, 8 September 2020, https://www.rand.org/blog/2020/09/abes-resignation-could-leave-japan-less-secure-and.html; and Robert Ward, 'Abe Resignation: A Full In-tray for His Successor', IISS Analysis, 28 August 2020, https://www.iiss.org/blogs/analysis/2020/08/abe-shinzo-resignation-japan-prime-minister-successor.

5   See Giulio Pugliese and Alessio Patalano, 'Diplomatic and Security Practice Under Abe Shinzo: The Case for Realpolitik Japan', *Australian Journal of International Affairs*, vol. 76, no. 4, 2020, pp. 615–32; Alessio Patalano, *Shinzo Abe and Japan's Strategic Reset* (London: Policy Exchange, 2020), https://policyexchange.org.uk/publication/shinzo-abe-and-japans-strategic-reset/; and Adam P. Liff, 'Japan's National Security Council: Policy Coordination and Political Power', *Japanese Studies*, vol. 38, no. 2, 2018, pp. 253–79.

6   See Andrew L. Oros, *Japan's Security Renaissance* (New York: Columbia University Press, 2017); Adam P. Liff, 'Japan's Security Policy in the "Abe Era": Radical Transformation or Evolutionary Shift?', *Texas National Security Review*, vol. 1, no. 3, 2018, https://tnsr.org/2018/05/japans-security-policy-in-the-abe-era-radical-transformation-or-evolutionary-shift/; Wilhelm Vosse and Paul Midford (eds), *Japan's New Security*

Partnerships: Beyond the Security Alliance (Manchester: Manchester University Press, 2018); and Alessio Patalano, '"Natural Partners" in Challenging Waters? Japan–NATO Co-operation in a Changing Maritime Environment', *RUSI Journal*, vol. 161, no. 3, 2016, pp. 42–51.

7   See Martin Fackler, 'Ex-premier Is Chosen to Govern Japan Again', *New York Times*, 26 December 2012, https://www.nytimes.com/2012/12/27/world/asia/shinzo-abe-selected-as-japans-prime-minister.html; and Richard J. Samuels and Corey Wallace, 'Introduction: Japan's Pivot to Asia', *International Affairs*, vol. 94, no. 4, 2018, pp. 703–10.

8   'Japanese Economic Slump Threatens to Tarnish Abe's Legacy', *Japan Times*, 18 August 2020, https://www.japantimes.co.jp/news/2020/08/18/business/japan-economic-slump-shinzo-abe/.

9   See Leika Kihara and Takaya Yamaguchi, 'Abenomics Fails to Deliver as Japan Braces for Post-Abe Era', Reuters, 28 August 2020, https://uk.reuters.com/article/us-japan-economy-abenomics-analysis/abenomics-fails-to-deliver-as-japan-braces-for-post-abe-era-idUKKBN25O0TT.

10 See Karl Gustaffson, 'Long Live Pacifism! Narrative Power and Japan's Pacifist Model', *Cambridge Review of International Affairs*, vol. 32, 2019, pp. 502–20; Karl Gustafsson, Linus Hagström and Ulv Hanssen, 'Japan's Pacifism Is Dead', *Survival*, vol. 60, no. 6, December 2018–January 2019, pp. 137–58; and Hugo Dobson, 'Is Japan Really Back? The "Abe Doctrine"

and Global Governance', *Journal of Contemporary Asia*, vol. 47, no. 2, 2017, pp. 199–224.

[11] See Thierry Balzacq, Peter Dombroski and Simon Reich (eds), *Comparative Grand Strategy: A Framework and Cases* (Oxford: Oxford University Press, 2019), pp. 7–8.

[12] See Christopher W. Hughes, *Japan's Foreign and Security Policy Under the 'Abe Doctrine': New Dynamism or Dead End?* (New York: Palgrave Macmillan, 2015).

[13] Abe Shinzo, 'Japan Is Back', remarks at CSIS, Washington DC, 22 February 2013, https://www.mofa.go.jp/announce/pm/abe/us_20130222en.html. 'Take back Japan' was an LDP slogan for the 2012 lower-house election: Jimintō, 'Nihon o Torimodosu: Jūten Seisaku 2012', Tokyo, 21 November 2012, https://jimin.jp-east-2.storage.api.nifcloud.com/pdf/seisaku_ichiban24.pdf.

[14] See Abe, 'Japan Is Back'; and Richard L. Armitage and Joseph S. Nye, 'The US–Japan Alliance: Anchoring Stability in Asia', CSIS, 2012, p. 1, http://csis.org/files/publication/120810_Armitage_USJapanAlliance_Web.pdf.

[15] Harris, *The Iconoclast*, pp. 47–58.

[16] See Christopher W. Hughes, 'Japan's Grand Strategic Shift: From a Yoshida Doctrine to an Abe Doctrine?', in Ashley J. Tellis, Alison M. Szalwinski and Michael Wills (eds), *Strategic Asia 2017–18: Power, Ideas and Military Strategy in the Asia-Pacific* (Seattle, WA: National Bureau of Asian Research, 2017), pp. 72–105.

[17] Abe Shinzō, *Utsukushii Kuni E* (Tokyo: Bunshun Shinsho, 2006).

[18] See Victor Cha, 'Abandonment, Entrapment, and Neoclassical Realism in Asia: The United States, Japan and Korea', *International Studies Quarterly*, vol. 44, no. 2, 2000, pp. 261–91; Eric Heginbotham and Richard J. Samuels, 'Japan's Dual Hedge', *Foreign Affairs*, vol. 81, no. 5, 2002, pp. 110–21; Kei Koga, 'The Concept of "Hedging" Revisited: The Case of Japan's Foreign Policy Strategy in East Asia's Power Shift', *International Studies Review*, vol. 20, 2018, pp. 633–60; and Adam P. Liff, 'Unambivalent Alignment: Japan's China Strategy, the US Alliance, and the "Hedging" Fallacy', *International Relations of the Asia-Pacific*, vol. 19, 2019, pp. 453–91.

[19] Kobayashi Yoshinori, *Kibō no Kuni Nihon: Kyūjin no Seijika to Shinken Shōbu* (Tokyo: Asuka Shinsha, 2010), p. 273.

[20] See Hughes, *Japan's Foreign and Security Policy Under the 'Abe Doctrine'*, pp. 15–19.

[21] See Michal Kolmaš, *National Identity and Japanese Revisionism: Abe Shinzō's Vision of a Beautiful Japan and Its Limits* (New York: Routledge, 2019), pp. 69–72; and Christian G. Winkler, *The Quest for Japan's New Constitution: An Analysis of the Visions of Constitutional Reform Proposals 1980–2009* (London: Routledge, 2011), pp. 50–8.

[22] See Christopher W. Hughes, 'Japan's Security Trajectory and Collective Self-defense: Essential Continuity or Radical Shift?', *Journal of Japanese Studies*, vol. 43, no. 1, Winter 2017, pp. 93–126.

[23] See Kenneth B. Pyle, *Japan in the American Century* (Cambridge, MA: The Belknap Press of Harvard

University Press, 2018), pp. 374–78.

24 Tokyo seemed at times to depart from this aim by courting authoritarian regimes.

25 See Dobson, 'Is Japan Really Back?', p. 204; and Christopher W. Hughes, 'Japan and the South China Sea Disputes: Emerging Power Politics and "Fake Liberalism"', in Huiyun Fung and Kai He (eds), *US–China Competition and the South China Sea Disputes* (New York: Routledge, 2018), pp. 82–97.

26 Japan Cabinet Secretariat, 'National Security Strategy', 17 December 2013, https://www.cas.go.jp/jp/siryou/131217anzenhoshou/nss-e.pdf.

27 See Aurelia George Mulgan, *The Abe Administration and the Rise of the Prime Ministerial Executive* (London: Routledge, 2017).

28 See Liff, 'Japan's National Security Council', pp. 253–79; and Japan Cabinet Secretariat, 'National Security Strategy'.

29 See Takako Hikotani, 'Trump's Gift to Japan: Time for Tokyo to Invest in the Liberal Order', *Foreign Affairs*, vol. 96, no. 5, pp. 21–7; and Reiji Yoshida, 'Japanese Officials Play Down Trump's Security Treaty Criticisms, Claim President's Remarks Not Always "Official" US Position', *Japan Times*, 2 July 2019, https://www.japantimes.co.jp/news/2019/07/02/national/politics-diplomacy/japanese-officials-play-trumps-security-treaty-criticisms-claim-remarks-not-always-official-u-s-position/#.Xh2licj7SUk.

30 See Liff, 'Unambivalent Alignment'.

31 See Ellis S. Krauss and Hanns W. Maull, 'Germany, Japan and the Fate of the International Order', *Survival*, vol.

62, no. 3, June–July 2020, pp. 166–7.

32 See Abe Shinzo, 'Asia's Democratic Security Diamond', Project Syndicate, 27 December 2012, http://www.project-syndicate.org/commentary/a-strategic-alliance-for-japan-and-india-by-shinzo-abe; and Jeffrey W. Hornung, 'Japan's Growing Hard Hedge Against China', *Asian Security*, vol. 10, no. 2, 2014, pp. 97–122.

33 See Yomiuri Shimbun Seijibu, *Abe Kantei vs Shū Kinpei: Gekika Suru Nicchū Gaikō Sensō* (Tokyo: Shinchōsha, 2015).

34 See Luis Simon, Alexander Lanoszka and Hugo Meijer, 'Nodal Defence: The Changing Structure of US Alliance Systems in Europe and East Asia', *Journal of Strategic Studies*, 2019, pp. 1–29.

35 See Paul Midford, *Overcoming Isolationism: Japan's Leadership in East Asian Security Multilateralism* (Stanford, CA: Stanford University Press, 2020), pp. 155–7.

36 See Tomohiko Satake and John Hemmings, 'Japan–Australia Security Cooperation in the Bilateral and Multilateral Contexts', *International Affairs*, vol. 94, no. 4, 2018, pp. 815–34.

37 See Patalano, '"Natural Partners" in Challenging Waters?'; and Michito Tsuruoka, 'Abe Shinzo's Legacy in Japan–Europe Relations', *Diplomat*, 14 September 2020, https://thediplomat.com/2020/09/shinzo-abes-legacy-in-japaneurope-relations/.

38 See Saori N. Katada, *Japan's New Regional Strategy: Geoeconomic Strategy in the Asia-Pacific* (New York: Columbia University Press, 2020), pp. 116–18; and Takashi Terada, 'Japan and TPP/

TPP-11: Opening the Black Box of Domestic Political Alignment for Proactive Economic Diplomacy in Face of "Trump Shock"', *Pacific Review*, vol. 32, no. 6, 2019, pp. 1,041–69.

39 See Prime Minister of Japan and His Cabinet, 'Address by Prime Minister Shinzo Abe at the Opening Session of the Sixth Tokyo International Conference on African Development', 27 August 2016, https://japan.kantei.go.jp/97_abe/statement/201608/1218850_11013.html; Ministry of Foreign Affairs of Japan, 'Japan's Efforts for a Free and Open Indo-Pacific', May 2020, available at https://www.mofa.go.jp/policy/page25e_000278.html; and Yuichi Hosoya, 'FOIP 2.0: The Evolution of Japan's Free and Open Indo-Pacific Strategy', *Asia-Pacific Review*, vol. 26, no. 1, pp. 18–28.

40 Prime Minister of Japan and His Cabinet, 'Statement by Prime Minister Shinzo Abe', 14 August 2015, https://japan.kantei.go.jp/97_abe/statement/201508/0814statement.html.

41 See Christopher W. Hughes, 'The Political Economy of Japanese Sanctions Towards North Korea: Domestic Coalitions and International Systemic Pressures', *Pacific Affairs*, vol. 79, no. 3, 2006, pp. 455–81.

42 See Richard J. Samuels, *Special Duty: A History of the Japanese Intelligence Community* (Ithaca, NY: Cornell University Press, 2019), pp. 205–8; Hitoshi Nasu, 'Japan's 2015 Security Legislation: Challenges to Its Implementation Under International Law', *International Law Studies*, vol. 92, no. 249, 2016, pp. 250–80; and National Institute for Defence Studies, 'Japan:

Revising Security Legislation and the Japan–US Defence Cooperation Guidelines', *East Asian Strategic Review*, 2015, pp. 39–57.

43 See National Institute for Defence Studies, 'Japan: Upgrading of National Security Policy', *East Asian Strategic Review*, 2015, pp. 312–13.

44 See Reinhard Drifte, 'The Japan–China Confrontation over the Senkaku/Diaoyu Islands: Between "Shelving" and "Dispute Escalation"', *Asia-Pacific Journal*, vol. 12, issue 30, no. 3, 27 July 2014, https://apjjf.org/-Reinhard-Drifte/4154/article.pdf.

45 White House, Office of the Press Secretary, 'Joint Press Conference with President Obama and Prime Minister Abe of Japan', Tokyo, 24 April 2014, https://obamawhitehouse.archives.gov/the-press-office/2014/04/24/joint-press-conference-president-obama-and-prime-minister-abe-japan.

46 See Alessio Patalano, 'Seapower and Sino-Japanese Relations in the East China Sea', *Asian Affairs*, vol. 45, no. 1, 2014, p. 48.

47 See Emma Chanlett-Avery and Ian E. Rinehart, *The U.S. Military Presence in Okinawa and the Futenma Base Controversy* (Washington DC: Congressional Research Service, 2016), pp. 16–17, https://fas.org/sgp/crs/natsec/R42645.pdf; and Ayako Mie, 'Obama Makes History, Confronts Past in Hiroshima', *Japan Times*, 27 May 2016, https://www.japantimes.co.jp/news/2016/05/27/national/politics-diplomacy/obama-pays-historic-visit-to-hiroshima/.

48 See Sam Nussey, 'Trump Asks Japan to Hike Payments for U.S. Troops to $8 Billion: Foreign Policy', Reuters,

16 November 2019, https://www.
reuters.com/article/us-japan-usa-
idUSKBN1XQ06F; and 'Trump
Pressed Japan's Abe to Build More
Vehicles in the U.S.', Reuters, 27 April
2019, https://www.reuters.com/article/
us-usa-japan-idUSKCN1S30KO.

49 See US Department of Defense, 'Indo-
Pacific Strategy Report: Preparedness,
Partnerships, and Promoting a
Networked Region', 2019, pp. 3–6.

50 See Zack Cooper and Hal Brands, 'It
Is Time to Transform the US–Japan
Alliance', *Nikkei Asia*, 25 October
2020, https://asia.nikkei.com/
Opinion/It-is-time-to-transform-the-
US-Japan-alliance.

51 See Takashi Shiraishi, 'Shinzo Abe Is
Redefining Japan's China Policy for a
Generation', *Nikkei Asia*, 12 February
2020, https://asia.nikkei.com/Opinion/
Shinzo-Abe-is-redefining-Japan-s-
China-policy-for-a-generation.

52 See Hosoya, 'FOIP 2.0', pp. 24–5.

53 See Alessio Patalano, 'What Is China's
Strategy in the Senkaku Islands?',
War on the Rocks, 10 September 2020,
https://warontherocks.com/2020/09/
what-is-chinas-strategy-in-the-
senkaku-islands/.

54 See Kentaro Furuya, 'Maritime
Security – The Architecture of Japan's
Maritime-security System in the East
China Sea', *Naval War College Review*,
vol. 72, no. 4, 2019, pp. 30–1.

55 See A. Patalano, 'Japan as a Maritime
Power: Deterrence, Diplomacy,
and Maritime Security', in Mary
M. McCarthy (ed.), *The Handbook of
Japanese Foreign Policy* (Abingdon:
Routledge, 2018), pp. 163–5.

56 Japan Ministry of Defense, *Defence
of Japan Digest* (Tokyo: Ministry of

Defense, 2020), p. 3, https://www.
mod.go.jp/e/publ/w_paper/wp2020/
DOJ2020_Digest_EN.pdf.

57 See, for example, Thomas Wilson
and Kiyoshi Takenaka, 'G7 Agrees
Need Strong Message on South
China Sea; China Says Don't
"Hype"', Reuters, 26 May 2016,
https://www.reuters.com/article/
us-g7-summit-idUSKCN0YH016.

58 See Patalano, 'What Is China's
Strategy in the Senkaku Islands?'

59 See Kentaro Iwamoto, 'Asia Forms
World's Largest Trading Bloc
RCEP After Years of Talks', *Nikkei
Asia*, 15 November 2020, https://
asia.nikkei.com/Economy/Trade/
Asia-forms-world-s-largest-trading-
bloc-RCEP-after-years-of-talks.

60 See John Wright, 'Abe Scraps Japan's
1 Percent GDP Defense Spending
Cap', *Diplomat*, 29 March 2017,
https://thediplomat.com/2017/03/
abe-scraps-japans-1-percent-gdp-
defense-spending-cap/.

61 See Robin Harding, 'Japan to Raise
Military Spending to New Record',
Financial Times, 20 December 2019,
https://www.ft.com/content/9e897000-
22ef-11ea-b8a1-584213ee7b2b;
Paul Kallender and Christopher
W. Hughes, 'Japan's Emerging
Trajectory as a "Cyber Power":
From Securitization to Militarization
of Cyberspace', *Journal of Strategic
Studies*, vol. 40, nos 1–2, 2017, pp.
118–45; and Paul Kallender and
Christopher W. Hughes, 'Hiding in
Plain Sight? Japan's Militarization of
Space and Challenges to the Yoshida
Doctrine', *Asian Security*, vol. 15, no. 2,
2019, pp. 180–204.

62 See Patalano, *Shinzo Abe and Japan's*

Strategic Reset, pp. 11–12; and Sheila A. Smith, *Japan Rearmed: The Politics of Military Power* (Cambridge, MA: Harvard University Press, 2019), p. 146.

63 See Tomohiko Satake and Yuji Maeda, 'Japan: New National Defense Program Guidelines', *East Asian Strategic Review*, 2019, pp. 205–32.

64 See Alessio Patalano, 'Beyond the Gunboats: Rethinking Naval Diplomacy and Humanitarian Assistance Disaster Relief in East Asia', *RUSI Journal*, vol. 160, no. 2, 2015, pp. 32–9.

65 See Patalano, 'Japan as a Maritime Power', pp. 155–72.

66 See Alessio Patalano, 'Commitment by Presence: Naval Diplomacy and Japanese Defense Engagement in Southeast Asia', in Jeff Kingston and James Brown (eds), *Japan's Foreign Relations in Asia* (Abingdon: Routledge, 2018), pp. 100–13.

67 See *ibid.*, pp. 107–11.

68 See Patalano, '"Natural Partners" in Challenging Waters'; and Axel Berkofsky et al. (eds), *The EU–Japan Partnership in the Shadow of China* (New York: Routledge, 2018).

69 See Luis Simón and Ulrich Speck (eds), 'Natural Partners? Europe, Japan and Security in the Indo-Pacific', Royal Elcano Institute Policy Paper, 2018, http://www.realinstitutoelcano. org/wps/wcm/connect/e1b07fbd-ac5f-4d8d-874c-1fe1b7ff1892/ Policy-Paper-2018-Natural-Partners-Europe-Japan-security-Indo-Pacific. pdf?MOD=AJPERES&CACHEID= e1b07fbd-ac5f-4d8d-874c-1fe1b7ff1892.

70 Data from Japan Ministry of Defense, 'Japan Defense Focus', 2013, p. 41; and Japan Ministry of Defense, 'Japan Defense Focus', 2015, p. 62.

71 See Japan Ministry of Defense, *Defense of Japan* (Tokyo: Japan Ministry of Defense, 2016), pp. 453–4; and Franz-Stefan Gady, 'India, US, and Japan to Hold "Malabar" Naval War Games This Week', *Diplomat*, 5 June 2018, https://thediplomat.com/2018/06/ india-us-and-japan-to-hold-malabar-naval-war-games-this-week/.

72 See Ankit Panda, 'India–Japan–US Malabar 2017 Naval Exercises Kick Off with Anti-submarine Warfare in Focus', *Diplomat*, 10 July 2017, https://thediplomat.com/2017/07/ india-japan-us-malabar-2017-naval-exercises-kick-off-with-anti-submarine-warfare-in-focus/.

73 See Michito Tsuruoka, 'Resetting Japan–Russia Relations: Challenges for a New Prime Minister', *Diplomat*, 7 October 2020, https:// thediplomat.com/2020/10/ resetting-japan-russia-relations/.

74 See James D.J. Brown, 'Japan and the Skripal Poisoning: The UK's Fair-weather Friend', *Japan Times*, 27 March 2018, https://www.japantimes.co.jp/ opinion/2018/03/27/commentary/ japan-commentary/japan-skripal-poisoning-u-k-s-fair-weather-friend/.

75 See Krishnadev Calamur, 'Japan Says Sorry for Its Crimes Against Wartime "Comfort Women"', *Atlantic*, 28 December 2015, https:// www.theatlantic.com/international/ archive/2015/12/japan-korea-comfort-women/422016/; and Ankit Panda, 'The "Final and Irreversible" 2015 Japan–South Korea Comfort Women Deal Unravels', *Diplomat*, 9 January 2017, https://thediplomat.com/2017/01/the-final-and-irreversible-2015-japan-south-korea-comfort-women-deal-unravels/.

76 See Alessio Patalano, 'Seoul, Tokyo Need to Move Beyond History to Grow Ties', *Business Times*, 27 December 2018, https://www.businesstimes.com.sg/opinion/seoul-tokyo-need-to-move-beyond-history-to-grow-ties.

77 See Joyce Lee and Kiyoshi Takenada, 'Japan to Skip Naval Event After South Korea Protests over "Rising Sun" Flag', Reuters, 5 October 2018, https://cn.reuters.com/article/us-southkorea-japan-flag/japan-to-skip-naval-event-after-south-korea-protests-over-rising-sun-flag-idUSKCN1MF0D7; and Mike Yeo, 'Accusations Fly Between South Korea and Japan over "Threatening" Maritime Manoeuvres', *DefenseNews*, 24 January 2019, https://www.defensenews.com/global/asia-pacific/2019/01/24/accusations-fly-between-south-korea-and-japan-over-threatening-aircraft-maneuvers-radar-targeting/.

78 See Jesse Johnson, 'Trump's De Facto Blessing of North Korean Missile Tests Sends Ominous Message to Japan', *Japan Times*, 28 August 2019, https://www.japantimes.co.jp/news/2019/08/28/national/trump-blesses-north-korea-tests-japan/.

79 See 'Trump and Kim Jong-un Meet at Korean Demilitarised Zone', BBC News, 30 June 2019, https://www.bbc.co.uk/news/av/world-asia-48815938; 'Kim Jong-un to Meet Moon Jae-in at Korean Border for Summit', BBC News, 26 April 2018, https://www.bbc.co.uk/news/world-asia-43903155; and 'Vladimir Putin and Kim Jong-un Meet in Vladivostok', BBC News, 25 April 2019, https://www.bbc.co.uk/news/av/world-48049166.

80 See Ministry of Foreign Affairs of Japan, 'The 12th Mekong–Japan Summit Meeting', 13 November 2020, https://www.mofa.go.jp/page3e_001078.html.

81 PM's Office of Japan (@JPN_PMO), tweet, 18 October 2020, https://twitter.com/JPN_PMO/status/1317828835732201474.

82 See '"Jiyū de Hikareta Indotaiheiyō" Bei Jiki Seiken Dō Suru', *Asahi Shimbun*, 8 December 2020, p. 4; and Shushō Kantei (@kantei), tweet, 14 November 2020, https://twitter.com/kantei/status/1327545525806108673.

83 'Suga Shushō "TPP Kakudai de Jiyū Bōeki o" APEC ni Messēji', *Nihon Keizai Shimbun*, 20 November 2020, https://r.nikkei.com/article/DGXMZO66453380Q0A121C2MM0000.

84 See 'Japan, Australia and India to Launch Supply Chain Initiative', Bloomberg, 1 September 2020, https://www.bloomberg.com/news/articles/2020-09-01/japan-australia-and-india-to-discuss-supply-chains-alliance.

85 IMF, 'World Economic Outlook, October 2020: A Long and Difficult Ascent', https://www.imf.org/en/Publications/WEO/Issues/2020/09/30/world-economic-outlook-october-2020.

86 See 'All Abe's Men: Japan's Economy Ministry Sidelined Under Suga', *Nikkei Asia*, 17 September 2020, https://asia.nikkei.com/Politics/Japan-after-Abe/All-Abe-s-men-Japan-s-economy-ministry-sidelined-under-Suga.

87 See 'Suga Seiken Ikkagetsu, Menkai Shita Minkan 70 Nin, Seisaku Ni Chiken Hanei', *Nihon Keizai Shimbun*,

15 October 2020, https://r.nikkei.com/article/DGXMZO64993140U0A011C2PP8000?s=5.

88 See Y.A., 'A View from Japan: The Virtues of a Confrontational China Strategy', *American Interest,* 10 April 2020, https://www.the-american-interest.com/2020/04/10/the-virtues-of-a-confrontational-china-strategy/.

89 See Suga Yoshihide, *Seijika no Kakugo* (Tokyo: Bunshun Shinsho, 2020), pp. 203, 210.

90 Japan Cabinet Office, 'Economic Policy Speech by Nishimura Yasutoshi, Minister of State for Economic and Fiscal Policy to the 201st Session of the Diet', 20 January 2020, https://www5.cao.go.jp/keizai1/2020/0120keizaienzetsu-en.pdf.

91 'Ryōshi, AI, Posto 5G Nado ni 1.7 Chō En, Seifu no 2020 Nen "Digitaru Yosan" o Sōzarai', *Nikkei xTECH*, 6 January 2020, https://xtech.nikkei.com/atcl/nxt/column/18/00001/03430/.

92 See 'Twenty Years On, Japan Government's Digital Ambitions Still Stuck in Piles of Paper', Reuters, 24 July 2020, https://uk.reuters.com/article/us-japan-economy-digital/twenty-years-on-japan-governments-digital-ambitions-still-stuck-in-piles-of-paper-idUKKCN24P0J0.

93 PM's Office of Japan (@JPN_PMO), tweet, 16 September 2020, https://twitter.com/jpn_pmo/status/1306264578137890816?lang=en.

94 See 'China Rises as World's Data Superpower as Internet Fractures', *Nikkei Asia*, 24 November 2020, https://asia.nikkei.com/Politics/International-relations/China-rises-as-world-s-data-superpower-as-internet-fractures.

95 'NEC Sees Huawei's Woes as Chance to Crack 5G Market', *Financial Times*, 1 July 2020, https://www.ft.com/content/502a3a39-4c3a-4ee0-a3a9-7ad734081537.

96 Abe Shinzo, 'Defeatism About Japan Is Now Defeated', World Economic Forum, 23 January 2019, https://www.weforum.org/agenda/2019/01/abe-speech-transcript/.

97 Suga Yoshihide, 'Building Together the Future of Indo-Pacific', speech delivered at the Vietnam–Japan University, 19 October 2020, https://www.mofa.go.jp/s_sa/sea1/vn/page3e_001070.html.

Dilemmas of Aiding Ukraine

Henrik Larsen

The election of Volodymyr Zelensky as Ukraine's president in 2019 marked the third time since its independence from the Soviet Union in 1991 that Ukrainian voters opted for a radical break with the past. They had tried twice before: in 2005 after the Orange Revolution, and in 2014 after the Maidan – or Dignity – Revolution. Zelensky appealed to the vast majority of voters who saw a political outsider as the best means of fighting the corrupt political and business establishment, and bringing Ukraine economic and social justice. As with the first two attempted departures, Western institutions stood ready to support Ukraine in its domestic reform efforts with billions of dollars of macro-financial and sector support.

Yet Ukraine's reform record calls for scepticism about any political elite's ability or willingness to reform the country. Historically, elites in all but a few areas have gotten away with delaying or merely feigning reform. After the Maidan Revolution, they depended on Western support for their political survival while steering Ukraine through a time of severe crisis. The developments during Zelensky's presidency could signal the beginning of a tragic replay of what Ukraine experienced under its previous president, Petro Poroshenko: the reassertion of vested interests at the expense of a broader state transformation that would benefit Ukrainian society and

Henrik Larsen is a Senior Researcher at the Center for Security Studies at the Swiss Federal Institute of Technology (ETH Zürich). He served as a political adviser with the European Union in Ukraine from 2014 to 2019.

Survival | vol. 63 no. 1 | February–March 2021 | pp. 161–178   https://doi.org/10.1080/00396338.2021.1881259

its citizens. Having missed several opportunities, Western institutions and governments can no longer settle for merely propping up Ukraine with money without ensuring that it can become self-sustaining.

To formulate a better approach, Western policymakers need a better understanding of why conditionality has failed to deliver. In particular, they must avoid keeping Ukraine artificially afloat without sufficiently incentivising the country to reform and establish resilience against external shocks. This requires rethinking the conventional wisdom about the external promotion of reforms, which ascribes success or failure to two basic structural determinants: 'leverage', defined as the difference in power between the outside actors and the target state; and 'linkage', defined as the density of the ties between them.[1] Ukraine scores high on both measures. Its political and financial dependency on the West was very strong after 2014 because it was facing insolvency, and it has considerable economic and social links to the European Union, which of course was the reason why the Maidan Revolution arose. Yet Ukraine can hardly be described as a successful example of external reforms promotion. The structural elements must be complemented with a more thorough appreciation of elite resistance.[2]

Western conditionality

Western conditionality after 2014 was premised on Ukraine's overhauling its criminal-justice system to build public trust in the state, and on its reforming the economy to stimulate growth. Meeting these two objectives was supposed to reduce Ukraine's domestic fragility and external-aid dependency. The total Western financing package for Ukraine amounted to $40 billion – a little more than half for macro-financial assistance and the rest for sector support.[3]

Ukraine's most powerful incentive was linked to the extensive agreement with the International Monetary Fund (IMF), which entered into force in early 2015, involving $17.5bn spread over four years. IMF conditionality targeted measures to improve both macro-financial stability (gas and heating tariffs, pension and banking reform) and the business climate (anti-corruption and privatisation).[4] The IMF sought to strengthen the rule of law to improve the investment climate and, in turn, economic performance. Both the EU and the United States decided to complement the IMF programme with additional monetary incentives. The United States during 2014–16 issued a total of $3bn in loan guarantees on condition that the Ukrainian government remain committed to an ambitious overhaul programme.[5] Since 2014, the EU has disbursed €4.4bn in macro-financial assistance to Ukraine, dividing it into five disbursements with different conditions. This is the highest amount the EU has ever disbursed to a single partner country.[6]

The EU incorporated additional structural incentives for rule-of-law and economic reforms. Apart from the symbolic importance for Ukraine's orientation toward Europe, its Association Agreement with the EU holds enormous potential for integrating Ukrainian exports into world markets via EU supply chains. It is more than a classical free-trade agreement because it not only removes import tariffs but also entails regulatory reform and opening up service sectors. The agreement requires Ukraine not only to reciprocate the removal of free-trade hindrances but also to incorporate the EU's vast trade-related legislation. To pull Ukraine closer to Europe, the EU in 2017 also allowed Ukrainians visa-free short-term travel in exchange for Ukraine's commitment to establish new specialised agencies to fight high-level corruption.

Ukraine's reform process is highly internationalised in the sense that the domestic legitimacy of its elected officials depends on their professed commitment to a pro-European course. A large and steady majority of Ukrainians see European integration as an appropriate template for the reforms that Ukraine has failed to deliver since independence and certainly as a better option than an economic union with Russia.[7] Even after 2014, however, Ukraine's political elites have remained largely self-serving and deeply enmeshed in business interests, including those of oligarchs. But they were also much more dependent on Western financial support than they were before 2014, and more sensitive to popular opposition to their deviation from Western aid conditionalities. These factors raised the political and financial costs of non-compliance and crucially forced the elites to make trade-offs against vested interests.

At the same time, Western sponsors had a geopolitical interest in keeping Ukraine economically viable. Their support for the Maidan Revolution, which favoured the West over Russia, made it more difficult to pressure the leadership. Soon enough, Western governments and institutions had invested so much money and political prestige in Ukraine's success that their level of tolerance for non-compliance with pre-agreed conditions increased, making it more and more difficult to establish and maintain a credible incentive structure for reform.

Serious initiatives

Between 2014 and the beginning of 2016, Western sponsors and Ukrainian elites enjoyed a largely cooperative relationship, with the elites adopting new legislation and setting up new institutions. Ukraine moved from severe economic contraction to economic growth and laid the foundations for increasing the professionalism of public institutions and reducing oligarchic rent. Western donors continued their disbursements in the belief that reforms had begun in earnest and in the hope that they would consolidate over time.

In late 2014, the Ukrainian government appointed a number of reform-minded figures to key positions, notably US-born Natalie Jaresko as minister of finance and Lithuanian-born Aivaras Abromavicius as minister of economy in charge of privatisation. The government also appointed deputy ministers for European integration in key ministries to ensure a natural entry point for international partners looking to assist in reform implementation. In a further gesture of goodwill, Poroshenko appointed the leader of the Rose Revolution in Georgia, Mikheil Saakashvili, as governor of Odessa region – an important trade hub infamous for corruption problems in the customs service. By granting Saakashvili Ukrainian citizenship to allow him to govern a part of the country, Poroshenko wanted to show a practical reform commitment to both Ukrainian voters and Western sponsors.

To demonstrate a willingness to fight the politicisation of public institutions, the government launched an overhaul of law-enforcement agencies known for selective justice, loyalty to the incumbent and corruption. The creation of a new national police service in 2015 to replace the Soviet-style militia was the key measure, implemented with significant Western assistance. Ukraine also pledged to reform the Public Prosecutor's Office and the

Security Service, and forged a stricter separation between bureaucracies and politically appointed ministers, passing the enabling legislation after the EU had made it a clear precondition of financial assistance.[8]

Ukraine's dependency on Western support immediately following Russian aggression meant that the elites had little choice but to comply with the reform conditionalities. In its early stage of recovery, Ukraine needed to show commitment by taking the initial reform steps, even though full implementation was not yet feasible.

The prime target of deep reform was corruption at the highest levels of state power. Ukraine is among the most corrupt countries in the world, and Ukrainians consider corruption one of the biggest barriers to public trust. Ukraine established a specialised anti-corruption infrastructure consisting of a number of new agencies, including the National Anti-Corruption Bureau of Ukraine and the Specialized Anti-Corruption Prosecutor's Office, which has exclusive competency to investigate and prosecute major, high-level corruption. Ukraine also set up the National Agency on Corruption Prevention, which oversees an electronic asset-declaration system whereby public officials had to declare their assets in an electronic database then freely available to the public, subject to verification against their income histories – a major increase in transparency.

Ukraine's economic and financial sectors constituted the second focus of deep reform. Of particular concern was the notorious banking sector, known for money-laundering, insider loans and chronic mismanagement. As a result of IMF demands, Ukraine imposed tighter controls over cash and transparency with respect to end beneficiaries, and made banks liable for losses due to fraud.[9] In a short period, the National Bank of Ukraine closed nearly 100 of 180 banks on account of insolvency. In 2016, the IMF compelled Ukraine to nationalise PrivatBank, the country's largest commercial bank, which threatened the stability of the financial system owing to $5bn in shaky loans to insiders and shell companies.[10] It was a bold move, and PrivatBank continues to be a focus of conflict between oligarchic interests and Western demands.

Furthermore, IMF demands in 2015–16 drove Ukraine to bring gas prices up to market levels. Though an unpopular move, it worked to preclude

opaque gas-marketing schemes exploiting the difference between subsi-
dised prices and market prices that produced large deficits that the state
would have to cover, freeing up revenues for social benefit. Of Ukraine's
more than 3,000 state-owned enterprises, only a third yielded profits despite
combined revenues equalling 20% of GDP.[11] IMF requirements prompted
Ukraine to improve the governance of corrupt and inefficient state-owned
enterprises. Naftogaz, the national oil and gas giant, has been a particular
success story.[12]

Stalling reforms

From early 2016 to early 2018, Ukraine entered into a new phase, in which
reforms stalled and pro-reformist figures resigned in protest as initiatives
started to endanger vested interests. Ukraine failed to generate annual
growth rates higher than around 2%, which is unusual for a country recov-
ering from armed conflict. Direct confrontation with international partners
was avoided. But the inability of reform figures to operate independently of
the politicised state bureaucracy was a strong indication that initiatives were
failing to consolidate. Abromavicius, the minister of economy, resigned in
February 2016, accusing Poroshenko of undue influence in appointments
within state-owned enterprises. Jaresko, the technocratic minister of finance
who had successfully negotiated Western macroeconomic assistance, was
eased out in a reshuffle in April 2016. Saakashvili resigned as governor of
Odessa in November 2016, citing Poroshenko's support for 'corruption
clans' in the region. Two deputy prosecutors-general had to leave office after
having accused their employer of perpetuating corruption and bending to
political pressure.

The IMF issued warnings to Ukraine that its failure to meet conditions
was jeopardising aid programmes.[13] In March 2016, Joe Biden, then the US
vice president, threatened to withhold $1bn in loan guarantees if it did not
remove the prosecutor-general, whom Western partners saw as an obsta-
cle to law-enforcement reform. Ukraine complied, but replaced him with
a Poroshenko loyalist, Yuriy Lutsenko, who had neither a legal education
nor any relevant experience. Meanwhile, the new National Anti-Corruption
Bureau of Ukraine was operating as an independent institution, opening

a number of investigations against heads of agencies, incumbent ministers and parliamentarians. The ruling coalition introduced legislation to
undermine the bureau's independence, while the Security Service and the
Public Prosecutor's Office joined forces to disrupt the bureau's operations.
Repeated diplomatic interventions by Ukraine's Western partners preserved
the bureau's independence, and induced the establishment to back off. But
political interference with the National Agency on Corruption Prevention
was more effective: the agency was unable to check unlawful enrichment
in the public sector because other state agencies refused to cooperate.
Presumably on account of bribes or threats, Ukrainian judges ultimately
declined to hear high-profile corruption cases.

Reform also stalled in key areas of economic regulation under IMF
and EU scrutiny. Confirming Abromavicius's warnings, the government
dragged out not only privatisation but also the introduction of independent
corporate governance in the remaining state-owned enterprises.[14] Recurrent
political interference similarly caused the Naftogaz supervisory board to
resign in 2017.[15] In addition, the government never took the final decision to
separate Ukraine's gas distribution and storage from production and supply,
which was required to reduce the oligarchs' grip on retail gas sales and to
win the EU's trust as an energy partner. World gas prices increased but the
government did not follow suit with a corresponding increase in domestic
gas prices, increasing leeway for dubious pricing schemes.[16] Finally, Ukraine
failed to lift a ban on wood exports – a long-standing breach of its free-trade
commitments under its Association Agreement with the EU – to protect the
domestic market against foreign competition.

The impairment of anti-corruption and economic-reform efforts put the
Western institutions in a difficult position. They were torn between imposing costs on Ukraine for non-compliance and keeping the macro-financial
programme on track to maintain leverage over Ukraine going forward. The
EU and the IMF decided to proceed with some scheduled payments while
delaying others. In 2017, the IMF disbursed $1bn but, concerned about inef-
ficient state-owned enterprises and a weak judiciary, refused to disburse
two further tranches.[17] In January 2018, the European Commission decided
for the first time not to disburse a planned tranche of aid, this one for €600

million, due to Ukrainian non-compliance with agreed criteria. Immediately thereafter, however, it started negotiations with Ukraine on a new €1bn programme with an eye to maintaining leverage.[18]

Preventing backlashes

The situation worsened by around mid-2018, when it was clear that Ukrainian political elites were not going to deliver on the promise of privatisation or follow through on anti-corruption unless extraordinary measures were taken. By late 2018, however, Ukraine was in dire need of financial assistance to service debts incurred in 2014–15. This was a renewed chance for the IMF to reassert conditionalities related to anti-corruption.

In October 2018, the IMF recognised the missed opportunity to fundamentally transform the economy and decided to abandon the existing commitment of $17.5bn (of which $8.6bn had actually been disbursed) in favour of a less generous stand-by arrangement totalling $3.9bn extending through the 2019 election year. Under this new agreement, Ukraine had to immediately raise gas tariffs to reflect market prices and effect improvements in the governance of state-owned banks to help lenders resist political pressure.[19] The IMF also required Ukraine to establish the High Anti-Corruption Court, which would create extraordinarily intense conflicts with domestic interests.

The IMF considered the High Anti-Corruption Court necessary because it deemed ordinary courts too weak to properly decide highly controversial cases, which scared off potential investors and therefore discouraged economic growth. Accordingly, the IMF demanded that international experts with veto powers be involved in the selection of the new court's judges to guard against political interference. Poroshenko publicly tried to fend off this requirement, citing the need to protect Ukraine's sovereign right to select its own judges, but lacked leverage and ultimately bowed to the IMF. The World Bank backed the IMF by offering Ukraine a $750m guarantee contingent on the swift operationalisation of the High Anti-Corruption Court and the selection of independent judges.[20]

In the Ukrainian context, the prospect of high-level convictions poses an enormous threat to oligarchic and other vested interests. Ukrainian lawmakers first tried to sabotage the process by introducing an amnesty for cases already under way, which the IMF thwarted by promptly threatening to withhold funds. But the Specialized Anti-Corruption Prosecutor and the Constitutional Court dropped several of the high-level cases before they could reach the High Anti-Corruption Court.[21]

US Ambassador Marie Yovanovitch publicly criticised these rulings during the run-up to Ukrainian elections in early 2019, but Lutsenko, the prosecutor-general, undermined her standing by alleging to US media that she had provided him a list of people who were not to be prosecuted during their first meeting.[22] Lutsenko later admitted this was untrue, but at the time it provided the Trump administration with a pretext for smearing and recalling Yovanovitch, who stood in the way of Donald Trump's own efforts to pressure the Ukrainian government into investigating Hunter Biden's conduct as a board member of Ukraine's Burisma energy company. Trump's aim was to politically damage Hunter Biden's father, Joe Biden, who had been the US vice president when his son was named to the board in 2014 and was running for president against Trump in 2020, by withholding $400m of congressionally authorised US military assistance. This effort on Trump's part would become the basis for his impeachment in late 2019.[23]

Lessons for dealing with Zelensky

The standstill in privatisation, the difficulties in eliminating fraudulent gas schemes and backlashes against anti-corruption showed the limitations of international pressure. Ukrainian officials and politicians skilfully evaded direct responsibility and direct confrontation, while putatively independent but in fact compromised courts and institutions undermined progress. The reformist members of parliament were marginalised. External technical assistance was insufficient to minimise the politicisation of law enforcement and the judiciary. Yet the relative success in cleaning up Ukraine's banking sector shows that international pressure can work when conditionality is properly weaponised.

Zelensky, a wildly popular actor-turned-politician, was easily elected president of Ukraine in 2019 and bolstered by another landslide victory for his Servant of the People party in parliamentary elections a few months later. Zelensky started his term promising a fresh start, as Poroshenko had when he took office after the Maidan Revolution in 2014. Zelensky named Abromavicius director-general of Ukroboronprom, a big state-owned enterprise infamous for the corrupt procurement of defence equipment. Parliament rebooted the National Agency on Corruption Prevention to increase transparency in the public sector, strengthened legislation curbing money-laundering and adopted a sweeping land-privatisation bill, which previous governments had been unable to push through.

But developments since Zelensky's rise to power have eroded the confidence he had initially inspired among international supporters. A reshuffle in March 2020 notably led to the departure of prime minister Oleksiy Honcharuk, perceived as a competent economic operator, as well as Ruslan Ryaboshapka, the prosecutor-general who during six months in office had initiated a comprehensive vetting of the prosecutorial corps. Meanwhile, the independence of the National Bank of Ukraine was put into question after governor Yakiv Smolii resigned in July 2020, citing systemic political pressure that impeded him in carrying out his duties.

Zelensky rose to power in 2019 with the substantial help of Igor Kolomoisky, one of Ukraine's most powerful oligarchs, whose television channel gave him indispensable airtime. Doubts about Zelensky's ability to withstand Kolomoisky's pressure to regain control over PrivatBank, which he owned when it was nationalised in 2016, caused the IMF to pressure Ukraine to adopt legislation to prevent former owners of recently nationalised banks from regaining ownership rights or receiving monetary compensation. Nothing guarantees, however, that Ukraine will be able to return suspected stolen assets from PrivatBank, believed to be worth several billion dollars, to the state. Under Zelensky's presidency, the oligarchic struggle for political influence intensified within the energy sector, with Kolomoisky favouring cheap electricity imports from Russia for his energy-hungry industries, and Rinat Akhmetov, Ukraine's richest oligarch, favouring national electricity generation from his thermal plants.[24]

In addition, the Constitutional Court now appears to function as an effective obstructer of reformist legislation intended to allow Ukraine to dismantle vested interests and fight high-level corruption. In August and

September 2020, the court overturned certain legal provisions establishing the National Anti-Corruption Bureau of Ukraine, including the director's appointment in 2015. Worse still, in October 2020, the court ruled against free public access to public officials' asset declarations and removed criminal liability for submitting false information.[25]

Red lines and deadlines

Ukraine's long history of unhealthy alliance between politics and business, and mixed indications about the susceptibility of the new political leadership to similar arrangements, calls for a calibration of conditionality. It should be clear that Ukraine and its Western supporters have an interest in strengthening the rule of law and free-market competition, because doing so would bolster economic growth and resilience against external shocks, including Russian aggression. But bolstering the rule of law and economic reform are in fact political struggles that demand the dismantling of vested interests, and the record has shown that elites will not voluntarily give up their privileges. Accordingly, the leverage of Western supporters to effect Ukraine's reform lies in their willingness to impose economic and political costs on those elites. They need to fine-tune conditionality so as to leave no doubt about their preparedness to react to non-compliance. Western supporters should impose unambiguous red lines and deadlines beyond which costs will be meaningfully severe.

Large-scale financial assistance remains the most powerful source of Western leverage. It should be used without toleration for creative attempts to circumvent agreed principles. Of course, external sponsors do need to be cautious about disrupting the existing system to the point of instability.[26] But they have considerable latitude with respect to Ukraine because it no longer has the option of seeking financial support from Russia. While a suspension or reduction of Western financial support would not mean that Ukraine would face immediate bankruptcy, it would force the government to go to the financial markets for loans with much higher interest rates. The need to balance the state budget could induce the government to prioritise external finance over domestic pressures to preserve the status quo. That said, a suspension or reduction should not work as a punishment but as an incentive with clear conditions that Ukraine needs to fulfil for assistance to resume in full. Certainty that Western commitments are not open-ended would cultivate staying power and resilience in the new, reformist political cadre, enabling it to sustain a commitment to change beyond immediate euphoria.

Similarly, the EU must respond to Ukraine's persistent breach of its free-trade commitments under the Association Agreement, which is symptomatic of its ingrained protection of vested interests. Ongoing discussions in Brussels and arbitration with Kyiv have been so dilatory and ineffectual that Ukrainian elites see no short- or medium-term incentive to remove the obstacles. The EU should raise customs tariffs targeting export sectors to a sufficient degree to compel them to do so.

Western supporters should also invigorate their public-diplomacy efforts. The oligarch-controlled mass media notwithstanding, Ukraine is a functioning democracy in which voters are demanding a higher degree of accountability and, as Poroshenko's political fate has vividly demonstrated, punishing incumbents for failing to provide it. Furthermore, the Ukrainian people's strong tilt towards the West in general and European integration in particular, and their opposition to endemic corruption and oligarchic control over the economy, make it politically uncomfortable for elites to ignore vocal Western demands for reform.

Western governments should be prepared to call out non-compliance. Diplomatic timidity out of fear that Ukraine may veer off its pro-Western course is misguided: in the light of Russia's persistent aggression since 2014, Ukraine has no economic or political choice other than to court the West. US outspokenness on anti-corruption shows the power of diplomatic pressure through public channels in an area that most citizens deem important. Similarly, the G7 ambassadors, when speaking with one voice, encouraged reforms and impeded setbacks. In this vein, the IMF too could move beyond a largely technical interaction with the government behind closed doors and highlight instances of partial or full non-compliance in public. The IMF needs to abandon its practice of not commenting on court decisions, which is a severe and self-imposed liability in a country with a dubious judiciary. The EU, for its part, should make its regular assessments of Ukraine's performance against conditionalities more politically accented than these essentially bureaucratic exercises currently are, especially with respect to the EU's anti-corruption criterion, which is directly linked to Ukrainian citizens' visa-free travel to Europe.[27]

Effective leverage requires maximum unity among Western sponsors to preclude the Ukrainian authorities from playing one off the other. Coordination among Ukraine's main Western sponsors – the IMF, the EU and the United States – as to which is best positioned to impose conditionality in which sectors, and how to ensure coherence and consistency in responding to non-compliance, is crucial. Individual sponsors also need to apply conditionality in a consistent and principled manner. When the White House criticised and then removed the US ambassador on the basis of unfounded allegations by the Ukrainian prosecutor-general, it weakened what had been forceful messaging on anti-corruption. More detrimental still was Trump's apparent advancement of a personal political agenda by pressuring Zelensky to start investigations that could hurt Joe Biden as a US presidential candidate on pain of the United States' withholding of military assistance. In the wake of the subsequent US impeachment proceedings and political imbroglio, the US Embassy in Kyiv became less confrontational with the Ukrainian authorities on anti-corruption issues.[28]

*   *   *

In view of the West's experience with Ukraine since 2014, governments and institutions considering extending major support to a state undergoing significant political change must make a sound assessment of the geopolitical importance of doing so and long-term sustainability of the effort. Approaches that are initially conservative or agnostic have the advantage of preserving the option of retraction, while a substantial commitment of financial aid and political prestige at the outset can lead to self-perpetuating frustration. Western intervention in Afghanistan, for example, involved a commitment that was both open-ended and without red lines for government abuses, and has proven intractable for almost 20 years despite massive expenditure and military involvement.[29]

The EU and the United States from an early stage showed solidarity with the Maidan Revolution, which gave them a stake in its success, especially in the face of Russian aggression. Ukrainian elites, however, perceived in Western benefactors a greater interest in bolstering Ukraine against Russia than in facilitating the country's political transformation. Since Ukraine needs the West more than the West needs Ukraine, the elites' opportunistic disregard for Western conditionalities were self-defeating for the country as a whole. Be that as it may, had Western benefactors sought political transformation rather than mere economic stabilisation from the beginning, and calibrated their conditionalities accordingly, they would not have incentivised their Ukrainian beneficiaries to backslide so cynically.

The IMF will have to consider the peril of perpetual sponsorship in weighing the Ukrainian government's request to disburse the remaining $2.9bn of a new stand-by arrangement, worth $5bn in total and lasting until the end of 2021.[30] The same holds for the EU, which has yet to disburse €600m of a new package of macro-financial assistance worth €1.2bn.[31] The economic recession precipitated by the COVID-19 pandemic affords the IMF and the EU new leverage and opportunities to test Ukraine's commitment to political reform. They should insist, as conditions of continued financing, that Kyiv restore the independence of the National Bank of Ukraine and greenlight the large-scale privatisation of state-owned enterprises. To effectively combat high-level corruption, it appears necessary for the Western sponsors to insist that Ukraine reform and strengthen the independence of the Constitutional Court, which otherwise will threaten any effort to break the status quo.

Meanwhile, the operationalisation of the High Anti-Corruption Court paves the way for high-level convictions. Such action would be unprecedented for Ukraine and could be taken as a confirmation of its amenability to external pressure to reform. Going forward, Ukraine's credibility will turn on continuing high-level prosecutions that steer clear of partisan reprisal and selective justice, or their appearance. On this score, Ukrainian prosecutors will have to be judicious and circumspect in their pursuit of Poroshenko, the previous president and now leader of the pro-Western opposition, for possible abuse of office.

The IMF, the United States and the EU continue to hold considerable sway over key aspects of Ukraine's transition. To retain it, they must provide consistent signals that their support is not open-ended but rather conditioned on socially and politically meaningful reforms, such as state accountability and the return of oligopolistic rent and stolen assets to the national treasury. Ukraine cannot afford more failure, and it falls to its international benefactors to devise the right incentives for avoiding it.

Notes

[1] See Steven Levitsky and Lucan A. Way, *Competitive Authoritarianism: Hybrid Regimes After the Cold War* (Cambridge: Cambridge University Press, 2010); and Steven Levitsky and Lucan A. Way, 'Linkage Versus Leverage: Rethinking the International Dimension of Regime Change', *Comparative Politics*, vol. 38, no. 4, July 2006, pp. 379–400.

[2] See, for example, Louis-Alexandre Berg and Naomi Levy, 'When Aid Builds States: Party Dominance and the Effects of Foreign Aid on Tax Collection After Civil War', *International Interactions*, vol. 46, no. 3, March 2020, pp. 454–80; Hadley J. Swedlund, *The Development Dance: How Donors and Recipients Negotiate the Delivery of Foreign Aid* (Ithaca, NY: Cornell University Press, 2017); and Jakob Tolstrup, 'When Can External Actors Influence Democratization? Leverage, Linkages, and Gatekeeper Elites', *Democratization*, vol. 20, no. 4, 2013, pp. 716–42.

[3] Laurence Norman and Nick Shchetko, 'Ukraine Bailout Set to Rise to Around $40 Billion over Four Years', *Wall Street Journal*, 12 February 2015, https://www.wsj.com/articles/ukraine-to-receive-40-billion-in-international-assistance-imf-says-1423730531.

[4] IMF, 'IMF Announces Staff Level Agreement with Ukraine on a New US$ 17.5 Billion Extended Fund Facility Arrangement', Press Release No. 15/51, 12 February 2015, https://www.imf.org/en/News/Articles/2015/09/14/01/49/pr1551.

[5] White House, Office of the Press Secretary, 'Fact Sheet: US Assistance to Ukraine Since February 2014', 15 June 2016, https://obamawhitehouse.archives.gov/the-press-office/2016/06/15/fact-sheet-us-assistance-ukraine-february-2014.

[6] See European Commission, 'Ukraine: Macro-financial Assistance', 2020, https://ec.europa.eu/info/business-economy-euro/economic-and-fiscal-policy-coordination/international-economic-relations/enlargement-and-neighbouring-countries/neighbouring-countries-eu/neighbourhood-countries/ukraine_en.

[7] See International Republican Institute, 'Public Opinion Survey of Residents of Ukraine', 13–23 June 2019, p. 60, https://www.iri.org/sites/default/files/july_2019_ukraine_poll.pdf.

[8] 'EU to Assist Ukraine in

Reforming the Civil Service – Tombiński', 112Ukraine, 2 November 2015, https://112.international/ukraine-and-eu/eu-to-assist-ukraine-in-reforming-the-civil-service-tombiski-1340.html.

9   See John Lough and Vladimir Dubrovskiy, 'Are Ukraine's Anti-corruption Reforms Working?', Research Paper, Chatham House, 19 November 2018, pp. 17–18.

10 See Mehreen Khan, 'IMF Welcomes Ukrainian Bank Nationalisation', *Financial Times*, 19 December 2016, https://www.ft.com/content/81f6cd38-eadd-38d8-81e5-9e0f729345eb.

11 Ukraine Ministry of Economic Development and Trade, 'TOP-100 ohliad naybilshykh derzhavnykh pidpryiemstv Ukrayiny' [Top 100 – Review of the largest state enterprises of Ukraine], 2016, https://www.kmu.gov.ua/storage/app/media/reforms/top-100-naybilshikh-derzhpidpriemstv-ukraini.pdf.

12 See Lough and Dubrovskyi, 'Are Ukraine's Anti-corruption Reforms Working?', pp. 10, 23.

13 See Neil Buckley, Roman Olearchyk and Shawn Donnan, 'IMF Warning Sparks Ukraine Pledge on Corruption and Reform', *Financial Times*, 11 February 2016, https://www.ft.com/content/44c1641e-cff7-11e5-831d-09f7778e7377.

14 See Organisation for Economic Cooperation and Development (OECD), 'Anti-corruption Reforms in Ukraine: Prevention and Prosecution of Corruption in State-owned Enterprises', 2018, https://www.oecd.org/corruption/anti-bribery/OECD-ACN-Ukraine-4th-Round-Bis-Report-SOE-Sector-2018-ENG.pdf.

15 Naftogaz, 'All Independent Directors of Naftogaz to Quit the Supervisory Board Because the Government Is Derailing the Reforms', Press Release, 19 September 2017, http://www.naftogaz.com/www/3/nakweben.nsf/0/6D7C544D5F376866C22581A0006883A0?OpenDocument&year=2017&month=09&nt.

16 See Lough and Dubrovskyi, 'Are Ukraine's Anti-corruption Reforms Working?', p. 11.

17 See IMF, 'Ukraine Receives IMF Support But Must Accelerate Reforms', IMF Country Focus, 4 April 2017, https://www.imf.org/en/News/Articles/2017/04/03/na040417-ukraine-receives-imf-support-but-must-accelerate-reforms; and Sujata Rao and Karin Strohecker, 'Ukrainian Finance Minister Confident of One More IMF Tranche in 2017', Reuters, 12 September 2017, https://www.reuters.com/article/us-ukraine-economy/ukrainian-finance-minister-confident-of-one-more-imf-tranche-in-2017-idUSKCN1BN10L.

18 European Commission, 'EU–Ukraine: Commission Proposes €1 Billion in New Macro-financial Assistance', Press Release, 9 March 2018, https://europa.eu/rapid/press-release_IP-18-1702_en.htm.

19 IMF, 'Request for Standby Agreement and Cancellation of Arrangement under the Extended Fund Facility', IMF Staff Country Report, 8 January 2019, https://www.imf.org/en/Publications/CR/Issues/2019/01/08/Ukraine-Request-for-Stand-By-Arrangement-and-Cancellation-

of-Arrangement-Under-the-Extended-46499.

20 World Bank, 'World Bank Guarantee Supports Vital Reforms in Ukraine', Press Release, 18 December 2018, https://www.worldbank.org/en/news/press-release/2018/12/18/world-bank-guarantee-supports-vital-reforms-in-ukraine.

21 See Anti-Corruption Action Center, 'Register of Dumped Cases', 2019, http://sapfails.antac.org.ua/engsap; and Constitutional Court of Ukraine. Decision 1-r/2019, 26 February 2019, http://www.ccu.gov.ua/en/docs/2541.

22 See 'Top Ukrainian Justice Official Says US Ambassador Gave Him a Do Not Prosecute List', Hill, 20 March 2019, https://thehill.com/hilltv/rising/434875-top-ukrainian-justice-official-says-us-ambassador-gave-him-a-do-not-prosecute.

23 See, for example, Dana H. Allin, 'Impeachment, Trump and US Foreign Policy', Survival, vol. 62, no. 1, February–March 2020, pp. 221–32.

24 See Bohdan Nahaylo, 'Ukraine's Energy Wars Continue', Ukrainian Weekly, 19 June 2020, http://www.ukrweekly.com/uwwp/ukraines-energy-wars-continue/.

25 See Roman Olearchyk, 'Ukraine's Constitutional Court Crisis Escalates', Financial Times, 30 December 2020, https://www.ft.com/content/733a91e2-6ec8-4c5a-9f52-8bd38dfebc5b.

26 See, for instance, Jonathan Stevenson,

Preventing Conflict: The Role of the Bretton Woods Institutions, IISS Adelphi Paper 336 (Oxford: Oxford University Press for the IISS, 2000).

27 See 'Report from the Commission to the European Parliament and the Council: Second Report Under the Visa Suspension Mechanism', 19 December 2018, https://ec.europa.eu/home-affairs/sites/homeaffairs/files/what-we-do/policies/european-agenda-migration/20181219_com-2018-856-report_en.pdf.

28 Author interview with EU official, 13 December 2019.

29 See, for instance, Stephen Watts and Sean Mann, 'Determining US Commitments in Afghanistan', Washington Quarterly, vol. 38, no. 1, Spring 2015, pp. 117–18.

30 See IMF, 'Ukraine: Request for Stand-by Arrangement – Press Release; Staff Report; and Statement by the Executive Director for Ukraine', 11 June 2020, https://www.imf.org/en/Publications/CR/Issues/2020/06/10/Ukraine-Request-for-Stand-by-Arrangement-Press-Release-Staff-Report-and-Statement-by-the-49501.

31 See European Commission, 'EU Disburses €600 Million in Macro-financial Assistance to Ukraine', Press Release, 9 December 2020, https://ec.europa.eu/neighbourhood-enlargement/news_corner/news/eu-disburses-%E2%82%AC600-million-macro-financial-assistance-ukraine_en.

Review Essay

Coffee and Communism

Russell Crandall

Coffeeland: One Man's Dark Empire and the Making of Our Favorite Drug
Augustine Sedgewick. New York: Penguin Press, 2020. $30.00.
448 pp.

On 13 January 1932, D.J. Rodgers, the British consul in El Salvador, fired off a diplomatic note to his superiors in London, describing his sense that a leftist insurrection was afoot in the lush, green coffee-plantation zones 80 or so kilometres from El Salvador's capital: 'The communist agitation among the plantation laborers is steadily increasing in seriousness' (p. 269).

For Rodgers, there was 'little doubt' that this was no routine labour agitation for higher wages, but rather an attempt to obtain a 'general division of lands and property and government by the proletariat'. A week later, he wrote another, more alarming note warning of an imminent Bolshevik offensive 'to blow up banks, take possession of railways and plantations, kill members of Government, Army officers and women, sack town and establish soviet republic [*sic*]' (p. 271).

Despite the hyperbole, Rodgers was spot-on in some respects: this was a bona fide communist insurrection. Seizing numerous provincial towns in and around the coffee-planted skirts of the Santa Ana Volcano, the vengeful leftists torched land deeds, killed scores of loathed local politicos, forced

Russell Crandall is a professor of American foreign policy and international politics at Davidson College in North Carolina, and a contributing editor to *Survival*. His latest book is *Drugs and Thugs: The History and Future of America's War on Drugs* (Yale University Press, 2020).

Survival | vol. 63 no. 1 | February–March 2021 | pp. 179–188   https://doi.org/10.1080/00396338.2021.1881260

plantation women to make tortillas for the peasants (*campesinos*) and distributed stolen provisions to them. In the mist-shrouded emerald hamlet of Juayúa, machete- and shotgun-wielding rebels raised a red flag in the *plaza central* while forcing locals to don red bands and refer to each other as 'comrade'. The organisers' manifesto, published two days before the uprising started, detailed their grievances:

> We the workers, they call us thieves ... and steal our wage, paying us a miserable wage, and condemning us to live in filthy tenements or in stinking barracks, or working day and night in the fields under rain and sun. We are labeled thieves for demanding the wages that they owe us, a reduction in the workday, and a reduction in the rents that we pay to the rich who take almost all of our harvest, stealing our work from us ... According to the wealthy, we do not have a right to anything, we shouldn't open our mouths. (p. 270)

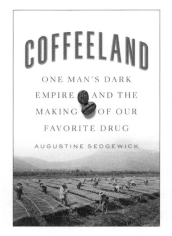

In his wonderfully imagined and exquisitely written book *Coffeeland*, historian Augustine Sedgewick describes how the counter-attack was immediate. 'Prominent banker' Rodolfo Duke – perhaps a member of the country's notorious oligarchy – urged his fellow conservatives to use 'rifles and revolvers' to 'shoot any Communist on sight'. Indeed, 'the Salvadoran aristocracy', the *New York Times* told its readers, 'were armed and turned loose to snare any radicals' (p. 275). Interestingly, key revolt instigators Miguel Mármol, founder of the Salvadoran Communist Party, and Farabundo Martí were already behind bars – the latter even before the fighting started.

Under the imperious eye of acting president Maximiliano Hernández Martínez, army and paramilitary units hunted down the rebels with machine guns, 'pacifying' the provincial towns before turning to the countryside. In a clear instance of genocide, state forces lumped together 'Indians' and 'communists' in what became a bloodbath – known as 'La Matanza' ('The Slaughter') – that killed up to 30,000 overwhelmingly defenceless peasants, only some of whom were outright communists or communist sympathisers.

One farmer who managed to elude the killers recounted his story after visiting a church near the capital: he answered no when asked by the authorities if he was a communist and was spared. Those who answered in the positive were given a check next to their names and later executed.

A century of coffee

As Sedgewick unpacks it, coffee's arrival in Latin America in the eighteenth century was via imperialism and slavery; but it was liberalism – defined as a mixture of freedom, equality and brotherhood inspired by the American, French and Haitian revolutions – that caused it to flourish, including in 'backwaters' such as El Salvador (p. 30). In terms of economics, Latin American liberalism became a 'vision of market-based national progress', which included a strong embrace of international trade (pp. 39–40). In efforts to catch up with neighbours who had already been producing coffee for many years (Brazil, Costa Rica, Haiti, Mexico), in 1846 the liberal Salvadoran government gave tax rebates to entities who seeded over 5,000 coffee trees and exempted coffee-estate workers from military conscription.

The author acknowledges that the Salvadoran government and planters were sincere in their vision of 'emancipation' and 'liberation' of the *campesinos*, but argues that over the ensuing decades this vision moved from 'incentives to demands' (p. 42). This entailed moving against the residents (and in particular the communal landholders) of 'virgin fertile lands' – lands that might have been bountiful in the pre-coffee monoculture era, but now were simply 'unproductive, no matter how many meals had grown there' (p. 42). To cement control of these lands, an 1882 law abolished the system of communal ownership. Five years later, a newly organised police force was established on the coffee estates. Coffee cultivation duly boomed from 2,100 acres in 1860 to 110,000 by 1890, while the total value of exports soared by a factor of 60 over the same period.

Sedgewick is scathing about this transformation from a communal and self-sufficient system to that of the capitalist plantation: 'The privatization of land; the militarization of commerce; the strict policing of work and social life: collectively these laws were the "liberal reforms." They were liberal to the extent that they concealed core racism behind the principle of opportunity in the marketplace – a principle that applied, of course, only to those who had money' (p. 45).

According to Sedgewick, this shift came with terrible consequences. In the pre-coffee era, El Salvador appears in the author's analysis as a kind of Eden: he quotes early European visitors to the country as being astonished by the 'absence of all extreme poverty' and the manifest bountiful soil growing all sorts of fruits (p. 2). Then came the privatisation of the garden in a manner familiar to readers of Karl Marx. Sedgewick explains: 'In principle, after common resources have been transformed into private property, the only way to eat is to sell labor in the market in exchange for a wage, and then spend that wage buying food. By this account, capitalism operates through a kind of economic deism: land privatization starts a clock on hunger that ticks away each working day.' The result? A 'plantation production of hunger itself' (pp. 159–60). To back up his point, Sedgewick provides the reader with an extended lesson on Marx's and Friedrich Engels's descriptions of global capitalism – especially the former's theory of 'surplus value' (the value added by workers in addition to their labour cost).

Dark empire?

While the situation got worse for workers, Sedgewick suggests that late-nineteenth-century El Salvador could have been a lucrative place for the foreigner with the right moxie: 'There were already plenty of workers – what El Salvador needed was bosses' (p. 45). Or, as Englishman Maurice Duke put it at the time:

> There are at this present time very first-rate opportunities offering to men of industry and sobriety who will put a little intelligent work into the land; men of this description, with a moderate capital of, say, five to fifteen thousand dollars, are the men required here; at the same time others with a much smaller capital have very great advantages of making money from the outset; but those who come merely seeking work will find themselves hopelessly miserable. (p. 45)

And come they did, founding new settlements in the coffee regions and giving them names such as California and Berlín to reinforce their global connection. Sedgewick expands: 'And to these new places came more and more migrants who had left the United States and Europe in search of a better life, who cast their economic exile as adventure, and who, unaccustomed to the steaming heat of their new country, took to dressing in "loose suits of white duck"' (p. 45).

One of those migrants was James Hill. Born in 1871 in an especially gritty neighbourhood of Manchester, England, a virtually penniless Hill sailed to El Salvador in 1889 'not for coffee' but to flee the 'gloomy skies and prospects that hung over his life' in his native city. But coffee was what he found. As one American tourist stated in 1928, 'the first thing that strikes the visitor is the apparent unanimity of thought: COFFEE. Everything is coffee, everyone is directly or indirectly engaged in coffee' (p. 3), an observation that could easily be applied to El Salvador in 1889. As Sedgewick notes, what 'cotton was to Manchester … coffee was to Santa Ana' (p. 58).

Within three decades, aided by marrying into a Santa Ana coffee-plantation family, Hill became a 'member of one of the world's most entrenched oligarchies' and 'king of coffee of El Salvador', running innovative and illustrious plantations (p. 7). But according to Sedgewick, this also meant that he 'did more than anyone else' to turn his adopted country 'into one of the most intensive monocultures in modern history' (p. 3). When he passed away in 1951, Hill's coffee investment had become a veritable 'archipelago' of nearly 20 plantations comprising more than 3,000 planted acres and 5,000 employees at peak harvest time, all providing the fruit to be milled at Las Tres Puertas, which produced 2,000 tons of export-ready beans in an especially strong year. Sedgewick reckons that, in part due to Hill's innovations by the latter half of the twentieth century, coffee now employed one in five Salvadorans and was grown on a quarter of the country's arable land. El Salvador's per-acre yield was 50% greater than Brazil's, while the crop contributed to almost all of its export revenue and a quarter of its GDP.

Hill is, of course, the subject of the book's subtitle: 'One Man's Dark Empire'. Yet Hill's empire specifically did not appear to be all that dark. Hill was no Boy Scout, and life for workers on his plantations was hard: they worked from sunrise to sunset, six days a week. Nevertheless, we do also learn that Hill at least attempted to make his working conditions more humane in order to attract the best harvesters from nearby rival owners, who were often inclined to use corporal punishment for putative infractions. 'He discouraged direct physical violence as a strategy for labor management on his plantations,' writes Sedgewick, 'and he specifically sought to hire managers who would not be rough with people under their charge' (p. 161).

Brewing trouble

Almost a half-century after the 1932 communist revolt, in 1979 oligarch-funded paramilitary death squads (often comprising moonlighting soldiers and National Guardsmen) were hunting down suspected communists on the streets and campuses of the capital, San Salvador; an October coup by reformist young officers removed a strongman general from the presidential office; and nascent Marxist guerrilla organisations were kidnapping businessmen and oligarchs to raise funds for arms so that they could begin the revolution that would topple the state – as had just happened in neighbouring Nicaragua, where the Sandinista guerrillas toppled the widely loathed Somoza ruling dynasty.

On 31 October, two weeks after the civil war began, Scotch-imbibing and polo-playing scion Jaime Hill, the 40-something grandson of James Hill, was kidnapped from his tony San Salvador neighbourhood by several gunmen, blindfolded and driven in a truck for several hours to the same coffee country where his grandfather had built his Las Tres Puertas plantation in the late nineteenth century. The culprits were the People's Revolutionary Army of El Salvador, one of the five rebel bands that months later would merge into the Farabundo Martí National Liberation Front (FMLN) – the largest and most potent Marxist-guerrilla insurgent group in Latin America's Cold War history. After four months of negotiations that included a public plea by the archbishop of San Salvador, Óscar Romero, the Hill family agreed to pay a ransom of $4 million ($14m today) to secure his release. The Hills also agreed to cover the expense of running full-page manifestos in regional and international newspapers, including *Le Monde* and the *New York Times*. Here is a sample:

> The Salvadorian people are at present confronting a crucial moment in history, in search of their final liberation. The struggle that is now taking place in our country, expresses a people's right to be the author of its own destiny ... It will not end until the people take in their hands what legitimately belongs to them, the huge plantations of coffee, sugar, cotton; the huge factories, the banks and all the properties belonging to

the oligarchy; this is the definitive solution and no other that would keep
us subjected to poverty and permanent repression is acceptable. (p. 347)

On 14 March 1980, the rebels kicked Jaime out of a vehicle on the outskirts of the capital. Over the next 11 years, the guerrillas, buoyed by military
aid supplied mainly by Cuba (usually via the Sandinistas), would fight the
US-backed Salvadoran military to a stalemate.

America's favourite drug

In the roughly 80 years that James Hill lived between the end of the American
Civil War and the onset of the Cold War, the world became exponentially
more interconnected. In this new world, Europe's and America's adept-
ness at 'constructing ports, rail lines, stringing telegraph cables, founding
banks and brokerages, developing plantations, ranches, and mines' (p. 33)
was 'rewarded' by the riches associated with booming exports from Latin
America and elsewhere. With global trade up 1,000% between 1850 and
1914, 'the world had never seen such a dizzying creation of wealth' (p. 12).

Of course, the boom in trade did not benefit all its participants equally.
Coffee production had become a 'virtual monopoly of the world's poorest
nations'. Accordingly, Sedgewick argues, coffee became one of the 'most
important commodities in the history of global inequality' (pp. 12–13).
Gringos (especially Americans) started drinking lots of it. Sedgewick
expertly details how coffee went from a 'coastal elite delicacy' to an essential
component of a rapidly urbanising United States (p. 61). And of course
there was ample retail promotion, which took off with the rapid expansion
of supermarkets in the twentieth century. With a quarter of the country's
food for sale, they allowed innovators such as San Francisco's Hills Bros.
(no relation to James Hill's empire) to display alluringly designed cans to
millions of American consumers who increasingly required caffeine.

Giving up Eden

Towards the end of his account, Sedgewick returns to El Salvador's
tumultuous years of the late 1970s and early 1980s, when the civil war
broke out. Unsurprisingly, given his broad Marxist lens, he connects the

dots between the coffee monoculture, the 1932 communist revolution quashed during La Matanza and the incipient Marxist insurgency in late 1979. Sedgewick makes a telling slip, however, writing that the counter-insurgency campaign to repel the FMLN 'deployed a small ground force to train the Salvadoran army to fight the Salvadoran people' (p. 348). In fact, especially after death-squad activity eased in the mid-1980s, the Salvadoran military's effort mainly targeted the guerrillas and not the 'Salvadoran people' – even if legions of civilians perished in this effort. Indeed, one of the great mysteries of the civil war was that, despite their stated allegiance to workers and the poor, the guerrillas never won the hearts and minds of this crucial population.

In addition, backed by a bipartisan consensus in a Washington fearful of another Cuba – but also wanting to avoid another Vietnam – the democratically elected Salvadoran government enacted a series of relatively radical measures, most critically land reform and bank nationalisation. Unlike in Cuba and Nicaragua, where brutal dictators such as Fulgencio Batista and Anastasio Somoza Debayle inspired mass hatred and drove the popular mobilisation that led to successful revolution, the relatively conservative Salvadoran population remained loyal to its leadership. In fact, the *campesinos* routinely voted for rightists, including Roberto D'Aubuisson, the death-squad leader. This state of affairs deeply concerned US policymakers committed to promoting centrist Christian Democratic figures.[1]

The FMLN was a Marxist–Leninist group, more intensely so than Fidel Castro's romantic and at least initially nationalist, bearded revolutionaries, or even Daniel Ortega's Sandinistas. Even so, the historic peace agreement in 1992 brokered by the United Nations that ended the 11-year stalemate required the guerrillas to give up their demand for power-sharing and the idea of a communist Eden, instead becoming just another a political party reliant on ballots. Now entirely democratic, the FMLN is El Salvador's main leftist political party. The experiences of China, Cuba, North Korea and Vietnam suggest that, had the FMLN won the civil war, El Salvador could well have become a far more repressive and unfree country – certainly not a workers' paradise.

As Sedgewick does mention, some of the key guerrillas not only entered democratic politics after the civil war, but also turned to capitalism. Jaime

Hill himself even advised some of them on how to start a business. Today in San Salvador, former revolutionaries and military officers are neighbours, friends and political adversaries. This suggests that Sedgewick might have foregone an exacting, multifaceted historical account in favour of an idealistic Marxist parable. That said, he is certainly not alone in being seduced by the tales of oppressed peasants and brutal rulers.[2]

Coffee's legacy

In the 1600s, coffee was an exotic Ottoman habit, and the bean was grown solely in Yemen. But it soon became a staple of 'society's privileged classes', fuelling 'ideas, conversation, art, politics, and culture' (p. 11). Today, coffee fills 'billions of cups' as the 'unrivaled work drug', while the word 'coffee' itself, Sedgewick notes, is one of the most used words on our planet. The industry employs 25m people in around 75 countries, although the benefits of this huge industry merit further discussion.

Sedgewick ends his ambitious book by returning to the Jaime Hill hostage story – and, implicitly, its broader moral and historical significance. As he recounted to the author in an interview, Jaime came to see his guerrilla captors as noble and valiant. In contrast to his own fecklessness, they were doing something admirable by 'fighting for social justice' (p. 361). This is what inspired him to dedicate his post-captive life to a San Salvador clinic treating citizens for traumas visited by the civil war.

Somewhat surprisingly, Sedgewick concludes on a moderately hopeful, positive note, citing a 2011 story by the *New Yorker*'s Kelefa Sanneh, who came to El Salvador to understand the origins of the country's red-hot coffee industry.[3] As Sanneh explained, there had previously been two distinct eras in US coffee-consuming history. The first featured Hills Bros., Folgers and Maxwell House arrayed in large supermarkets, the second retail chains such as Starbucks and Peet's. But a third, ultra-high-end coffee market has emerged. 'In a small but growing number of cafes, you can order coffee more or less the way you might order wine, specifying the varietal and the region and the farm … And perhaps you will find it difficult to go back to whatever you used to drink' (p. 349). In a twist of fate, Santa Ana became a leading player in this new, niche market. During the chaos of the civil war, the plantations had mostly been abandoned and planters failed to replace Bourbon trees with improved hybrids. But these once-marginalised Bourbons became a 'sort of heirloom varietal' (p. 350). Now El Salvador is exporting less than half the amount of coffee it did 40 years ago, but its high-quality beans are fetching record prices.

Sanneh profiled coffee-plantation heir Aida Batlle, a Salvadoran coffee planter and 'something of a coffee celebrity in the United States' who had moved to El Salvador from Nashville, Tennessee, to give back to her ancestral country. After trundling along the vertiginous slopes of the Santa Ana Volcano in a four-by-four to see the plants that produce coffee sold for $14 per pound, Batlle took Sanneh to see her mill in Las Tres Puertas. What would Marx say? He might have been confused by high-price luxury coffee harvested according to fair-trade practices. At this stage, global coffee is arguably making the world a slightly better place.

Some contend that capitalism has reformed itself enough (for example, through child-labour reforms, social security and pensions) to ensure that most people – including workers – buy into it. While a Marxist lens frames powerful instances of social injustice, capitalism has helped integrate El Salvador into the global economy and boost its revenues. Coffee has played a complex role in the country's history. The oligarchs gave Salvadoran coffee cultivation a terrible name, but the recent shift suggests that coffee can still be a force for good. Perhaps nothing better illustrates this than the Las Tres Puertas mill: built by a Victorian English maverick, taken over by a grandson-turned-social-reformer, and now operated by Batlle and her fair-trade concern. The 'dark empire' might just have a bright side after all.

Notes

[1] For a discussion of all these issues related to the Salvadoran civil war, see Russell Crandall, *The Salvador Option: The United States in El Salvador, 1977–1992* (Cambridge: Cambridge University Press, 2016).

[2] See, for example, filmmaker Oliver Stone's noble but cartoonish *Salvador* (1986); and US journalist Mark Danner's widely assigned but reductionist *The Massacre at El Mozote* (New York: Vintage, 1994).

[3] Kelefa Sanneh, 'Sacred Grounds: Aida Batlle and the New Coffee Evangelists', *New Yorker*, 14 November 2011, https://www.newyorker.com/magazine/2011/11/21/sacred-grounds.

Book Reviews

War, Conflict and the Military
Rosa Brooks

Un-American: A Soldier's Reckoning of Our Longest War
Erik Edstrom. New York: Bloomsbury, 2020. £18.99/$28.00.
304 pp.

Part memoir and part polemic, *Un-American* fits squarely into a long tradition of anti-war narratives. Enchanted by America's militarist mythologies – by a childhood of plastic GI Joe figurines, Boy Scout merit badges and hours spent listening to his step-grandfather's stories of the Second World War – young Erik Edstrom applies to the US Military Academy at West Point, entering the first West Point class to apply after 9/11. He envisions a life of heroism, status and pride: he would come home someday, he imagines, as 'the returning war hero … wearing badass combat boots' with a 'hot chick' whispering sexy words in his ear against a backdrop of Fourth of July fireworks (p. 29).

West Point culture shakes up his romanticised view of the military. En route to a 'motivational spirit briefing', his cadet platoon sergeant marches Edstrom and his fellow new cadets to a cadence that glorifies war crimes: 'Left right, left right, left right, KILL! … I went to the playground where all the kiddies play / I pulled out my Uzi and I BEGAN TO SPRAY!' (p. 36). Despite these discordant notes – which include the hazing and sheer relentless stupidity of many of West Point's rules, and newspapers that are increasingly full of stories about Abu Ghraib, torture and civilian deaths — Edstrom buys into the full fantasy of a life ennobled by war. He chooses infantry as his service branch; he goes through Ranger School and Special Forces assessment and selection; and he looks forward to proving himself in combat.

Survival | vol. 63 no. 1 | February–March 2021 | pp. 189–195   https://doi.org/10.1080/00396338.2021.1881261

But the discordant notes grow louder. A close friend from the West Point class above Edstrom's is grievously wounded, burned and disfigured when his vehicle hits an anti-tank mine in Kandahar, Afghanistan. Other friends die, and Edstrom attends their funerals. He sees Afghan civilians wounded and killed, watches lucrative US contracts go to corrupt and brutal warlords, and sees his own soldiers grow more and more cynical and numb. 'You can't think of the Afghans as humans', one of his soldiers tells him. 'They aren't people. They're stupid, selfish, animals. Fuck yeah, I'd kill a kid to see my wife again' (p. 138). The Afghan war, he begins to suspect, is nothing but pointless cruelty. 'Not only were we not winning, no one knew what we were doing. Everything we did was a derivative, regurgitated version of a failed approach' (p. 119). The war, he writes, 'had strip-mined my soul' (p. 110).

Finally, he cracks; when his company commander suppresses evidence of civilian deaths, Edstrom requests a transfer to a non-combat staff position. 'I didn't want to lead troops in a war I would never believe in' (p. 181). Predictably, this enrages his company commander, but eventually Edstrom is sent home and diagnosed with PTSD. He serves out the remainder of his five-year post-West Point military commitment as a member of the Honor Guard in Washington DC, becoming, in effect, 'a stage prop … All you had to do was stand completely still, sweating for dignitaries who rarely acknowledged your existence, and bury your best friends in Arlington National Cemetery' (p. 187).

As a memoir, *Un-American* is a moving and often painful story of a young soldier's soul-shattering experiences. But Edstrom goes beyond this to deliver a blistering critique of American militarism and militarisation. Everyone supporting a war, he asserts in the book's powerful opening lines, should first contemplate three visions: 'The vision of your own death in that war; the vision of experiencing the war from the other side; and the opportunity cost – what could have been *but was not*, because of the war' (p. vii, emphasis in original).

The book's least interesting – and least persuasive – sections are those that move beyond memoir to a critique of the causes, costs and consequences of America's post-9/11 wars. Imagine, demands Edstrom, the lives that would not have been lost if the US had not launched a 'global war on terror'; imagine the money that could have been invested instead in education, in countering climate change or in reducing income inequality. It's a critique that is certainly fair, but it is neither unique nor compellingly made in *Un-American*.

This is, in large part, because Edstrom's polemic is oddly ahistorical. He blames American culture and politics for all his woes: 'Military service in other countries is not romanticized' as it is in the US, he insists (p. 22). But this statement – breathtaking in its naivety – ignores most of human history. After all,

Edstrom is hardly the first soldier embittered by his previous susceptibility to 'the old Lie; Dulce et decorum est / Pro patria mori'. Indeed, his book lies squarely in the tradition of Stephen Crane's *The Red Badge of Courage*, Robert Graves's *Goodbye to All That*, Erich Maria Remarque's *All Quiet on the Western Front*, Wilfred Owen's poetry (as quoted here), and a thousand other works from a thousand other wars. America undeniably has its unique pathologies, but although Edstrom's personal story is wrenching and well told in *Un-American*, it does not, in and of itself, offer much support for his sweeping arguments about US culture and foreign policy.

Why We Fight
Mike Martin. London: C. Hurst & Co., 2018. £20.00. 311 pp.

It's not politically correct to say so, but for many soldiers, war is fun. In *Why We Fight*, Mike Martin, a former British officer, recalls his own experiences in Afghanistan: 'When I saw action … it was the most exhilarating thing that I have ever done in my life.' In talking to other soldiers and veterans, he found that this was 'the most common response to the act of going to war' (p. 10). For some veterans, war is a source of moral injury, memorable for the death and destruction it visits upon soldiers and civilians alike. For others, including Martin, war is memorable for its joys; he recalls his fellow soldiers 'grinning' with excitement in the middle of Taliban firefights, and concludes that combat was, 'hands down, the greatest rush of positive emotions that I have ever experienced' (pp. 43–4).

In *Why We Fight*, Martin offers an evolutionary explanation for what seems, on the surface, to be an evolutionarily baffling phenomenon. In many respects, the attraction of war seems profoundly 'anti-evolutionary' (p. ix), for what could be the evolutionary function of something that has, historically, killed off countless fit young males before they even have time to reproduce? Martin guides readers of *Why We Fight* through recent anthropological and political-science theories, and through research on cellular, animal and human evolution. Along the way, he explores concepts of human consciousness, the material underpinnings of our illusion of free will, the origin of moral codes and the evolutionary purpose of human beliefs in the supernatural.

Why We Fight is an ambitious book. (Perhaps a little too ambitious: this lay reader couldn't help wondering what a professional evolutionary biologist would make of some of Martin's arguments). In the end, however, Martin's argument boils down to something straightforward: humans fight, he tells us, 'to achieve status or belonging' (p. 1). As individuals, we find violence and war appealing because they offer us opportunities to gain status and power within our social groups, and because they are a way to affirm or lay claim to group membership. In this view, ideology, morality and religion do not 'cause' wars; they are simply mental constructs humans develop or adopt to explain and justify our evolutionary quest for status and belonging. The evolutionary drive to achieve these is, for most of us, strong enough to overcome our awareness, as individuals, that war may leave us dead.

Martin's argument is compelling, but sometimes reductionist. While it offers a powerful counter to simplistic claims that 'ideas' drive people to kill and die, it is less satisfying as applied to the vast array of laws, practices and bureaucratic institutions that support and enable human wars. True, groups – even large nation-states – are nothing more than collections of individuals, but it is hard to see how millions of individual drives to achieve status and belonging come together, collectively, to produce such behemoths as, say, the military–industrial complex.

Similarly, Martin struggles to explain conscription, which takes individual preferences entirely out of the equation, and forces into battle many who might prefer a longer life over status and belonging. 'Undoubtedly,' he admits, 'in specific wars [conscription] has worked as a mechanism to raise armies'. But, he wonders, if conscription truly forced people to fight against their will, shouldn't humans 'have evolved behaviors that enable them to escape the selection pressure of war?' Regardless, he concludes, 'conscription is far from ubiquitous, and there are countless instances of huge armies being raised without forcing people to fight' (p. 9).

This seems too pat. There are also countless instances of men literally maiming themselves to avoid conscription, and of large-scale anti-conscription riots and resistance. Nor does Martin wonder about mercenaries, or the many historical instances of mercenary armies refusing to fight in the absence of higher pay.

One might explain even these acts of apparent unwillingness to fight as efforts to achieve status and belonging: opposition to state conscription could reaffirm an individual's status and membership in a group that defines itself in opposition to the state, and a refusal to fight in the absence of higher pay could represent an effort by individual mercenaries to gain status among their fellow mercenaries and affirm their group cohesion. But if the evolutionary drive to seek status and belonging can explain refusal to fight as well as eagerness to fight, it becomes less useful as an explanation for war. Would it not be simpler to argue that if evolutionary pressures produced, in humans, a species that seeks status and belonging, this drive can propel humans in virtually any direction – sometimes towards war, but sometimes away from it?

This, of course, brings us back to the same questions about ideology, religion and morality that Martin wants to move past. If the quest for status and belonging can push individuals either towards war or away from it, we need to understand the 'something else' that makes some eagerly seek out war even as others take extreme measures to avoid it. If the 'something else' is merely that different people seek status and belonging in different groups, it still raises the same question: what makes a group define itself as a group? Why are some groups more appealing than other groups to any given individual? Is it mere accident? Or do we need to restore some role for ideology, narrative and institutions?

Despite these unresolved questions, *Why We Fight* is a worthwhile and thought-provoking read, and Martin's framework offers a useful corrective to the 'war of ideas' school of thought that has driven so much Western counter-terrorism policy. If terrorism is 'caused' by jihadist ideology, anti-radicalisation programmes that focus on countering such ideologies make sense, and tactics such as counter-terrorism drone strikes may advance Western goals. But if terrorism is fuelled not by ideology but by a desire to gain status, redress perceived humiliation and affirm group identity – as Martin persuasively argues – then much of what passes for counter-terrorism policy will be profoundly counterproductive, and will indeed (as many critics have charged) create more terrorists than it eliminates.

As Martin notes, this also has profound implications for how governments and civil society respond to the rising tide of nationalism and right-wing populism so evident today in both Europe and the United States. If we want to reduce right-wing extremist violence, we would do well to heed his advice.

Military Waste: The Unexpected Consequences of Permanent War Readiness

Joshua O. Reno. Oakland, CA: University of California Press, 2020. £19.00/$34.95. 288 pp.

War, we often hear, is wasteful: it wastes money that could be more constructively spent at home than on dubious military adventures abroad; it wastes the lives of the human beings it kills, preventing them from becoming doctors or physicists or teachers or parents or beloved friends; it reduces land and buildings and whole cities to rubble. In *Military Waste*, however, anthropologist Joshua Reno eschews these common ways of understanding war's wastefulness, turning instead to a quirky ethnographic exploration of other forms of military waste. Reno looks at material objects – the damaged, obsolete or surplus planes, ships and guns left over from war and preparations for war (and the toxic chemicals that sometimes leach from them) – and also at war-making's less concrete detritus: the narratives, ideologies and explanatory tropes (some toxic, some possibly liberating) that emerge as relics and by-products of militarism and militarisation.

Military Waste takes us first to the Boneyard – formally, the 309th Aerospace Maintenance and Regeneration Center on the outskirts of Tucson, Arizona – where old US military airplanes go to die. Except, it turns out, they don't necessarily die. The Boneyard is less cemetery than 'open-air garage', a place where planes are 'tinkered with [and] stripped for parts' (p. 52). It's also a museum, a restoration venue and, sometimes, an artists' studio and supply store. Some of the more than 4,000 planes at the Boneyard will be restored and fly again; others will have their nose cones turned into enormous canvasses for street artists. The Boneyard introduces the primary theme of Reno's book: that 'waste' can be viewed as both failure and opportunity, as both loss and a chance to create new objects, new stories and new ways of representing the world. It is not just that one man's trash is another man's treasure – the detritus of war-making can, Reno notes, cause literal, physical harm to landscapes and people, but it can also be used to subvert and challenge the militarism and militarisation that produce it.

From the Boneyard, Reno takes readers on a tour of various other manifestations of military waste, from obsolete warships sunk to create artificial reefs to the space debris that litters extra-terrestrial space. We learn of the imperialist policies that turned nitrate-rich guano islands in the South Pacific – islands covered by the waste of sea birds – into objects to be bought, sold, exploited and defended. We explore islands rendered toxic by practice bombings, and islands once used by the military that have now been converted into conservation and environmental-research sites.

As we go, we move further and further from the obsolete and damaged physical objects that litter the Boneyard towards an examination of the cultural refuse of militarism, including school shootings (and, to a lesser extent, police shootings) as the detritus of war-making. Physical objects still play some role here: if the United States is awash in guns, this is to some extent a direct result of war-making, which leads to the production of weapons that will, at some point, cease to be of use to the military and pass into civilian hands. But the ubiquity of guns, and the mythologies that propel their manufacture and sale, are also 'waste products' of a particularly American brand of militarism and militarisation. 'Militarism', notes Reno, 'is a way of being, of thinking and acting, that privileges violent confrontation as a way to resolve conflict and, more broadly, as a way to demonstrate strength' (p. 141). In the US, militarism is deeply intertwined with a long history of racialised violence and an understanding of white masculinity as perpetually under threat, and defensible – redeemable – only through violence. (So much so, notes Reno, that a would-be school shooter who, after an encounter with a compassionate schoolmate, changed his mind about carrying out his lethal plans was depicted in the press and even by his defence attorney as someone who 'chickened out' – p. 166.)

Military Waste is ethnography, not polemic. Reno's interest lies mainly in showing the richness and complexity of how military waste is conceptualised and used, both materially and culturally. His book is an academic one, and at times uses too much abstruse scholarly jargon (such jargon, it might be said, is a waste product of modern scholarly culture). But it is nonetheless a fascinating read, and Reno succeeds in bringing us into the worlds of his subjects: retired aerospace engineers, artists, entrepreneurs, environmentalists and more. In the end, Reno is making an argument, albeit a subtle one, that is reflexive and reflective of the tensions he so ably documents: military waste is a by-product of a vast global military machine designed to inflict death and destruction, but it is also, at the same time, something that can be imaginatively 'demilitarized or re-worlded' – and used, in the end, to question and challenge the logic of perpetual war-making (p. 211).

Russia and Eurasia
Angela Stent

Russia
Dmitri Trenin. Cambridge: Polity Press, 2019. £12.99. 212 pp.

Dmitri Trenin provides a succinct account of Russia's turbulent twentieth-century history in this informative book. He explains how the Russian state has twice collapsed and resurrected itself in the space of less than 100 years, and why it endures. The 'new' Russia, he argues, does not represent a break with the past, but is a 'continuation state of the Soviet Union, the Russian Empire, and the tsardom of Muscovy' (p. 8).

Trenin highlights the centrality of victory in the 'Great Patriotic War' for contemporary Russia, a theme that President Vladimir Putin continually emphasises. Victory in the Second World War 'is regarded in Russia as its biggest contribution to humanity' (p. 88). This explains why Josef Stalin remains so popular among many Russians. The war represents a crucial part of Russian national identity, and any attempt to question the USSR's role in it is interpreted as anti-Russian. Indeed, the new 2020 Russian constitution makes it a punishable offence to criticise the official version of what happened during the war.

The Soviet system, Trenin argues, was ultimately less able to meet the challenges of peacetime than of war and upheaval. By the time Mikhail Gorbachev came to power in 1985, the system was in crisis and he was determined to renew it. But according to the author, Gorbachev did not really understand the country he had inherited, nor did he have a vision of what the new system should look like. Gorbachev himself admits that he underestimated the nationalities question and this, finally, led to the USSR's demise.

Could a different leader have saved the Soviet Union? Trenin points to an alternative path that could have been taken: Deng Xiaoping's policy of reforming the economy while maintaining tight political control. Gorbachev opted for political liberalisation over economic reform, which ultimately led to his political demise – a lesson not lost on the current Russian president.

Putin, says Trenin, has been a stabiliser who has restored order after the chaotic 1990s and has also 'become the godfather of contemporary Russian capitalism' (p. 14). He has restored Russia's status as a great power and kept the country geographically intact. He initially sought to integrate Russia into the West but, argues Trenin, was rebuffed by the United States and Europe. The year 2014, with Moscow's annexation of Crimea and launch of a war in southeastern Ukraine, marked the end of that quest and a turn toward China, the Middle East and countries elsewhere.

Survival | vol. 63 no. 1 | February–March 2021 | pp. 196–202   https://doi.org/10.1080/00396338.2021.1881262

Although Trenin gives Putin credit for stabilising Russia and bringing it prosperity and international influence, he admits that corruption has become the essence of the system. Moreover, 'the secret of Putin's Russia is that it is a regime posing as a state' (p. 15). According to the author, there will inevitably be a political crisis following Putin's departure from the Kremlin, one that will involve a redistribution of wealth. The central challenge for his successors will be to build a functioning state with the rule of law, an independent judiciary and a modernised economy.

Contemporary Russian Conservatism: Problems, Paradoxes, and Perspectives
Mikhail Suslov and Dmitry Uzlaner, eds. Leiden: Brill, 2020.
€109.00. 426 pp.

Promoting conservative values at home and abroad has become a central theme in Putin's Russia over the past 15 years. The ruling United Russia party espouses conservatism, the Russian Orthodox Church extols its virtues and Putin has committed himself to promoting 'traditional family values', as opposed to those of a decadent West. Indeed, the contributors to this informative book stress that the rise of Russian conservatism is closely related to the growth of anti-Western rhetoric and actions.

According to Mikhail Suslov, conservatism arose in response to the need to redefine Russian identity after 1991, when a 25-million-strong Russian-speaking diaspora suddenly found itself separated from the motherland. The Yeltsin-era vision of this 'Russian world' was to embrace the idea that diaspora Russians, with their hybrid identities, could become agents of globalisation to Russia's advantage. But, after Putin came to power and following the first 'colour' revolutions, Kremlin official Vladislav Surkov announced the theory of 'sovereign democracy': 'The "Russian world" was now understood as an instrument of state, facilitating Russia's "soft power" abroad' (p. 94).

A major challenge for Russian conservatives is how to deal with the Soviet past. After all, the USSR persecuted the Church, banned private property and forced peasants to give up their land. Yet today's conservatives feel nostalgia for the Soviet Union's status as a feared superpower, and for its scientific and technological achievements. Accordingly, in 2017 the Kremlin supported a low-key commemoration of the 1917 revolution. Putin highlighted the problematic legacy of what could be described as the mother of all colour revolutions, which split the country in two. Putin sees himself as the Russian leader who has finally reconciled 'Red' and 'White' Russia.

Russian conservatives have recently exported their doctrines to the West, argues Marlene Laruelle. While they have focused on Europe, their links with like-minded American groups are growing. During a violent, racist march in Charlottesville, Virginia, in 2017, American white supremacists chanted 'Russia is our friend'. Members of the radical right, such as former Ku Klux Klan grand wizard David Duke, see post-Soviet Russia as a place where the 'white race' has been reborn. Representatives from American white-power groups participate in the annual nationalist Russian March.

The links between Russian and American conservatives extend to the alt-right movement, which includes the more radical supporters of Donald Trump. Its main website, Breitbart News, has praised Putin for his rejection of 'decadent' American liberalism and embrace of nationalism. Alexander Dugin, one of Russia's leading conservative theorists, appears on alt-right media. Furthermore, the US 'Christian right' has welcomed contacts with the Russian Orthodox Church, supporting its stance on 'traditional family values' and opposition to abortion and LGBT rights.

The main spokesman for Russian conservatism's international role has been Foreign Minister Sergei Lavrov, who stresses Russia's exceptionalism – a result, argue the authors, of the inconsistency between Russia's status ambitions and the way the West has treated it. Lavrov has also warned that 'historical attempts to isolate Russia have always brought catastrophe upon Europe' (p. 226).

This Is Not Propaganda: Adventures in the War Against Reality
Peter Pomerantsev. New York: PublicAffairs, 2019.
$28.00. 237 pp.

After the Soviet collapse, many in the West hoped that Russia and other post-communist countries would democratise, introduce the rule of law and integrate into the liberal-international order. That did not happen. In the twenty-first century's brave new world of electoral authoritarianism, pervasive disinformation and 'alternative facts', argues Peter Pomerantsev in this panoramic book, the West is beginning to look more like Russia than vice versa.

Pomerantsev travelled the world to interview people about how they propagate disinformation, and he assigns Russia a central role in this new order: 'precisely because they had lost the Cold War, Russian spin doctors and media manipulators managed to adapt to the new world quicker than anyone in the entity once known as the "West"' (p. xiv).

The most infamous of these Russian operations was the Kremlin-connected 'troll factory' in St Petersburg, which recruited English-speaking trolls in Russia and other countries to flood social media with disinformation. Their most successful endeavour came during the 2016 US presidential-election campaign, when they created thousands of fake accounts and groups in an effort to make Americans hate each other and doubt the integrity of their electoral system. As Pomerantsev points out, 'lies are not illegal', and it has proven difficult to prosecute people for these activities (p. 24).

Russia's goal is to cause the consumers of its social-media fabrications to question the veracity of anything presented as fact. Nowhere is this more evident than in the duelling narratives about the Russo-Ukrainian War. As one of the investigators into the deadly 2014 fire that started during clashes between pro- and anti-Maidan protesters in Odessa, Ukraine, observed: 'Everyone lives in their own reality, everyone has their own truth, there is no reconciliation' (p. 99). Ukrainians and Russians continue to argue over who was responsible for igniting the blaze.

Pomerantsev interviewed Gleb Pavlovsky, a former Kremlin spin doctor, to understand how post-communist Russia became a prime purveyor of disinformation. Pavlovksy describes the 1990s as a period when Russia was a blank canvas: communist ideology was gone and there were no principles or structures to replace it. As the decade wore on, polling suggested that Russians wanted 'an intelligent spy as their leader' (p. 173). After Putin entered the Kremlin, Pavlovsky's mission was to cement a 'Putin majority' by invoking an image of Russia besieged by internal and external enemies, with a wise leader who could protect them. Pavlovsky believes that the West today is itself imitating a form of 'pro-Putinism' (p. 176).

Interspersed with Pomerantsev's analysis of a post-factual world is the personal story of his parents – Soviet dissidents who faced interrogation and prison, and who were forced to emigrate when he was a baby. His father eventually worked both for the BBC's and for Radio Free Europe/Radio Liberty's Russian-language services – his mission was to present real news to Soviet citizens who had no other source of objective information. The irony of this story is that, once again, objective facts remain elusive not only in Russia but also now in the West.

How to Lose the Information War: Russia, Fake News, and the Future of Conflict
Nina Jankowicz. London and New York: I.B. Tauris, 2020.
£20.00/$27.00. 259 pp.

Nina Jankowicz's wide-ranging book explains how different countries have responded to Russian disinformation campaigns and what they have learned from their experiences. The Kremlin, she argues, 'divides and deceives populations around the world – Russian deceptions exploit fissures in targeted societies to sow doubt, distrust, discontent and to further divide populations and their governments' (p. xvii).

Her first case study is Estonia, which in 2007 experienced a massive three-week cyber attack – attributed to Russia – after relocating a statue of a Soviet soldier from the centre of Tallinn to the suburbs. Relations between the Estonian and Russophone population had been deteriorating, and Estonia was forced to temporarily close its embassy in Moscow after the nationalist youth group Nashi attacked diplomatic personnel. Jankowicz explains that the Estonian authorities came to understand that they needed to improve educational and professional opportunities for their country's Russophone population. Today, the younger generation of Russian speakers is better integrated into Estonian society and, she argues, Russian disinformation is less problematic.

For Poland, the challenge of Russian disinformation was particularly acute after the 2010 Smolensk plane crash that killed the Polish president, Lech Kaczyński, and nearly 100 other members of the country's political elite. The crash was caused by pilot and air-traffic-control errors, but conspiracy theories began to circulate almost immediately – exacerbated by Russia's refusal to return the plane wreckage. Rumours that this was an assassination attempt and that Kaczyński's political rivals colluded with the Russians to bring down the plane have flourished, aggravating Poland's deep political divisions. Jankowicz emphasises that Russia has sought to manipulate these divisions to its own benefit, but argues that the Poles can only push back against Russian interference if they begin to address their own domestic polarisation.

The Netherlands has also been a target of Russian disinformation. In 2016, the Dutch held a referendum on whether to ratify Ukraine's Association Agreement with the European Union. In the lead-up, there was active campaigning against Ukraine, replete with negative stereotypes about Ukrainian corruption being imported into the EU and Ukrainian 'fascists' running the government in Kyiv. Russians were actively involved in supporting Dutch opponents of Ukraine's bid. The referendum failed, but the parliament eventually ratified the agreement.

The Czech Republic is the only European country to have created a centre to counter hybrid threats. A Russian disinformation campaign highlighting the alleged threat from Muslim migrants to the country had exacerbated political tensions on this issue, prompting Czech officials to act. They realised that any successful campaign to counter hybrid threats must be multi-pronged, targeting online covert and overt disinformation as well as the money that supports domestic groups on opposite sides of polarising issues.

Jankowicz provides some suggestions for combatting fake news and disinformation: Western societies need to build resilience to limit their vulnerability

to outside manipulation by better monitoring social media, improving education and following the money.

Rigged: America, Russia, and One Hundred Years of Covert Electoral Interference
David Shimer. New York: Knopf, 2020. $29.95. 367 pp.

A persistent question dogged Donald Trump's presidency after 2016: how far
was Russia responsible for putting him in the White House, given what is now
known about its social-media manipulation and cyber interference during
the election campaign? And how much did Russia continue to interfere in
US domestic politics during his presidency and into the 2020 presidential
race? These issues have made Russia a uniquely toxic subject in American
politics because, for many of Trump's opponents, Russia and Trump are
virtually synonymous.

David Shimer addresses the 2016 campaign by situating the issue of electoral
interference in the broader context of a century of covert US and Soviet/Russian
attempts to influence voting outcomes around the world. He stresses that, while
Russian interference in the 2016 election represented continuity with previous
practices, 'the digital age has irrevocably enhanced the weapon of covert electoral interference' (p. 10).

The first half of the book covers accounts of electoral interference that are
well known to those familiar with Cold War history, such as the CIA's support
for the victorious Christian Democrats during the pivotal 1948 elections in Italy,
while the USSR supported the Communists. Shimer points out that the Soviets
were at a disadvantage compared to the Americans, because they did not really
understand how competitive elections worked.

Nevertheless, the KGB, in cooperation with the East German Stasi, pulled
off a spectacular coup in 1972, when two West German politicians were bribed
to abstain in a crucial vote in the Bundestag that could have ousted chancellor
Willy Brandt and ended his policy of reconciliation with the Soviet bloc, thereby
changing the course of history.

The second half of the book focuses on contemporary Russia. Despite the
formal abolition of the KGB after the Soviet collapse, the Russian intelligence
services have remained strong and were never reformed. Once Putin, a former
KGB case officer, came to power, the intelligence services resumed their former
modus operandi. Putin, convinced that the United States was behind the mass
opposition demonstrations in Russia in 2011, determined that it was appropriate to interfere in US elections. The Obama administration had difficulty in
comprehending the full scope of the multi-pronged interference in 2016 and,

according to officials from his administration whom Shimer interviewed, was too slow to respond.

The 2019 Mueller report detailed how Russia used both social media and cyber penetration against Hillary Clinton's candidacy in 2016. Shimer postulates that Russian actions might have affected the election outcome by influencing how people viewed her presidential bid. What is indisputable is that Russia was able to take advantage of the deep divisions in American society to exacerbate its fissures.

Shimer reminds us that, once in office, Trump never showed any interest in securing America's elections, concluding that the president was 'the newest member of a distinct club: leaders who came to power psychologically indebted to foreign actors and insecure about their electoral legitimacy' (p. 228).

Asia-Pacific

Lanxin Xiang

Thucydides's Trap? Historical Interpretation, Logic of Inquiry, and the Future of Sino-American Relations
Steve Chan. Ann Arbor, MI: University of Michigan Press, 2020.
$75.00. 268 pp.

This book is a direct rebuke of Graham Allison's much-publicised argument in *Destined for War: Can America and China Escape Thucydides's Trap?* (2017), which asserts that the danger of a great-power war increases when a rising power overtakes an incumbent hegemon. Allison popularised this theory to project a scenario of war between the United States and China.

Steve Chan points out a fundamental flaw in Allison's theory: the misleading concept of one power being 'overtaken' by another during a hegemonic-power transition. A latecomer's capability to overtake an incumbent can not necessarily be measured simply by data such as GDP. 'Gauging national power based on physical size, quantitative volume and stockpile of tangible material', says Chan, 'tends to exaggerate China's relative international position' (p. 112). Moreover, focusing 'primarily or even exclusively on states' as the basic unit of analysis overlooks the additional strengths states might possess by virtue of their alliance relationships (p. 30). While the US has throngs of allies, China has but one: North Korea.

Allison used case studies of great-power wars in history to make his argument, but neglected many cases in which an upstart power had a war with a dominant one for reasons other than an ambition to 'overtake' or replace the incumbent. A case in point is the Korean War (p. 33). China's decision to enter the war was hardly driven by the idea of establishing a new world order, but rather by concerns of national security and domestic stability if the US military were allowed to unify the Korean Peninsula on its own terms.

Instead of relying on Allison's rather pessimistic and fatalist outlook, it is useful to consider the full picture of China's intentions. The power-transition theory argues that wars break out only when a rising power is driven primarily by revisionist ambitions. Thus, 'power shifts alone do not produce war' (p. 121). Western international-relations (IR) theories tend to assign the status quo orientation to the dominant power, and the revisionist orientation to the rising power. This approach makes it difficult to explain why China has emerged as a defender of the existing liberal-international order based on globalisation and multilateralism, at the same time that the US seems to be rejecting it (p. 123).

Survival | vol. 63 no. 1 | February–March 2021 | pp. 203–208   https://doi.org/10.1080/00396338.2021.1881263

Chan believes that China has not yet displayed a revisionist impulse, but cautions that its intentions may change in the future (p. 129). So far, China has not launched an ideological war or sought military alliances against the United States. Nor is there much evidence to suggest that China is imitating a young United States in establishing an 'Asian Monroe Doctrine'. China has been an active participant in international organisations and conventions. In contrast, the United States, during the Trump years at least, broke with many international organisations and impeded their work. 'Considering the record of their participation in international organizations and accords … it is difficult to argue that China has manifested a more revisionist inclination than the United States', writes Chan (p. 138). This is an interesting book that succeeds in debunking the Thucydides Trap theory within the logical framework of Western IR theories.

Taming Sino-American Rivalry
Feng Zhang and Richard Ned Lebow. Oxford and New York: Oxford University Press, 2020. £64.00/$99.00. 274 pp.

In this ambitious book, Feng Zhang and Richard Ned Lebow try to explain how Sino-American rivalry can be 'tamed'. The authors appear to be more interested in conflict management than in the question of why two major powers should go down the path of dangerous rivalry at all, especially given that 'they have every reason to live in harmony and benefit themselves and the world' (p. 2).

The basic assumption of this study is that the two countries are fighting over international prestige rather than real interests. The prevailing analysis in the US is that China is the 'inheritor of the Japanese mantle, as a threatening rising challenge to American hegemony' (p. 13). Chinese analysts reject this American argument and refuse to be drawn into the Thucydides Trap debate. The leadership in Beijing seems confident that China can avoid falling into the trap described by Allison (p. 23).

According to the authors, there are two schools of thought in international relations that affect policymaking. The dominant school in the US is the 'power transition' school, which believes that any shifts in hegemonic power will inevitably lead to war. According to this school, China is a classic case of a challenger to the incumbent hegemon. The realist school holds that the China threat to the United States has been invented by the national-security establishment in Washington. It is not a genuine security threat, but rather a threat to America's self-esteem, insofar as China's rapidly growing economic, military and political power affects the United States' relative global position (p. 201).

It is not surprising that Western scholars have tended to rely upon the logic of balances of power to explain Sino-American relations, given the experience of the Cold War. But China, unlike the Soviet Union, does not have any serious desire to seek global hegemony, nor even regional hegemony. Zhang and Lebow conclude that the 'alleged competition between China and the United States for hegemony or dominance of East Asia is largely hype' (p. 148). The US is unnecessarily obsessed with military superiority in maritime Asia, pushing China to seek control over sea lanes.

The authors believe the Trump administration has been wrong-headed in treating China primarily as a security threat so that the US does not 'appear weak in the eyes of the adversary' (p. 199). This approach promises to unleash a vicious cycle in which the danger of military clashes increases dramatically. Since the US will maintain military superiority in Asia-Pacific for some time to come, it is still possible to avoid conflict. Priority should be given to strategic reassurance rather than deterrence as a way of reducing tensions between the two powers (p. 150). 'If America and China were able to reconcile their respective quests for self-esteem through *hegemonia*-based authority sharing,' write the authors, 'other contentious issues would be much easier to manage' (p. 203). If the incoming Biden administration breaks with the approach of the Trump administration as critiqued in this book, this may well demonstrate the wisdom of the authors' findings.

In the Dragon's Shadow: Southeast Asia in the Chinese Century
Sebastian Strangio. New Haven, CT: Yale University Press, 2020. £20.00/$30.00. 360 pp.

Southeast Asian states have viewed a rapidly rising China with alarm, but 'China's economic centrality to the region makes it something they cannot ignore, as much as they might wish to', writes Sebastian Strangio (p. 8). At the same time, he cautions against overgeneralising about the region, since each country's perceptions will have been shaped by its own unique history of interacting with China.

The author believes that while China has no intention of replacing the United States as a global hegemon or even as a guarantor of Asia's regional order, 'it does want to reclaim something of the centrality it enjoyed in East Asia prior to its subjugation by the Western empires and imperial Japan in the nineteenth and the twentieth centuries' (p .12). Southeast Asia therefore occupies a pivotal position in China's rejuvenation project.

'Seen from Beijing,' observes Strangio, 'Asia is a claustrophobic place' (p. 12). China is enclosed on three sides by land borders with 14 nations. On its east coast, China faces an island barrier stretching from Russia's Kamchatka

Peninsula to the island of Borneo. The main part of this island chain is controlled by three formal US allies: Japan, the Philippines and South Korea. As the Chinese economy has grown, its heavy reliance on the Malacca Strait, both as an importation route for energy supplies and as an exportation route for Chinese goods, has compelled Beijing to build a strong navy, which has upset the regional balance.

Strangio places particular emphasis on the pivotal role played by China's southwest Yunnan Province as the bridgehead of China's Belt and Road Initiative. The transportation links that have been built under the initiative have fundamentally changed the landscape of Southeast Asia, a region once characterised by inaccessible geographic terrain that prevented economic interaction with China. In 1991, it took six weeks to travel by sea from Kunming, capital city of Yunnan, to Bangkok. Today, it takes only 24 hours to travel between the two cities via an expressway completed in 2013 (p. 47). The author details the many projects – roads, bridges, dams, train lines, casinos – that have connected regional countries with China in what promises to be an enduring way.

The author concludes that China 'presents each of the Southeast Asian states with a similar challenge: how to benefit from its booming economy while safeguarding its sovereignty from the perils of overdependence' (p. 37). It is not surprising that some countries have become deeply worried about a possible showdown between Washington and Beijing, worries that have been stoked by the behaviour of the Trump administration. 'Southeast Asia is too economically intertwined with China to enlist in a US-led coalition aimed at curbing its rise' (p. 279), says Strangio. This is, of course, the same kind of complex balancing act which has played out in many corners of the globe, including Africa, Latin America and the Middle East.

The Deer and the Dragon: Southeast Asia and China in the 21st Century
Donald K. Emmerson, ed. Stanford, CA, and Washington
DC: Walter H. Shorenstein Asia-Pacific Research Center and
Brookings Institution Press, 2020. $29.99. 386 pp.

The contributions to this edited volume cover a wide range of topics, but several interesting themes emerge. Editor Donald Emmerson characterises Southeast Asia as a 'mousedeer' that is continually subject to the influence and coercion of the Chinese 'dragon', a traditional symbol of Chinese imperial divinity and power. Asymmetries between China and its neighbours – the Chinese economy is four times that of Southeast Asia, and its population more than twice as big (p. 2) – allows China to thwart any strategic autonomy and consensus against it. Moreover, the preference of the Association of Southeast Asian Nations (ASEAN) for consensus-building and its avoidance of winner–loser votes (the so-called 'ASEAN way') may help the organisation to endure but also provides leverage for China to divide the group. ASEAN countries also face a dilemma in managing the Thucydides Trap between the US and China. On the one hand, they dread the thought of these two powers getting into a deadly fight as the power gap between them closes. On the other hand, they are eager to see that gap close to the extent that it creates a balance of power in which each side is able to check the other's ambition of dominating Southeast Asia (p. 3).

Thomas Fingar contributes a brilliant chapter on 'Security and Development in Historical Context'. According to him, from 1949 to the 1990s, China's policy towards Southeast Asia was primarily focused on security and the threats posed by US military engagement in the region and increasing Soviet influence in the wake of the Sino-Soviet split. Development started to become a priority in the 1990s, largely due to fundamental changes in the regional security environment and the economic opening of China and the surrounding countries. 'As security concerns decreased, economic opportunities grew' (p. 53). The 1990s also spelled the end of the Soviet Union, but the US was too busy elsewhere to fill the strategic vacuum its collapse created in Southeast Asia. It was around this time that China began to change its image among neighbouring states.

The chapter by See Seng Tan – 'Vulnerability and Engagement in Singapore–China Relations' – is especially interesting. It offers a balanced analysis of the delicate Singapore–China relationship. It is a multifaceted relationship that provides Singapore with opportunities as well as vulnerabilities. According to the author, Singapore's policy of autonomy 'has survived both despite and because of its close ties with China' (p. 211). At present, however, Singapore does not perceive China as a security threat. There is therefore no need for the city-state to make a clear choice between the United States and China. The leadership continues to adhere to late prime minister Lee Kuan Yew's judgement that China is not in a position to, and perhaps would not even want to, replace the United States as a security guarantor in Asia. Thus, the indispensability of the US presence in the region does not necessarily pose a security dilemma for Singapore.

The overall finding of this volume, which also presents analyses of Chinese engagement in Cambodia, Indonesia, Laos and Myanmar, is that ASEAN as an institution is too weak, and that regional states' national autonomy must be strengthened in order to 'remind Beijing not to rely too heavily on its success in neutering ASEAN as a strategic actor capable of standing up to China' (p. 30). This may be wishful thinking, but the book is certainly useful for understanding the various dimensions of China–Southeast Asia relations.

Indonesia: State and Society in Transition
Jemma Purdey, Antje Missbach and Dave McRae. Boulder, CO:
Lynne Rienner Publishers, 2019. $89.95. 261 pp.

At the beginning of this volume the authors ask why Indonesia has not been a significant player on the global stage, and whether it is underrated by other actors (p. 10). Indonesia is a big country with a sizeable population of 270 million, a stable democracy and a dynamic economy. Twenty years after the end of General Suharto's authoritarian regime, it still faces numerous political, economic and social challenges, but when compared with countries of similar historical trajectories – particularly other members of the 'third wave' of democratisation after the Cold War – Indonesia's overall performance is no worse, and in some spheres even better, than its cohorts'.

Nevertheless, there are some fundamental tensions within the country's democratic system. Decentralisation in 1999 shifted power from the central government to subnational ones, introducing 'de facto federalism' in the country's political system (p. 83). While decentralisation helped to stabilise centre–periphery relations, it has also raised the spectre of disintegration – a typical problem for multiethnic archipelagoes – as local political elites and corrupt interests have become entrenched. Another problem is persistent social and ethnic inequality, particularly in health, education and employment opportunities. The gap between the poorest and the richest has been growing faster in Indonesia than in any other Southeast Asian country (p. 107). Moreover, protecting individual rights, including minority rights, remains a daunting task. In the early reform period after Suharto, Indonesian civil society flourished and many new laws were passed to curtail human-rights abuses, but enforcement of the legislation remains problematic.

The authors imply that Indonesia's domestic weaknesses have rightfully influenced the way it is perceived by other states. But Indonesia has the potential to become a major player, not only because of its size and demography, but also because of its strategic position within the maritime and trading domains. This volume presents a useful survey of a country that is already a member of the G20 and a leading member of ASEAN.

Letter to the Editor

Brexit and the UN Security Council: Much Ado About Not Much?

Sir,

As the United Kingdom's ambassador to the United Nations and representative on the UN Security Council in December 1991, when the Soviet Union ceased to exist and the Russian Federation rose like a phoenix from the ashes to succeed it, I read Professor Dombey's article 'Brexit, Scotland and the UN Security Council' with considerable interest, but also some puzzlement at his account and at the implications he drew from the Russian case about how the UN might dispose of the UK's membership on the Security Council following a vote for independence by Scotland.

In December 1991 there was in fact no consultation, within either the UN General Assembly or the Security Council, following the receipt by the secretary-general (still Javier Pérez de Cuéllar in the last days of his mandate before Boutros Boutros-Ghali took over at the beginning of 1992) of the letter from Russian Federation president Boris Yeltsin asking that the Russian Federation be treated in all respects as the successor state to the Soviet Union. The only consultation that did take place consisted of discreet soundings of the four other permanent members of the Security Council (China, France, the UK and the United States), all of whom advised responding positively to Yeltsin's letter without more ado. So it was that, at the first meeting of the Security Council after Christmas (and before the New Year), I found myself sitting, as usual, next to Yuli Vorontsov, whose place at the table was marked by a nameplate inscribed 'Russian Federation', put there by the Secretariat. A little over a month later, Yeltsin attended the Security Council summit called by British prime minister John Major and no word of criticism was heard from any member state.

Why did the four other permanent members come to that unanimous position? Principally, I would suggest, because they did not wish to see the issue of the future membership of the Security Council, which was already the object of much fevered speculation, brought into play with unpredictable consequences; and because they wished to ensure that Yeltsin's Russia would be a source of stability.

Survival | vol. 63 no. 1 | February–March 2021 | pp. 209–212   https://doi.org/10.1080/00396338.2021.1881264

As to the matter of nuclear weapons, which Professor Dombey drags into the equation, that surely is a complete red herring. When the UN Charter was negotiated, signed, ratified and brought into operation in 1945, only one of the five permanent members (P5) of the Security Council possessed nuclear weapons. But all five held a veto on Security Council decisions.

So much for the precedent of 1991, which does not, I would suggest, provide an opening for the General Assembly to get involved as Professor Dombey speculates. No doubt, in the event of Scotland becoming independent, political considerations, rather than purely legal ones, would again predominate. As of today, there would seem to me no basis for believing that the other four permanent members would reach a different view from the one they did in 1991, nor that the secretary-general would act in a different manner.

David Hannay
House of Lords

In Reply

I am grateful to Lord Hannay for telling us about the discreet consultations among the four other permanent members of the UN Security Council in December 1991 following Yeltsin's letter to the UN secretary-general after the Soviet Union's collapse. I am also pleased that he agrees with me that there is no logical connection between the P5 and the nuclear-weapons states recognised by the Non-Proliferation Treaty, and that 'political considerations, rather than purely legal ones' would dominate at the UN.

I don't agree, however, that nuclear issues are a red herring. In December 1991, the most urgent issue for the United States and its allies was how to secure the thousands of Soviet nuclear weapons in Belarus, Kazakhstan and Ukraine. This meant, as a corollary, that it was also urgent for Russia to be recognised as the Soviet Union's successor at the UN and its agencies. Given the practical impossibility of revising the UN Charter in order to replace the Soviet Union with the Russian Federation, Yeltsin requested that the UN consider his letter 'confirmation of the credentials to represent the Russian Federation in United Nations organs for all the persons currently holding the credentials of representatives of the USSR to the United Nations'. That dispensation allowed Russia to take control of all the Soviet nuclear weapons without violating the Non-Proliferation Treaty.

The letter was cunningly worded so that the question of the Soviet Union's successor at the UN became a matter of credentials, such that any member state's objection would become a matter for the Credentials Committee of the General Assembly, thereby avoiding Charter amendment and bypassing the Security Council. Had any objection arisen, the Credentials Committee would have voted and then passed the matter to the General Assembly to decide, as it did in Cambodia's case. The General Assembly would then probably have determined that the matter was important because the question of the representation of a founder member who is named in the Charter of the United Nations should be deemed an important question, as it did in the case of China, and thus require a two-thirds majority. But no member state objected, so there was no need to discuss credentials. The Russian Federation then took the Soviet Union's place on the P5, as Lord Hannay says.

If Scotland becomes independent and follows the Yeltsin precedent, its leadership and that of the residual UK (England–Wales–Northern Ireland) would jointly write a letter to the secretary-general requesting that the credentials of the England–Wales–Northern Ireland representatives be recognised in place of UK representatives. I have suggested that, in contrast to the treatment of Russia in 1991, there probably would be objections to permanent Security Council membership for England–Wales–Northern Ireland, and that the matter would go to the Credentials Committee and then to the General Assembly. If the secretary-general were to consult China, France, Russia and the US for advice, following the 1991 precedent, the only conceivable outcome that they would be able to agree on would be to follow precedent and to ask member states for objections. If no letter were written, any member state could object to the Credentials Committee and the matter would be determined by the General Assembly.

Norman Dombey

Closing Argument

In Paranoid Style: The Last Days of Trump

Benjamin Rhode

I

In September 2020, as the COVID-19 pandemic's second wave began its ascent and soon after the president of the United States claimed that his electoral opponent was controlled by 'people that are in the dark shadows', I sought refuge in a sunlit bicycle ride through London's Hyde Park.[1] An unexpected association appeared in my mind: a memory of long hours in the French national library spent squinting at microfilmed works of an obscure *fin de siècle* writer, L-A Aubry. Few details are known about Aubry, other than that he was a staffer at the French Ministry of War and that, from 1895 to 1898, while the Dreyfus affair convulsed France, he published under various pseudonyms several screeds arguing that the English, Americans and Jews were in fact one race.[2] While many of his contemporaries agonised that Frenchmen were unmanly compared to their 'Anglo-Saxon' counterparts and that this might explain France's relatively poor colonial performance, Aubry asserted that the English/Jews were a 'feminine race' that employed subterfuge and seduction to subjugate 'male' races such as the French.[3] The eventual goal of this conspiracy was to colonise France, 'assimilate' the French and inflict periodic starvation and pestilence to cull the native population; England's cruel treatment of the Irish and Indians served as templates.[4] Aubry argued that Britain's and France's divergent fortunes since the early eighteenth century were explained not

Benjamin Rhode is IISS Senior Fellow for Transatlantic Affairs and Editor of the *Adelphi* book series.

Survival | vol. 63 no. 1 | February–March 2021 | pp. 213–230   https://doi.org/10.1080/00396338.2021.1881265

by Anglo-Saxon 'superiority' but by a conspiracy of England's agents, their infiltration of French government and the Jewish 'yoke' over France. Indeed, history's repeating patterns were a function of the unchanging tendencies of 'occult Semites'.[5] He revealed a cosmic yet covert war between good and evil, with the English – 'the terrestrial incarnation of Satan' – the Manichaean inverse of a 'good race' like the French. 'Since the two nations have existed,' he wrote, 'France and anti-France, as [England] is called, this war continues', but 'slyly' and seductively, 'through Jewish kisses'.[6]

What prompted these *fin de siècle* fever dreams to intrude upon an idyllic excursion in a London park? It was a particular detail of Aubry's intense interest in what he perceived as Victorian England's satanic sexual perversions. Protestant clergymen were, he argued, 'the organisers of Vice on Earth'.[7] Britain and America were rife with child prostitution. Aubry imagined recently discovered X-rays one day revealing how, behind their 'closed shutters', the English celebrated the Sabbath through the 'Bacchic and venereal cult offered … to their god'. Thousands of couples fornicated in Hyde Park to the rhythm of military bands: state-sanctioned pagan devotions to Lucifer.[8]

Aubry only ever enjoyed a limited readership, and only a small fraction of French society would have subscribed to the totality of his world view.[9] Yet he echoed and amplified the arguments of more popular writers, including the anti-Semitic polemicist Édouard Drumont. Drumont argued that the Jews, helped by a compliant education system, had infected the French with physical and mental illnesses, hypnotised them and through mental subversion left them primed for enslavement.[10] His work blended biologically racist and religious fixations, drew upon contemporary medical, social-scientific and psychological terminology, and added a hefty dose of the occult.[11] This was a wildly successful combination: Drumont's *La France juive* (1886) was among his country's top-five best-selling books during the nineteenth century. At the height of the Dreyfus affair in 1898, he was elected as the deputy for Algiers, where anti-Semitic riots had occurred.[12]

More generally, conspiracy theories attributing France's travails to treasonous internal forces – typically Jews, Freemasons or Protestants

– were at least as old as the French Revolution, and featured across the political spectrum. The royalist Charles Maurras would name these internal enemies 'anti-France', suggesting that such 'internal foreigners' could be connected, sometimes implicitly, to the external enemy Britain, which the renowned republican historian Jules Michelet had also labelled 'anti-France'.[13] Aubry, as we have seen, deployed Michelet's term, although in a more overtly primitive and Manichaean context. Drumont and other nationalists charged Freemasons and Protestants with treasonous acts; some argued that Protestants had instigated the Dreyfus affair on Britain's behalf to weaken France and thus prepare the way for its colonial humiliation in late 1898 at Fashoda, where its troops were forced to withdraw in the face of superior British force. In 1897, the writer known as Léo Taxil had supposedly uncovered Freemasonry's monstrosities, featuring satanic orgies, English high priestesses and stores of biological weapons at Gibraltar. Taxil's large and avid readership generally maintained its faith in the ultimate truth of his exposés, despite his later revelation at a press conference that they had been a hoax.[14]

On one level, this conspiratorial discourse, and the credulousness of its adherents, can appear comical. It can certainly appear bizarre to those who juxtapose Hyde Park's tranquil beauty with its role in Aubry's mind as a site for state-sponsored satanic mass copulation. Yet these fantasies and the milieu that generated them bequeathed a poisonous legacy. The historian Norman Cohn has shown how *The Protocols of the Elders of Zion*, the document posing as the record of a diabolical Jewish world-conspiracy, was very likely forged in Paris sometime between 1894 and 1898, at the behest of the head of the foreign branch of the Imperial Russian intelligence service. Like much other nineteenth-century anti-Semitism, the *Protocols* adapted or reformulated medieval anti-Jewish fantasies and tropes. More directly, its authors plagiarised a variety of anti-Semitic (and more benign) works from earlier in the century; marginalia in copies of certain works held by the French national library are suggestive of the forgers' dubious scholarship. Cohn noted one scholar's estimate that, by the time of the Second World War, the *Protocols* had become the most widely disseminated book worldwide after the Bible. It helped to inform the Nazi world view of a Jewish world-conspiracy that demanded extirpation, a myth that served, in Cohn's phrase, as a 'warrant for genocide'.[15]

Reaching the southern side of Hyde Park, one passes alongside Rotten Row, where members of London's high society once conducted their matinal social life on horseback. Overlooking the Row is the French Embassy. In late 1898, around the same time that Drumont and others were raving about Jewish hypnosis and black magic, and weeks after France and Britain had come close to war over Fashoda, the thoughtful and accomplished diplomat Paul Cambon arrived at the embassy as his country's new ambassador. He was in mourning. During his previous posting as ambassador to the Ottoman Empire, he had sent his consumptive wife, 'the love of [his] heart', letters full of tenderness and encouragement, sometimes accompanied by a pressed flower from the garden.[16] His wife, still in her forties, succumbed to tuberculosis a few months before he arrived in London. Despite his grief, within a few years Cambon had helped to broker the Entente Cordiale, the agreement that defused long-standing colonial disputes with Britain. He spent subsequent years doing his best to ensure that the British Empire would side with France in any eventual war with Germany. While he spent an agonising period in 1914 fearing that the British would abandon his country, he was ultimately successful. It is arguable, therefore, that Cambon played a significant role in modern European history.[17] Yet his status as a player in the corridors of power did not prevent his remarking in a private letter to his younger brother, also a senior ambassador, that *The Times* newspaper was 'in the hands of the Rothschilds'. Their favourable attitude towards France's government was 'a guarantee of peace for us' and was reflected in *The Times*'s coverage, illustrating 'the tremendous international influence of the Jews; they are masters of war and peace. It is not to be astonished or indignant about, it is a fact and it is necessary to take account of it.'[18] A belief in the epoch-shaping power of world Jewry was not just the preserve of the powerless, the ignorant or the insane.

Rounding the corner northwards, one approaches Speakers' Corner, long a source of British pride in a liberal political culture that allows one and all to stand up and shout out their views in the public square. On the day of my September ride the crowd was thicker than usual. There was a large gathering of protesters whose banners declared their opposition to vaccines and measures to contain COVID-19. Two women with determined expressions arriving at the protest's edge carried placards that sought to educate bystanders about the paedophilia practised by senior politicians and elderly members of the royal family, declaring that **WE KNOW THE TRUTH**.

II

In his classic 1964 essay 'The Paranoid Style in American Politics', Richard Hofstadter identified the 'paranoid style' and its 'central preoccupation': 'the existence of a vast, insidious, preternaturally effective international conspiratorial network designed to perpetrate acts of the most fiendish character'. While Hofstadter highlighted episodes in American history in which the paranoid style was particularly prominent, such as the fears over Illuminati, Masonic or Catholic conspiracies in the eighteenth and nineteenth centuries, or the panic about a communist conspiracy in his own time, he made clear that this 'style' was a universal phenomenon and attempted to abstract some of its key attributes.[19]

These included the apocalyptic tone of the 'paranoid spokesman' who, 'like religious millenarians … expresses the anxiety of those who are living through the last days' in which 'time is forever just running out' to defend against the diabolical danger, yet holds out the lingering opportunity of redemption if the warning is seized in time. There is a Manichaean, total war against 'absolute evil': an enemy who 'is a perfect model of malice' and whose personal schemes, rather than any impersonal forces, dictate history's course. There is often a special emphasis placed on defectors from 'the enemy cause' since, 'in the spiritual wrestling match between good and evil which is the paranoid's archetypal model of the world struggle', this figure 'brings with him the promise of redemption and victory'. The enemy might control the public mind through the press, education or some other seductive technique of mind control. Hofstadter realised that this fiendish enemy appeared 'to be on many counts a projection of the self: both the ideal and unacceptable aspects of the self are attributed to him'. In particular, lurid condemnations of the supposed sexual and sadistic perversions of the enemy allow 'exponents of the paranoid style an opportunity to project and freely express unacceptable aspects of their own minds'. Aubry's imagined satanic escapades in Hyde Park appear in sharper focus.

So too does his insistence on history's underlying engine being a Semitic conspiracy; for, as Hofstadter notes, while there have indeed been conspiracies throughout history, the exponents of the paranoid style see history not merely as riddled with conspiracies, but as driven by one unifying conspiracy: 'history is a conspiracy'. Hofstadter argued that the paranoid lacked what the historian Lewis Namier called 'the crowning achievement of historical study ... an intuitive sense of how things do not happen'. It is true that a historical education confers both an understanding that significant events are more often driven by contingency than conspiracy, and an inclination to favour explanations that value complexity over simplicity. Yet, as Hofstadter's elegant analysis demonstrates, a grounding in history also carries with it the knowledge of how prevalent the predilection to uncover supposed conspiracies has been. If there is a pattern to history, it is less endless conspiracy than endless conspiracy theories.

Hofstadter was correct to distinguish the experience of the clinically paranoid (who might form elaborate delusional structures) from that of most people and also, conversely, to note that 'paranoid modes of expression' could be used by 'more or less normal people'.[20] Yet the division between the clinical paranoiac and the 'normal' person may not be as sharp as he implied. The psychiatrist and psychoanalyst David Bell has observed how psychoanalysis has 'undermine[d] apparent discontinuities between the normal and the abnormal. The ideas of the insane ... can be shown to have in their content much more in common with ordinary human concerns than at first glance might be the case.' Paranoid anxiety, a more transient mental state than more permanent paranoid structures, is a more frequent feature of human experience than often supposed, and results from the commonplace psychological projection of intolerable internal feelings into the external world. Although these alarming thoughts or emotions have been safely attributed to others, the external world now appears more frightening. Something primitive and powerful within all of us makes us prone, to greater or lesser degrees, to project our own complex, conflicted feelings or inclinations onto external individuals or groups categorised as wholly good or wholly bad. In Bell's words, 'the interminable struggles between good and evil forces, so basic to religious doctrine … derive from our projection onto the heavens of the division in our own minds'. This simplistic division of the world can have profound consequences when it is a dominant mode of thought in individuals or groups.[21]

Sigmund Freud's insight into the more vivid paranoid delusional structures found at one end of the pathological spectrum was that they themselves are not the mental illness, but 'a process of reconstruction' attempted by an individual, who is on one level aware that they are experiencing a catastrophic mental collapse and seeks relief by imposing some form of explanatory system. Anxiety is reduced when, for example, a sense that the individual's world is collapsing is converted into a conviction that the entire world is nearing its end. More broadly, paranoia also serves as a psychological defence against an awareness of loneliness and insignificance. Rather than being ignored, others are taking an intense interest in you, albeit a sinister one. 'If you are paranoid', as Bell puts it, 'you are never alone. Intolerance of the indifference of the material world to our fate underlies our wish to believe in powerful gods and devils who are determining our fate.'[22]

It is important not to reduce all paranoid movements, whether religious or political, to issues of individual psychology, ignoring other political, economic or sociological factors.[23] Hofstadter argued that paranoid movements appeared in waves rather than continuously because they were stimulated by 'social conflicts that involve ultimate schemes of values', 'catastrophe or the fear of catastrophe' and the sense of a lack of political representation.[24] Cohn emphasised the interdependence of 'the sociological and psychopathological aspects' in explaining how, for instance, the Holocaust occurred, as well as the fact that medieval 'revolutionary millenarianism' tended to erupt in the context of broader socio-economic cataclysm or plague.[25] But while we should be cautious of overstating the role of individual psychology, we should be careful not to downplay it either.

Nor should we ignore the role that paranoia plays not only on the level of the individual but on that of larger groups. Hofstadter sought to distinguish the clinical paranoid's belief that he personally was the subject of persecution from that of the 'spokesman of the paranoid style', who discerned hostility and conspiracy against larger national or cultural groupings to which he belonged rather than against himself alone.[26] To some extent, Hofstadter may have overstated this distinction. There is a threat to the individual inherent in any larger threat to his group, and his fantasies of an enemy attack along a broader front may allow for his individual anxieties to be sublimated into these larger concerns. More generally, primitive, projective and paranoid mechanisms appear to operate just as much in larger groups as in individuals, if not more so. There appears to be a broader human, tribalistic need to attribute bad characteristics to an 'out-group', if only to promote the cohesion of the 'in-group'.[27]

Drawing on Cohn's work, Hofstadter highlighted the similarities between the world view of the paranoid style in its political context and that of the religious millenarian and apocalyptic traditions.[28] Cohn's study of 'revolutionary millenarianism' in the Middle Ages and early-modern era had alerted him to certain recurrent patterns in the narratives these groups promulgated. He argued that these narratives and tropes – of a great battle that will see the total triumph of good over evil, the punishment of evil's oppressive human agents, and 'the elect … thereafter [living] as a collectivity, unanimous and without conflict, on a transformed and purified earth' – originally derived from developments in Zoroastrianism which were reflected in Jewish apocalyptic traditions and thence strands of Christian millenarianism, most famously represented in the Book of Revelation. Cohn argued that the 'tradition of apocalyptic fanaticism' had endured and, in a secularised form, been 'inherited by Lenin and Hitler'.[29]

Channelling Cohn and the arguments of the philosopher André Glucksmann, the writer Paul Berman has drawn out the similarities between the 'ur-myth' found in the narrative of the Book of Revelation and those of so many totalitarian political movements in the modern age. 'There was always a people of God', Berman notes, 'whose peaceful and wholesome life had been undermined':

> They were the proletariat or the Russian masses (for the Bolsheviks and Stalinists); or the children of the Roman wolf (for Mussolini's Fascists); or the Spanish Catholics and the Warriors of Christ the King (for Franco's Phalange); or the Aryan race (for the Nazis). There were always the subversive dwellers in Babylon, who trade commodities around the world and pollute society with their abominations … [These] were always aided by Satanic forces from beyond, and the Satanic forces were always pressing on the people of God from all sides … Yet no matter how putrid and oppressive was the present, the reign of God always beckoned in the future … The coming reign was always going to be pure – a society cleansed of its pollutants and abominations … The coming reign was going to last a thousand years … It was going to be the one-party state … a society that had achieved the final unity of mankind. And every one of those states was governed … by a great living symbol, who was the Leader … who, in his statements and demeanour, was visibly mad, and who, in his madness, incarnated the deepest of all the anti-liberal impulses, which was the revolt against rationality … And every one of those Leaders behaved as God behaves, dealing out what God deals out, which is death. For … before the Reign of God could be achieved, there was always going to be the war of Armageddon – the all-exterminating bloodbath.[30]

The paranoid world view and its related millenarian narrative, both of which resonate on a primitive level of human psychology, were thus integral to the totalitarian movements.[31] Even adopting a more instrumentalist analysis, the close connection between the paranoid world view and authoritarian political systems is evident as, even more than in most human groupings, these systems require the spectre of internal and external enemies to justify the nature of their rule.

III

The QAnon movement emerged online in late 2017 following a series of posts by the anonymous 'Q', purportedly a renegade from the heart of the 'deep state' that was supposedly controlling America. People wearing the movement's branded garb or bearing its banners soon began to appear at rallies for Donald Trump. Like many cults and paranoid movements before it, its adherents revelled in the details of their enemies' all-encompassing evil; in this instance, the enemies' supposed sexual perversion, corruption and occasional murder of children have been particularly prominent. The revealed truth is of a vast global network of sinister elites engaging in satanic worship, cannibalism (echoing the historical 'blood libel' that accused Jews of drinking the blood of Christian children) and the trafficking of children for sex. This international 'globalist' elite includes members of the 'deep state', prominent Democrats, and Jewish financiers such as George Soros and the Rothschilds. President Trump, representing the forces of light, has been engaged in a covert, cosmic war against the evildoers. Apparent setbacks to Trump's agenda have been explained as only feints or diversions before his ultimate triumph: 'the Great Awakening' will see the eyes of the masses opened to the conspiracy, followed by 'the Storm', a resplendent victory over the forces of darkness, in which figures such as Hillary Clinton will be put to death, and in whose final outcome the elect must put their trust.[32] By late 2020, 41% of Republicans who had heard of QAnon believed it was a 'somewhat' or 'very' good thing for the United States.[33]

In the 1960s, Hofstadter observed that the paranoid style had enjoyed varying degrees of success worldwide, capturing the heights of power in Germany but thus far relegated to 'minority movements' in the US.[34] Yet today, as others have noted, the 45th US president – whose political career was born in the 'birther' conspiracy movement that claimed president Barack Obama was a secret foreigner – is himself an exponent of theories once restricted to the fringe.[35] During his presidency, the most power-ful man in the world frequently trafficked in fact-free fantasies typically associated with powerless outsiders. When questioned about the QAnon phenomenon, Trump described its adherents as people who 'love our country', adding that 'I understand that they like me very much, which I appreciate', and later saying that 'what I do hear about [QAnon] is they are very strongly against paedophilia. And I agree with that.'[36] On 6 January 2021, Trump directly incited his supporters to march on the Capitol, presumably in the hope that they would intimidate lawmakers into overturning the election results. Reality would be forced to conform with the delusion that he had triumphed.

Even before that tragic day, QAnon dogma had already had fatal results. One of its intellectual precursors was the 'Pizzagate' theory of 2016 which claimed, improbably, that Clinton and her associates directed a paedophile network from a Washington pizza restaurant; in December 2016, Edgar Welch was charged (and later imprisoned) for firing his rifle inside the restaurant, which he was 'self-investigating'.[37] In a 2019 sequel of sorts, a QAnon adherent attempted a citizen's arrest of a Staten Island Mafia don whom he believed to be part of the 'deep state'; this episode ended with the mobster shot dead outside his home.[38] Thus, in a twist perhaps too implausible for fiction, a member of a very real, centuries-old international criminal conspiracy was murdered due to fantasies of his participation in a non-existent conspiracy. Before the Capitol assault, the FBI had considered QAnon followers to pose a risk of domestic terrorism, and a considerable number of them had been arrested, charged or imprisoned for real or attempted violent crimes.[39] While the exact composition of the mob that stormed the Capitol was unconfirmed when this issue went to press, it is clear that it included a number of QAnon adherents, alongside far-right activists and neo-Nazis. Perhaps the most photogenic rioter was a prominent QAnon 'shaman' from Arizona.[40] An intruder shot dead by police, Ashli Babbitt, was an Air Force veteran and former Obama voter; yet photographs showed her wearing QAnon merchandise, and her final tweet declared that 'the storm is here and it is descending upon DC in less than 24 hours … dark to light!'[41]

Perhaps even more significantly, at least in terms of body counts, there has been a notable overlap between QAnon and proponents of theories that COVID-19 is a conspiracy or hoax.[42] These theories have indisputably caused thousands of unnecessary deaths – sometimes including those of their proponents – and, if they encourage a widespread refusal to accept COVID-19 vaccines, could potentially kill hundreds of thousands more, possibly preventing any meaningful social or economic recovery from the pandemic.

Hofstadter identified the 'mass media' as one factor distinguishing McCarthyite America from earlier periods when less vivid or widely known fantasies of Masonic or Catholic conspiracies were prevalent.[43] Yet the capabilities of the mass media and information networks of Hofstadter's time now seem like small beer. We live in an era of all-pervasive and instantaneous distribution of misinformation and disinformation. The internet and social media – partly thanks to their eradication of many traditional news organisations' business model – have engendered an information environment in which shared authoritative sources, along with the notion of objective truth itself, are increasingly hard to find. At the same time, these networks, driven by algorithms designed to maximise users' engagement by providing them with increasingly extreme versions of the information in which they have previously shown interest, have helped to reinforce in their users a binary interpretation of world events. This has had political consequences beyond what would have typically been labelled the 'lunatic fringe'.[44] Former president Obama has warned of 'an epistemological crisis' threatened by unregulated social media, conspiracy theories and 'deepfake' technology, arguing that 'if we do not have the capacity to distinguish what's true from what's false, then by definition the marketplace of ideas doesn't work. And by definition our democracy doesn't work.'[45]

On one level, Joe Biden's victory in the 2020 presidential election represents a rejection by the majority of Americans of Trump's conspiratorial discourse. Trump's defeat seems to have unsettled many QAnon adherents, who were already impeded by widespread (if belated) bans of their content across several social-media channels. Following the Capitol assault, Trump himself was permanently suspended from Twitter to prevent 'further incitement of violence'. Yet the new US Congress will also seat two QAnon-supporting Republicans, and it seems likely that the movement will adapt, with many QAnon followers moving sideways into other conspiratorial causes.[46] Such causes are by no means a minority phenomenon. Two weeks after the election, 88% of Trump voters believed Biden's victory was illegitimate.[47] It is unclear what consequences the decision by more than a third of the US electorate to inhabit a parallel reality may have on the future of the Republican Party, Biden's ability to serve as president or the longer-term viability of the US system of government. The violent storming of the Capitol by Trump supporters, determined to thwart what they considered was a stolen election, was suggestive of the powerful hold their delusions had over them, and the lengths to which they might be willing to go to impose those delusions on others.

We should avoid the trap of considering paranoid thought the preserve of any one group or political tradition. We are all, to varying degrees, susceptible to it. It is easy for anyone – including the author – to imagine a clear split between an enlightened, sunlit version of themselves and the oddness of 'them', outside in the darkness, thereby attributing alarming internal tendencies wholly to others.

Certainly, while it is indisputable that the United States is home to a large number of Christians with apocalyptic beliefs – in 2010, 41% of Americans polled believed it was definite or probable that Jesus would return by 2050 – the predisposition towards conspiratorial thinking is not peculiarly American.[48] A September 2020 survey suggested that 6% of Britons polled supported QAnon, 17% believed that COVID-19 was intentionally released to depopulate or control the world, and 25% believed that 'secret Satanic cults exist and include influential elites'.[49] In 2020, there were 60 attacks against 5G masts in Britain, and some politicians belonging to mainstream parties have supported claims that 5G presents a health risk.[50] Even before the pandemic, it was estimated that 79% of French people subscribed to at least one conspiracy theory, with 34% believing in at least four.[51] In December 2020, a survey suggested that only 40% of French people would accept a COVID-19 vaccine if offered one.[52]

False beliefs and Manichaean world views can have real and profound consequences. It is tempting to laugh away those who, like Aubry, Drumont or the adherents of QAnon, spin lurid tales of conspiracy, perversion and plot – the inhabitants of that 'subterranean world', in Cohn's words, 'where pathological fantasies disguised as ideas are churned out by crooks and half-educated fanatics for the benefit of the ignorant and the superstitious'. This would be unwise. For, as Cohn warns us, when economic, political or cultural conditions are propitious, 'there are times when this underworld emerges from the depths and suddenly fascinates, captures and dominates multitudes of usually sane and responsible people, who thereupon take leave of sanity and responsibility. And it occasionally happens that this underworld becomes a political power and changes the course of history.'[53] We must acknowledge that people can be captivated by beliefs that are irrational and terrifying; and that they tend to act on their beliefs.

Notes

1   Trump made this claim on 31 August 2020. David Smith, 'Donald Trump Makes Baseless Claim that "Dark Shadows" Are Controlling Joe Biden', *Guardian*, 1 September 2020.

2   These pseudonyms included Louis Martin, Louis Martin-Chagny and Louis Marthin-Chagny. The most extensive treatment of Aubry's work is Francesco Germinario's *Costruire la Razza Nemica: La Formazione dell'Immaginario Antisemita Tra la Fine dell'Ottocento e gli Inizi del Novecento* (Turin: UTET libreria, 2010), pp. 306–34, which examines several of the themes discussed here; see also Emmanuel Kreis, *Les Puissances de l'Ombre: Juifs, Jésuites, Francs-Maçons, Réactionnaires: La Théorie du Complot dans Les Textes* (Paris: CNRS, 2009), pp. 179–87; Bertrand Joly, 'Déroulède et l'Angleterre', in Philippe Vervaecke (ed.), *À droite de la droite* (Villeneuve d'Ascq: Presses Universitaires du Septentrion, 2012), p. 44; Ian Buruma, *Anglomania: A European Love Affair*

(New York: Vintage, 1998), pp. 190–1; and Fabrice Serodes, *Anglophobie et Politique: de Fachoda à Mers el-Kébir: Visions Françaises du Monde Britannique* (Paris: Harmattan, 2010), p. 52.

3   Louis Marthin-Chagny, *L'Angleterre Suzeraine de la France par F. . M. .* (Paris: Chamuel, 1896), pp. 217–18.

4   Marthin-Chagny, *La Sémitique Albion* (Paris: Henri Jouve, 1898), pp. 159–75, 224–6.

5   *Ibid.*, pp. 292, 353–9.

6   *Ibid.*, pp. 114, 192–3; and Louis Martin, *L'Anglais est-il un Juif?* (Paris: Savine, 1895), pp. 44–5.

7   Marthin-Chagny, *La Sémitique Albion*, pp. 99, 215–21.

8   *Ibid.*, pp. 8–15, 102–6, 109–28. For broader French impressions of British sexual hypocrisy and depravity, see Robert and Isabelle Tombs, *That Sweet Enemy: The French and the British from the Sun King to the Present* (London: William Heinemann, 2006), pp. 403, 454–6.

9   Joly, 'Déroulède et l'Angleterre', p. 44. That said, the notion of an Anglo-

Jewish nexus found royal adherents across Europe. Tsar Nicholas II claimed that 'an Englishman is a Jew'. See Barbara Tuchman, *The Guns of August* (New York: Macmillan, 1962), p. 8. Later in life, his cousin, the half-English former Kaiser Wilhelm II, railed against the 'Antichrist Juda' needing to be removed from 'Juda-England', whose Freemason ruling class was 'thoroughly infected' by Jews. He also believed in an Anglo-Jewish plot to kill his German father. See John C.G. Röhl, *The Kaiser and His Court: Wilhelm II and the Government of Germany* (Cambridge: Cambridge University Press, 1994), pp. 190–212, especially pp. 202, 211; and Buruma, *Anglomania*, pp. 203–4. For a discussion of the significance of Aubry's writings and a critique of the claim that they are simply psychotic delusions, see Germinario, *Costruire la Razza Nemica*, pp. 318–19.

10 See Pierre Birnbaum, *Jewish Destinies: Citizenship, State, and Community in Modern France* (New York: Hill & Wang, 2000), pp. 101–4, 108–11; and Frederick Busi, *The Pope of Antisemitism: The Career and Legacy of Edouard-Adolphe Drumont* (Lanham, MD: Rowman & Littlefield, 1986) p. 123.

11 See Ruth Harris, *Dreyfus: Politics, Emotion, and the Scandal of the Century* (New York: Picador, 2010), pp. 172–81; and Birnbaum, *Jewish Destinies*, pp. 103–15.

12 See Frederick Brown, *For the Soul of France: Culture Wars in the Age of Dreyfus* (New York: Anchor Books, 2010), pp. 74–5; and Busi, *The Pope of Antisemitism*, pp. 138–46.

13 See Robert Tombs, *France, 1814–1914* (London: Routledge, 1996), pp. 88–94; Robert O. Paxton, *Vichy France: Old Guard and New Order* (New York: Columbia University Press, 1982), p. 171; M. Anderson, 'The Myth of the "Two Hundred Families"', *Political Studies*, vol. 13, no. 2, June 1965, pp. 163–78; and Harris, *Dreyfus*, p. 169.

14 See Harris, *Dreyfus*, pp. 176–7, 179; Joly, 'Déroulède et l'Angleterre', pp. 43–4; Busi, *The Pope of Antisemitism*, pp. 72–3; and Robert Gildea, *Children of the Revolution: The French, 1799–1914* (London: Allen Lane, 2008), pp. 355–6.

15 Norman Cohn, *Warrant for Genocide: The Myth of the Jewish World-conspiracy and the Protocols of the Elders of Zion* (London: Eyre & Spottiswoode, 1967).

16 The flowers are still attached to some of these letters: see Centre des Archives diplomatiques du ministère des Affaires étrangères, France, PA-AP 42, Volume 101.

17 For more on Cambon's life and outlook, see M.B. Hayne, *The French Foreign Office and the Origins of the First World War, 1898–1914* (Oxford: Oxford University Press, 1993); Margaret MacMillan, *The War that Ended Peace* (London: Profile Books, 2013); Laurent Villate, *La République des Diplomates: Paul et Jules Cambon, 1843–1935* (Paris: Science Infuse, 2001); and Henri Cambon ('Un Diplomate'), *Paul Cambon, Ambassadeur de France* (Paris: Plon, 1937).

18 See Paul Cambon to Jules Cambon, 19 March 1900, in Paul Cambon, *Correspondance*, vol. 2 (Paris: B. Grasset, 1940–46), p. 38; Villate, *La République des Diplomates*, pp. 209, 384, n. 17; and David Pryce-Jones, *Betrayal: France, the Arabs, and the Jews* (New York: Encounter Books, 2006), p. 23.

19 The preceding and following quota-
tions and analysis are drawn from
Richard Hofstadter, *The Paranoid
Style in American Politics and Other
Essays* (London: Jonathan Cape,
1966), pp. 3–40.

20 *Ibid.*, pp. 3–4.

21 David Bell, *Paranoia* (Cambridge:
Cambridge University Press, 2003),
pp. 3–30.

22 *Ibid.*, pp. 15–20, 50–1.

23 See *ibid.*, pp. 64–5.

24 Hofstadter, *The Paranoid Style*, p. 39.

25 See Cohn, *Warrant for Genocide*, pp.
18, 267; and Norman Cohn, *The
Pursuit of the Millennium* (London:
Pimlico, 1993).

26 Hofstadter, *The Paranoid Style*, p. 4.

27 For Freud's observation of this point,
see Bell, *Paranoia*, pp. 65–6.

28 See Hofstadter, *The Paranoid Style*, p. 38.

29 See Cohn, *The Pursuit of the
Millennium*, in particular the
'Conclusion'; and Norman Cohn,
*Cosmos, Chaos and the World to Come:
The Ancient Roots of Apocalyptic Faith*
(London: Yale University Press, 1993).

30 Paul Berman, *Terror and Liberalism*
(New York: W.W. Norton & Co.,
2004), pp. 22–51.

31 For a recent essay discussing the
themes of paranoia, conspiracy and
totalitarianism, see Sarah Churchwell,
'Can American Democracy Survive
Donald Trump?', *Guardian*, 21
November 2020.

32 Primers on the QAnon movement
include Laurence Arnold, 'QAnon,
the Conspiracy Theory Creeping into
U.S. Politics', Bloomberg, 21 August
2020; Kevin Roose, 'What Is QAnon,
the Viral Pro-Trump Conspiracy
Theory?', *New York Times*, 19 October

2020; Mike Wendling, 'QAnon:
What Is It and Where Did It Come
From?', BBC News, 20 August 2020;
Ben Sales, 'QAnon an Old Form of
Anti-Semitism in a New Package, Say
Experts', *Times of Israel*, 20 September
2020; and Adrienne LaFrance, 'The
Prophecies of Q', *Atlantic*, June 2020.

33 Pew Research Center, '5 Facts About
the QAnon Conspiracy Theories',
16 November 2020. Some polls had
higher estimates, such as that 56%
of all Republicans believed that
the QAnon theory was mostly or
partly true: see Civiqs/Daily Kos
National Politics Survey, September
2020, https://civiqs.com/documents/
Civiqs_DailyKos_monthly_banner_
book_2020_09_klw74f.pdf.

34 Hofstadter, *The Paranoid Style*, pp. 6–7.

35 See Churchwell, 'Can American
Democracy Survive Donald Trump?'

36 See Katie Rogers and Kevin Roose,
'Trump Says QAnon Followers Are
People Who "Love Our Country"',
New York Times, 19 August 2020; Matt
Perez, 'Trump Refuses to Denounce
QAnon After Conspiracy Theory Is
Described to Him', *Forbes*, 19 August
2020; and Philip Bump, 'Rather than
Condemn the QAnon Conspiracy
Theory, Trump Elevates Its Dangerous
Central Assertion', *Washington Post*, 16
October 2020.

37 See Roose, 'What Is QAnon, the Viral
Pro-Trump Conspiracy Theory?'; and
Aria Bendix, '"Pizzagate" Shooter to
Serve Four Years in Jail', *Atlantic*, 22
June 2017.

38 See Ali Watkins, 'He Wasn't Seeking
to Kill a Mob Boss. He Was Trying to
Help Trump, His Lawyer Says', *New
York Times*, 21 July 2019.

39 See Perez, 'Trump Refuses to Denounce QAnon After Conspiracy Theory Is Described to Him'; and Lois Beckett, 'QAnon: A Timeline of Violence Linked to the Conspiracy Theory', *Guardian*, 16 October 2020.

40 See 'Capitol Riots: Who Broke into the Building?', BBC News, 8 January 2021.

41 See 'Ashli Babbitt: The US Veteran Shot Dead Breaking into the Capitol', BBC News, 8 January 2021.

42 See Marianna Spring and Mike Wendling, 'How Covid-19 Myths Are Merging with the QAnon Conspiracy Theory', BBC News, 2 September 2020.

43 Hofstadter, *The Paranoid Style*, p. 14.

44 For an overview of this large topic, and a discussion of other problems exacerbated by social media, see Jonathan Haidt and Tobias Rose-Stockwell, 'The Dark Psychology of Social Networks', *Atlantic*, December 2019; Center for Humane Technology, 'Ledger of Harms', https://ledger. humanetech.com/; and Katherine J. Wu, 'Radical Ideas Spread Through Social Media. Are the Algorithms to Blame?', NOVA, 28 March 2019.

45 Jeffrey Goldberg, 'Why Obama Fears for Our Democracy', *Atlantic*, 16 November 2020, https://www. theatlantic.com/ideas/archive/2020/11/ why-obama-fears-for-our-democracy/617087/.

46 See Kevin Roose, 'Shocked by Trump's Loss, QAnon Struggles to Keep the Faith', *New York Times*, 10 November 2020; Hannah Murphy and Siddharth Venkataramakrishnan, 'Twitter Permanently Bans Donald Trump's Account Citing Risk of Violence', *Financial Times*, 9 January 2020; and Siddharth Venkataramakrishnan, '"Rudderless" QAnon May Reinvent Itself after US Election, Warn Experts', *Financial Times*, 26 December 2020.

47 Jochen Bittner, '1918 Germany Has a Warning for America', *New York Times*, 30 November 2020.

48 Pew Research Center, 'Jesus Christ's Return to Earth', 14 July 2010.

49 Ben Quinn, 'One in Four Britons Believe in QAnon-linked Theories – Survey', *Guardian*, 22 October 2020.

50 Nick Cohen, 'Lib Dems Hook Up with 5G Cranks and Give a Boost to Wild Conspiracy', *Observer*, 26 December 2020.

51 '79% des Français croient au moins à une "théorie du complot"', *Le Figaro*, 7 January 2018. My thanks to Lionel Laurent for bringing this to my attention.

52 'Coronavirus: French Government Vows to Speed Up Vaccinations', BBC News, 4 January 2021.

53 Cohn, *Warrant for Genocide*, pp. 18–19.

Correction

Article title: Saving Strategic Arms Control
Author: Alexey Arbatov
Journal: *Survival*
Bibliometrics: Volume 62, Number 5, pages 79–104
DOI: http://dx.doi.org/10.1080/00396338.2020.1819640

When this article was first published online, the fifth sentence of the second paragraph on page 79 read as follows:

Russia suspended the Conventional Armed Forces in Europe Treaty in 2015, and the United States will leave the treaty in November.

This has now been corrected to read:

Russia suspended its implementation of the Conventional Armed Forces in Europe Treaty in 2007, and the United States and its NATO allies ceased carrying out treaty obligations with respect to Russia in 2011.

These corrections have been made to the online article.